Representative Americans

THE COLONISTS

REPRESENTATIVE AMERICANS

The Colonists

The Revolutionary Generation

FORTHCOMING:

The Romantics

The Civil War Generation

Representative Americans

The Colonists

Norman K. Risjord
University of Wisconsin–Madison

SECOND EDITION

A MADISON HOUSE BOOK
ROWMAN & LITTLEFIELD PUBLISHERS, INC.
Lanham • Boulder • New York • Oxford

To my brother

JOHN C. RISJORD

A Madison House Book

Rowman & Littlefield Publishers, Inc.
4720 Boston Way
Lanham, MD 20706
www.rowmanlittlefield.com

Norman K. Risjord,
Representative Americans: The Colonists

LIBRARY OF CONGRESS CATALOGING-IN-PUBLICATION DATA

Risjord, Norman K.
Representative Americans, the colonists / Norman K. Risjord.—2nd ed.
p.cm.
Includes bibliographical references and index.
ISBN 0-7425-2072-2 (cloth: alk. paper)
ISBN 0-7425-2073-0 (pbk.: alk. paper)
1. United States—History—Colonial period, ca. 1600–1775—Biography.
2. United States—Biography. I. Title: Colonists. II. Title.

E188.R5 2001
973.2'0922—dc21
[B]   00-056637

Designed by William Kasdorf

Printed in the United States of America on acid-free paper

SECOND EDITION

Contents

Preface to the Second Edition

The purpose of this series on "Representative Americans" is to make history human, to put some tissue on the skeletal framework of names and dates. By using a biographical approach, I hope to make the past more concrete and vivid, to recover a heritage that today's reader can feel and experience.

The series is directed at the interested but inexpert dilettante, whose memory is taxed and attention is exhausted by lengthy textbooks and scholarly tomes. Representative life stories are morsels to be tasted and sampled without overfilling. They hint of greater delights beyond, when knowledge beckons and leisure time permits.

My selections are not "representative" in the sense of average or common, but neither do they depict heroes of the sort chosen by Emerson or Carlyle in their "great men" approach to history. Rather, I have searched for human beings with whom the reader can identify without attempting to emulate. Among heroes or heroines I prefer those whose lives are made poignant by tragedy, such as Pocahontas, George Rogers Clark, or Osceola. Antiheroes, too, such as Jay Gould or Huey Long, enrich and enliven the fabric of American history. I have also chosen people who illustrate elusive concepts. In this volume, for instance, Anne Hutchinson offers a passage through the labyrinth of Calvinism, and James Logan's varied interests help us explore the Enlightenment.

For purposes of arousing an interest in history, the antithesis of the Napoleonic hero admired by Emerson may be the most useful. The biographical approach permits access to what some have called the "underside" of history: racial and ethnic minorities, the poor, and women. Political/diplomatic history—and that is necessarily the focus of most surveys—is essentially the story of white males, for it was they who served as presidents and popes, generals and diplomats. Conscientious scholars who seek to rescue women and minorities from the obscurity of a biased past unfortunately find only a scant literary record with which to work. As a result, such groups commonly enter the historical narrative in one of two ways: either as statistics (e.g., the percentage of poor in Boston over five decades) or through a heavy emphasis on "rights" movements. The first approach is dull, and the second risks stereotypical distortion. The biographical method provides an easy avenue to the contributions of an Eliza Pinckney, an Abigail Adams, a Margaret Fuller, or an Amelia Earhart; of a Sequoia, a Jackie Robinson, or a Cesar Chavez. Such people, though intensely concerned with their "rights," enriched the American past in other ways as well.

The focus of this volume is on the colonial generations, the men and women who founded America, shaped its society, and coined its traditions. They lived in an age of adventure and exploration, as well as of deep-seated piety and meditation. They laid the foundations of modern politics and modern science. In my sketches I have tried to include the adventurous and the meditative and some who were both. The result, I trust, is a wide-angle view of a portion of the American past.

Norman K. Risjord
University of Wisconsin–Madison

Introduction

Unlike the other volumes in this series, this book does not attempt to portray a generation as a reflection of a particular epoch in American history. The colonial period spanned at least three generations (in some families, such as the Winthrops, one might even count four). The concept of a generation, beyond that of a single family tree, is at best a fuzzy one. There is no particular indicator to mark where one generation ends and another begins, nor have I tried to find one. Yet there are changing interests and attitudes that can best be described as generational. The Mathers—Richard, Increase, and Cotton—whose collective life-span (1596–1728) roughly parallels the contour of this book, are a case in point. Richard was one of the founders of New England; Increase was preoccupied with the preservation of New England, spiritually and politically; and Cotton was caught up in the intellectual and pietistic awakenings of the eighteenth century. These varieties of experience are represented in the three divisions of *The Colonists*. The divisions are not intended to reflect generations, but in some sense they do.

The first section, entitled "Pathmarkers of Empire," focuses on the founders, their hopes, and their accomplishments in the American environment. The founding of the colonies was not a generational phenomenon, since it required more than a century to complete. Yet the experiences, over time, were comparable. Captain John Smith and Nathaniel Bacon, though their lives were separated by a half-century, were both soldiers of the frontier. Their thoughts and actions shaped relations between the two conflicting cultures, Native and European, and each left a lasting imprint on the history of Virginia. William Bradford and William Penn came to America, also a half century apart, each hoping to found a community of the righteous. In differing but parallel ways, each saw his ideals compromised in the American environment.

The second section on "Swords of Empire" explores the triangular contest among Britain, France, and Spain for supremacy in the New World. In addition, it provides a good adventure story as well as an introduction to the histories of Canada and the West Indies, which are too often neglected in United States texts. To readers who have been imbued with the Anglo-American view of history, the life of Le Moyne d'Iberville is a reminder that the "other side" produced heroes of its own. James Oglethorpe, "Pathmarker" as well as "Sword" of empire, ties this section to the first one.

The "Bridges of Empire" are that in every sense. The principals in this section span the psychological spectrum from transplanted Englishmen to prideful Americans. They managed also the intellectual leap from universe of mystery and revelation to universe of physical law, mathematical symmetry, and scientific experiment. And finally, they gathered at the still uncompleted—and for many unimagined—bridge to revolution and nationhood. Completion of that structure was left to the Revolutionary generation, the subject of the second volume in this series.

PART 1

Pathmarkers of Empire

"Having undertaken, for the glory of God and advancement of the Christian faith and honour of our king and country, a voyage to plant the first colony in the northern parts of Virginia, do, by these presents, solemnly and mutually in the presence of God and of one another, covenant and combine ourselves together into a civil body politic for better ordering and preservation and furtherance of the ends aforesaid."

—*The Mayflower Compact* (November 17, 1620)

Captain John Smith and Pocahontas:
The Meeting of Cultures

To his Indian captors he cut a strange figure. Smaller than they by several inches and heavily bearded, he wore a strange costume with metallic plates that seemed both too heavy for the trail and too hot for the season. Strangest of all, he seemed to accept his plight without sign of fear. Warriors were expected to suffer danger with impassive courage, but this ship-borne invader was too much at ease for one who faced a likely death. Did he have some powerful and unseen medicine that protected him? Indian medicine or modern charm, Captain John Smith certainly had it. Quick wits. Physical prowess. Commanding presence. Luck.

John Smith (1580?–1631). By an unknown artist after an engraving of 1617. After founding Virginia and mapping the North American coast, Smith received the grand title, Admiral of New England. This portrait suggests the title fit the man. Commanding eyes, the flicker of a smile, a relaxed pose, all bespoke a confident leader of men. (National Portrait Gallery, Smithsonian Institution.)

He had them all. Only a few months before his current misadventure began—that is to say, some time in the summer of 1607—Smith had been taken by another tribe of Virginia Indians, and he had charmed his way to freedom by impressing the chief with the magical powers of his compass. In one way or another his medicine in years past had enabled him to survive warfare in Eastern Europe, piracy in the Atlantic, and slavery at the hands of the Turks. In all his adventures, fortune accompanied him in the way that the goddess Athena watched over the roving Ulysses. His current status was a case in point. His Indian captors, having seized him while he was exploring the falls of the James River (killing his companions in the process), marched him overland some eighty miles to the Rappahannock, where Smith was to be interviewed by a tribe wronged some years earlier by an unnamed white explorer. Since all white men looked essentially alike to Indians, Smith stood little chance in his wilderness docket. Yet he escaped death again, this time because of his diminutive size. The earlier wrongdoer was remembered, despite the passage of some years, as a man of uncommon height. And fortunately for Smith, the Indians' sense of justice superseded their desire for revenge.

With that formality attended to, Smith's captors had taken him to their own capital, the village of Werowocomoco, to present him to their chief, Powhatan. That august being had governed the Powhatan tribe (and had even taken for his own the name of the tribe) for more than a quarter of a century. In that time he had extended his dominion over the neighboring tribes of eastern Virginia. His woodland empire extended from the Potomac River to the Great Dismal Swamp. The English, in their naive assumption that America was built in the image of Europe, commonly addressed Indian leaders as king or emperor. In the case of Powhatan they were not far off the mark. He had gained most of his territory by conquest, and he governed each village and clan through lieutenants, called *werowances*. Every village paid him tribute, in the form of corn, beans, or deerskins.

Powhatan received his captive in a large ceremonial house. He lay on a small platform of mats, garbed in a robe of raccoon pelts. A young woman sat at his head, another at his feet. Squatting in rows on either side of him were the principals of the tribe, each with a woman behind him. All wore ceremonial beads; faces and bodies were decorated with bloodroot paint.

A great shout greeted Smith on his entrance. Then an Indian woman presented him with a bowl of water to wash his hands and a towel of turkey feathers. Trays of food were brought in, and then, at last, Powhatan greeted him. His tone was reassuring; he spoke of friendship and promised Smith his freedom within four days. Then they exchanged military intelligence. Smith described the power of the English, what their ships and cannons could do. Powhatan countered with a summary of his dominions and the allies he could command. The vocabulary was limited—Smith as yet had only a few words of Powhatanese—but the meaning was clear.

Then the mood in the council house changed. Priests entered and began a ritual chant. The fire blazed forth, and two large stones were placed before it. Smith was suddenly grabbed and his head placed on the improvised altar. The invocations of the priests grew louder, and two executioners stood forth with raised clubs. For the first time in his captivity, he knew fear.

At that critical moment Powhatan's favorite daughter, eleven-year-old Pocahontas, rushed forth with a cry and threw herself on Smith, daring the executioners to club her first. All eyes turned to Powhatan, who, after a tense moment, nodded solemnly. It was a commutation of sentence, a redemption from death.

To the end of his life Smith believed that he had been saved by the Indian maiden. Instead, what he had undergone was in all likelihood a symbolic ritual. Pocahontas, explains a modern-day anthropologist, was acting in a role of cultural mediator, symbolically saving Smith's life so that he could, in effect, be reborn into a new world of cultural relationships. This interpretation of the event is reinforced by an incident that occurred two days later. Smith recalled the scene vividly:

> Powhatan, having disguised himself in the most fearfulest manner he could, caused Captain Smith to be brought forth to a great house in the woods, and there upon a mat by the fire to be left alone. Not long after, from a mat that divided the house, was made the most doleful noise he ever heard. Then Powhatan, more like a devil than a man, with some two hundred more as black as himself, came onto him and told him now they were friends, and presently he should go to Jamestown, to send him two great guns, and a grindstone, for which he would give him the country of Capahowasick, and forever esteem him as his son Nantaquoud.

Powhatan, the emperor, had decided to incorporate Jamestown into his realm. Smith would embody the transition, serving as friend, loving son, and dutiful *werowance*. Through this ritual process the Jamestown settlers had become fellow countrymen of the Powhatans. Peace, friendship, and obedience were among their new responsibilities. At least, in the eyes of Powhatan. Smith never understood this and apparently never related the event to his fellow colonists. The story first appeared in print almost twenty years later in Smith's *Generall Historie of Virginia, New England, and the Summer Islaes* (1624). The mutual misunderstanding symbolized the clash of cultures, the mixture of love and hate, apprehension and fear that would scar Indian-white relations for the next three centuries. At the same time the tender friendship that developed between Pocahontas and John Smith symbolized the common interest that did exist, the need to coexist on the same continent.

John Smith, World Soldier

Historians were long inclined to disbelieve the Pocahontas rescue story, in part because everything Smith wrote about himself seemed so incredible. And few men have written as much about themselves. Smith's adventures were certainly strange, but most of his autobiography can be tied to actual historical events. Smith was given to exaggeration and he no doubt enriched his own role in history, but recent scholars are inclined to credit his story, fantastic though it seems.

He was a self-made man in a society that frowned on such. Smith's father was a yeoman farmer of Lincolnshire, a county that bordered on the North Sea. In the highly stratified society of Elizabethan England, Smith was expected to work contentedly his father's modest plot of land. Excessive ambition, it was felt, was dangerous to the social order.

Of ambition he had plenty; it was his glory and his undoing. At village schools in Lincolnshire he learned some grammar and a little mathematics. At fifteen he was apprenticed to a merchant in the coastal town of King's Lynn. But neither formal education nor vocational training satisfied his drive. In the year 1597—he was about eighteen then—he entered "that university of war," as he called it, the Netherlands. For a quarter century the Dutch had been fighting to rid themselves of Spanish rule. The English had been slowly drawn into the conflict, and after the Armada of 1588 they became a formal ally of the Dutch. More than a struggle for independence, it was a war of Protestants against Catholic Spain.

Whatever he learned of the art of war, Smith returned from that "university" convinced that he must become a gentleman. Since gentlemen were normally born to their station, this was no easy task, but Smith went about it with systematic devotion. He retired to his Lincolnshire fields with books on war and social behavior, built himself "a pavillion of boughs," and concentrated on self-improvement. A mysterious Italian companion taught him fencing, horsemanship, and a little Italian. How Smith financed all this he does not say. His autobiography never dwells on such mundane details as monthly income.

His education completed, Smith set out again to find a war. War, after all, was one of the few avenues to success available to a low-born fortune seeker. This time he directed his steps toward eastern Europe. The neverending struggle between Holy Roman Empire and Ottoman Turks offered infinite opportunities for glory and plunder, and the cause at issue—Christianity versus Islam—was stark enough for any professional crusader.

Confident that the war would always be there, Smith proceeded to the front at a leisurely pace. He rode across France to the Mediterranean and took ship for Rome. It turned out to be full of Catholic pilgrims, who, discovering that he was a Protestant, threw him overboard. That he was himself embarking on a crusade against Turkish infidels apparently made no difference. Smith swam to a nearby island where he was rescued by a French merchant vessel. Taking a liking to the captain, he signed on as a partner in the Mediterranean trade. The Frenchman proved to be a parttime pirate, and Smith cooperated in this side of the venture as well. He emerged with a modest fortune of 500 zecchini (a gold Venetian coin) in his purse "and a little box God sent him worth near as much more."

This windfall enabled him to resume his education. He toured Italy in gentlemanly style, acquainting himself with the "rarities" of Italian culture. He also made some important political acquaintances, one of whom mapped a route for him through the Balkans to Vienna, seat of the Holy Roman Empire. There this "English gentleman," as he now styled himself, became a captain in the imperial army.

Courage and ingenuity soon made Smith a hero of the Hungarian war theater. In his first operation he showed his commander how to coordinate an attack by the use of signal fires, a system apparently picked up from books read in his "pavillion of boughs." Given command of a cavalry troop, he besieged a town on his own and captured it with some home-made bombs—clay pots filled with gunpowder, musket balls, and pitch, which he ignited and slung over the walls. In a later campaign he answered a challenge from a Turkish commander for one-on-one combat, slew him, and in successive days defeated two more challengers. After each victory he cut off the head of his opponent, presenting the trophies to his commander. The Prince of Transylvania rewarded him for this exploit with an insignia bearing three Turk's heads and an annual pension of 200 ducats. With a coat of arms and a pension, Smith at last had the trappings of a gentleman.

Good fortune soon gave way to bad. The Transylvanians lost a battle, and Smith was taken prisoner. Chained to twenty other prisoners, he was marched 500 miles to Constantinople to be sold into slavery. From there he was shipped to Tartary on the north shore of the Black Sea. He escaped and walked back to Hungary across Russia and Poland. Many years later, when setting down his life story for posterity, he still had fond memories of the kindness with which Russian farmers had treated him.

In Leipzig, where he finally found his former commander, he obtained a formal discharge from the imperial army and 1500 gold ducats in lieu of an annual pension. He then toured Germany, France, Spain, and North Africa before returning to England.

Four years had passed since Smith began his search for gentility. The war with Spain had ended. Elizabeth had died, unwed and childless, leaving the crown to her distant cousin, James Stuart, king of the Scots. With peace, England's merchant-adventurers were ready to resume their quest for a foothold in the New World, a quest begun by Elizabeth's "sea dogs" before the Armada.

In April, 1606, King James I issued charters to two companies and authorized them to build settlements in Virginia, the English name for North America. The Plymouth Company received a patent to the northern part of Virginia; the London Company got the southern part. Smith played no part in the proceedings, nor did his name appear in the king's grant. But when the London Company dispatched three shiploads of colonists the following December, Smith was on board, and he was prominent enough to be included in the list of councillors who were to govern Virginia on arrival. No doubt the story of his eastern adventures—which Smith was never shy about recounting—earned him a place. For Smith the choice was natural. He had seen virtually all of the civilized world. It was time to try "uncivilized America."

The voyage was uneventful nautically and tense politically. In the Canary Islands, where the fleet stopped for water, Smith was accused of plotting a takeover and arrested. That he actually planned to "murder the Council and make himself king" is unlikely to the point of being preposterous. What probably happened is that Smith the soldier forgot his common origins and offended with impertinent suggestions one or more of the aristocrats who commanded the company. Tempers flared again when the fleet touched land in the West Indies; only the intercession of the fleet commander, Admiral Christopher Newport, saved Smith from the gallows. It was probably Newport too who set him free when the three vessels arrived at last in Chesapeake Bay. The shower of arrows that greeted the first landing party doubtless convinced the bluebloods that a man with military experience, even a commoner, might be of value. The tension nonetheless portended ill for the colony and for Smith.

Clash of Cultures

To the native residents of Virginia, the tiny squadron of ships was neither surprise nor mystery. A party of Indians, possibly scouts or fishermen, spotted the sails as soon as they rounded Cape Henry. Wilderness telegraph informed Powhatan within hours; his scouts carefully monitored the English progress up the river. Nor were the ships an unfamiliar sight. Several explorers had peeked into Chesapeake Bay in past years. One or two, including the tall roughneck who abused the Rappahannocks, had made landings. Powhatan also knew of the spurious Roanoke Colony on the North Carolina coast. He even hinted at one point in his talks with Smith that a couple survivors of the "lost colony" were living among his people.

Powhatan regarded the English not as gods but as invaders. He wanted to know how many there were and how long they planned to stay. Until he gained this intelligence, Powhatan prudently bided his time. Others were less patient, among them the tribe that owned the finger of land that the English took for their village. That tribe became an early and unforgiving foe of the Jamestown colonists.

Pocahontas, on the other hand, was more tolerant of the strangers. In her a natural curiosity blended with youthful innocence and friendly disposition. "God made Pocahontas," John Smith declared in later years. It can certainly be said that no being ever worked harder in the cause of harmony among people.

She was born in 1596 or 1597, about the time that John Smith was going to the "university of war," the Netherlands. Her father, who originally had gone by the name of Wahunsonacock, had become chief of the Powhatan tribe some twenty years earlier. Shortly after his accession, Wahunsonacock took for his own the name of the tribe and began a policy of imperial expansion. He conquered neighboring clans and annexed their lands. Peoples too large to be absorbed were placed under subjection, often with one of Powhatan's brothers or sisters as titular head, or werowance. By the time Pocahontas was born, Powhatan's hegemony extended from the Potomac River to the Carolina capes.

We know nothing of her mother. One of Powhatan's first actions upon taking office was to decree polygamy for the tribe. He himself took many wives, though most lasted only a short time before being given to someone else. And we know little of Pocahontas's girlhood other than the clues implicit in her names. Like all the Powhatans, she had both a public and a secret (or spiritual) name. Pocahontas, the public name conferred by her father, was translated by John Smith as "little wanton one." It suggests a sprightly personality, playful, a bit adventurous. Her secret name was Matoax (or Matoaca), "Little Snow Feather." A lithe girl comes instantly to the imagination, clad perhaps in the ceremonial gown of a princess, tanned buckskin decorated with goose feathers. (The Canada goose, which wintered in the Chesapeake marshes, was an important feature of the Indian economy.)

Her entry into the historical record lends substance to either name. While Powhatan's scouts crept furtively through the woods, gathering information on the armed strangers who had landed on their shores, Pocahontas marched boldly into the settlement. One English diarist described her in prepubescent nakedness doing cartwheels with three of the ships' cabin boys. When adults approached her, she placed her left hand over her heart and raised her right in sign of greeting. The colonists took the gesture to mean, "I am your friend" or "I speak the truth." She soon discovered John Smith, or, most likely, Smith approached her. His eastern adventures had taught him the value of interracial communication, and Smith seems to have had a knack for languages. From her he learned a rudimentary Powhatan vocabulary, and rather quickly at that. When he began his explorations of Virginia in the fall of 1607, there is no indication that he had any difficulty communicating with the Indians. He in turn taught her some English words and gave her "jewells," probably trinkets brought over especially for Indian trade. The two became fast friends, though never more than that. Smith's attitude toward her seems to have alternated between avuncular tenderness and brotherly playfulness. She may have been more involved romantically—there is a hint to that effect in her behavior when they met years later in England—but they were never lovers.

In any case, the friendship certainly benefited Smith, especially when Powhatan captured him and put him to the trial/initiation death test. And their friendship benefited the entire colony. Unaccustomed to the climate and inexperienced in planting colonies, the English were in trouble from the start. Hunger and disease stalked the colony. The London Company had never intended that its Virginia plantation be a farming community; it was to be a trading post, a way station on the route to the Orient. Nor did any of its settlers know much about farming or have the initiative to learn. Hired by the London Company to engage in the venture, the typical Jamestown settler was much like the average recruit into the English army: "out of work and rather ne'er-do-well."

The intent of the London investors was to keep the colony supplied from England. Unfortunately, most of the food was consumed on the voyage over, and the first relief supply did not arrive until January 1608. Weakened by hunger, the colonists succumbed one by one to malaria and other fevers borne by the mosquitoes that swarmed in the tidal swamps. Half of all the English people who went to Virginia in the early years died within a few weeks after their arrival. Small wonder that Powhatan regarded the Indians as a superior people, or that he might view Jamestown as a potential "colony" of his own.

Because of her frequent visits to Jamestown, Pocahontas was aware of the colonists' plight, and she did her best to help. She told Smith which of the tribes in her father's confederacy were the least unfriendly, and thus helped direct his summer foraging expeditions. When the Indians' corn crop matured in September, she persuaded some of her people to bring their surplus into the fort. Her half-brothers, werowances of small clans along the river, sold Smith corn, fish, and wild game. Summarizing his experiences ten years later, Smith flatly declared that Pocahontas was "the instrument" that saved the colony "from death, famine, and utter confusion."

The Rule and Ruin of Captain John Smith

Smith exaggerated, for no outside instrument could have saved that particular band of Englishmen from confusion. Government by a council of twelve was an awkward method at best, and the characters named to the council by the London Company ensured divisiveness and intrigue. The President of the Council, Edward Maria Wingfield, was a haughty aristocrat possessed of neither charisma nor common sense, two essential qualities of leadership. With a few exceptions his eleven associates, gentlemen all, varied from helpless weaklings to ambitious schemers.

Being gentlemen, the members of the council did not expect to have to work, and the rest of the settlers followed their example. Two months after Admiral Newport's ships returned to England, no houses were completed and no land was tilled. Wingfield did not even erect a fort for fear of offending the Indians. A few enterprising souls scoured the woods for nuts and berries, but most were content to sit around and consume the dwindling stores left by Newport. That such a group survived at all was due more to Indian forbearance than God's mercy, since it seems unlikely that God would have taken special interest in so contentious and self-centered a band of mortals.

John Smith, whose credentials as a gentleman were weak at best, had little standing among other members of the council, but his courage and vigor soon commanded attention. It was Smith, partly through the intercession of Pocahontas, who first opened trading relations with the Indians. And it was Smith who first explored the river on which they resided and the Chesapeake Bay. The exploration was demanded by the London Company, whose main hope for profit rested on the discovery of either gold or the Northwest Passage to the Orient. (The notion of a waterway across the continent was not as absurd as it seems. For all the English knew, the entire continent was as slim as the Isthmus of Panama where the Spanish explorer Balboa first glimpsed the "South Sea.")

His tour of the upper reaches of the James River led to his capture and ordeal at the hands of Powhatan. On his first expedition up Chesapeake Bay he discovered and explored the Potomac River. On a second expedition in the summer of 1608 he reached the mouth of the Susquehanna River at the head of the bay. There he encountered and somehow overawed a tribe of "giants," who spoke an utterly foreign tongue and traveled by birchbark canoe. (The Susquehannocks, many of whom reached seven feet in height, spoke an Iroquoian language.) Working through an interpreter, Smith mined them for geophysical intelligence. They spoke of "a great water beyond the mountains," which Smith took to mean (correctly, of course) a great lake or perhaps a broad river, rather than the Pacific Ocean. The intelligence, in any case, seems to have discouraged further search for a Northwest Passage.

Smith capped his diplomatic initiative with an exchange of goods, swapping beads for an assortment of spears and tomahawks. On the way home he displayed his weapons collection at various stopovers, giving the impression that it was the spoils of battle. The Virginia Indians, who lived in dread of the ferocious Iroquois, were duly impressed. Hastening to align themselves with so redoubtable a warrior, they offered food and friendship. Loaded to the gunwales with corn, Smith returned to Jamestown on September 7, 1608. His six-week tour of the bay was a blazing success. He had mapped the colony's environs and neutralized its neighbors, at least for the moment. And he had a precious stock of grain for

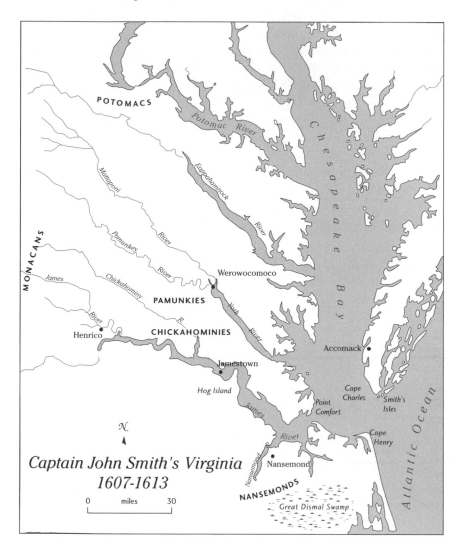

POTOMACS

Potomac River

Chesapeake Bay

Mataponi

Rappahannock

River

MONACANS

Pamunkey

River

River

Werowocomoco

James

Chickahominy

PAMUNKIES

R.

Henrico

River

CHICKAHOMINIES

York

River

Accomack

Jamestown

Hog Island

Cape
Charles

Smith's
Isles

Point
Comfort

James

River

Cape
Henry

Atlantic Ocean

𝒩

▲

Captain John Smith's Virginia
1607-1613

Nansemond

Nansemond

0　　miles　　30

NANSEMONDS

Great Dismal Swamp

the winter. The council rewarded him by electing him president; for the next year Smith ruled the Virginia colony.

Smith's first task was the care and handling of Christopher Newport, who had returned that same month, September, 1608, with the "second supply." Of supplies Newport had brought little, though the colony was in dire need of food, clothing, and tools. Instead, he brought seventy more mouths to feed, twenty-eight of whom were gentlemen with neither the skills nor temper for survival in the wilderness. Of even greater burden, in the short run, were new instructions Newport brought from the London Company. He was ordered to resume the search for gold and/or a passage to the South Sea. Smith had already satisfied himself that there was no access to the Pacific from Chesapeake Bay and that gold was not available in commercial quantities. He scoffed openly at the three-piece barge that Newport proposed to carry across the mountains to a westward-flowing river, but he could do nothing to deter the visionary admiral. While Newport cruised futilely around Chesapeake Bay, alienating Indians with his importunities, Smith put the colonists to work sawing lumber, shingles, and barrel staves, so the supply ship would have some sort of cargo for the London Company. If the London merchants were not satisfied with such mundane returns on their imperial venture, they had only themselves to blame.

Equally silly—and in Smith's view more damaging—were the company's instructions to give Powhatan a royal crown. The London investors evidently hoped to co-opt Powhatan by making him a prince of the empire. Smith feared it would only inflate his ego and raise the price of corn. Told of the impending award, Powhatan insisted that the ceremony be held in his own capital. His reply to Smith was quite revealing:

> If your king have sent me presents, I also am a king, and this my land. Eight days I will stay to receive them. Your father [Captain Newport] is to come to me, not I to him; nor yet to your fort: neither will I bite at such a bait.

The English obliged and journeyed up to the York River for the occasion. Melodrama quickly yielded to low comedy. Smith described the scene: Powhatan accepted the gifts, "but a foul trouble there was to make him kneel to receive his crown. He, neither knowing the majesty nor the meaning of a crown, nor bending of the knee, endured so many persuasions, examples, and instructions, as tired them all. At last, by leaning hard on his shoulders, he a little stooped, and Newport put the crown on his head." As with his earlier encounter with Powhatan, Smith again misjudged his man. Powhatan knew full well the significance of kneeling to receive a crown, and he was not going to go along with it.

Newport departed for England with the supply ship a few weeks later, leaving Smith to cope with his strong-willed neighbor. In command of the colony at last, Smith instituted his own Indian policy. He kept Powhatan off balance and at peace by a mixture of friendly gestures and quick reprisals for wrongdoing. He kept close control of the corn trade, hoarding his dwindling supply of copper trinkets and beads, and he made sure that no firearms fell into Indian hands. He also exchanged hostages with the Indians as security against surprise attack. But psychology remained his best weapon. On one occasion that winter some Chickahominies, who were sociable but light-fingered neighbors, stole a pistol. Smith promptly arrested two of the tribe, who turned out to be brothers. He put one in jail and sent the other to retrieve the pistol, threatening to hang the incarcerated one if the weapon was not returned within twelve hours. Because the weather was chill, the prisoner was allowed a fire in the tightly closed jail, and by morning he was unconscious from the fumes. His brother, who had returned on time with the missing pistol, set up a howl. Smith, though he was not sure how far gone his prisoner was, promised to revive the "dead" one if the Chickahominies would end their thievish ways. Smith then brought his prisoner around with a good dose of brandy, too liberal a dose, as it turned out, for the frightened warrior woke up so drunk "that he seemed lunatic." This distressed his brother even more, so Smith extracted further promises of good behavior before agreeing to restore his prisoner's sanity. He then put his prisoner to bed and let him sleep it off.

Word of Smith's magical powers spread swiftly through the piney woods. For months thereafter stolen goods were returned as soon as the loss was discovered. Thieves—including some who stole from other Indians—were brought to Smith for judgment. So long as Smith remained in charge of the colony's foreign policy, the two races remained generally at peace. Yet he laid the groundwork for future trouble. Realizing that one of the reasons for the colony's high mortality rate was its compact population, Smith set out to disperse the colonists. In early 1609 he founded a settlement at the falls of the James, not far from Powhatan's home village. This contravened the arrangement Powhatan thought he had made with Smith—to keep the English confined to one community within his realm. By mid-1609, even before Smith departed for England, the Powhatans were attacking the settlers whenever they found them in isolated groups.

In domestic affairs Smith seemed equally effective, but again only in the short run. Unwillingness to work had been the colonists' chief fault from the beginning. The London Company was in part to blame. It retained title to all lands, treating the colonists as mere employees; they labored for the company's profit, taking their necessities from a common storehouse. Instead of imperial drive, the company got communal sloth.

When food supplies were gone they bought corn from the Indians. Some colonists even sold their weapons and clothing for Indian corn, a short-sighted behavior doomed to disaster.

After Admiral Newport departed, Smith assembled the Jamestown settlers and told them they had to work or starve. He himself would keep the keys to the storehouse; only the "honest and industrious" would get to eat. Then he divided the colonists into work bands. Some cleared ground for spring planting, others prepared tar and pitch for shipment home. Smith also erected a blockhouse on the neck that connected Jamestown island with the mainland so he could monitor the Indian trade. By the spring of 1609 some forty acres of land were cleared. Three pigs brought in on the ships had multiplied to sixty and were housed on an island of their own, named, appropriately enough, Hog Island. The colony at last seemed to have some prospect of success.

Smith's rule was not without its troubles, however. In early summer it was discovered that some of the corn purchased the previous autumn from the Indians had spoiled, probably because it had been stored before fully dried, and rats had eaten much of the rest. Until late-summer harvest, the colony had to subsist on berries and herbs garnered from the forest. Hunger shortened tempers and spurred discontent. Smith suppressed at least one mutiny that summer and threatened to hang anyone who tried to escape in the colony's lone fishing vessel. Somehow he hung on until a new supply fleet rode into the river on August 11, 1609.

The supply of 1609 represented a prodigious effort by the London Company. Earlier that year the company had obtained a new charter from the king, one that clarified the colony's boundaries and sharpened the company's authority. Then, responding in part to a lengthy critique of its policies which Smith had sent back with Newport in 1608, the company reorganized the government of Virginia. For the unwieldy council it substituted a governor with full powers, appointed by the company. The new governor was Sir Thomas Gates, a professional soldier with experience in the Netherlands. Beneath him was a chain of command. Second in line was Sir George Somers, designated Admiral of Virginia, and third was Smith, who was put in charge of land defenses. To be placed so high in the hierarchy (two knights, as designated by "Sir," inevitably stood above him), was a signal honor for Smith, and indicated the company's growing respect for his leadership. Technically, it was a comedown from his current rank of "president," but he had obtained that position only by the accidental death or departure of all other members of the council.

Given a chance, he would certainly have accepted the new order of things.

Bad luck intervened. The company had put together a fleet of nine ships that spring with more than 500 prospective colonists, including the first sizable batch of women. In mid-Atlantic a tropical storm scattered the fleet, damaging ships and ruining provisions. The flagship, carrying Gates, Somers, and several other officers of the colony, became wrecked on Bermuda, thereby giving Britain a claim to that island paradise. It took the governor nine months to build a new ship from the wreckage and renew his voyage to Virginia. The remainder of the fleet straggled into Jamestown in August. Instead of supplies, they dumped on the sick and hungry colony a new burden of sick and hungry travelers.

The London Company's instructions of 1609 were stranded on Bermuda with its governor. The new arrivals could tell Smith only that he had been deposed. New administrators were on the way. Smith obligingly turned over the reins of power and retired into the wilderness. He purchased some land from the Indians at the falls of the James and started building a house. But fate again intervened. A sack of gunpowder blew up on him accidentally, burning him badly. As he lay abed tending his wounds, a cabal of enemies (old mutineers and ambitious newcomers) tried to murder him. That stunt and his need for medical attention changed his plans. In October, 1609, he sailed for England and never again returned to Virginia. But, by an ironic twist, ill chance was also his good fortune. Nine-tenths of those he left behind in Jamestown failed to survive the winter.

Tragic Rebecca

Before surrendering power Smith told the colonists the only way they could survive was to spread out and live like Indians, hunting, fishing, growing corn, and picking berries. Powhatan felt betrayed, and before Smith left the colony his warriors began attacking isolated settlements. The massacres were so sudden and so widespread that they must have been coordinated by Powhatan's war council. Seventeen men from the Nansemond settlement south of the James went in search of food and were never seen again. The outpost at the falls came under attack and had to fight its way back to Jamestown, losing another eleven. Any who sneaked out of Jamestown to trade for corn disappeared, only to turn up later floating in the river, their throats stuffed with bread. A band of fifty armed men was sent to Powhatan to negotiate a truce and purchase corn; sixteen returned. The leader was captured, strapped naked to a tree, and lived long enough to see his flesh scraped off his bones with clamshells.

Confined to their island, the colonists could not hunt or fish. When the corn that Smith had planted gave out, they lay down and starved. By spring the population of the settlement had shrunk from 500 to 60. The survivors were preparing to abandon the whole enterprise when Gates, Somers, and the others finally sailed in from Bermuda. Gates persuaded the group to stay, and they held on until summer brought a new supply and a new governor, Thomas West, Lord De La Warr.

La Warr reimposed some discipline in the colony and even managed an occasional counterattack. But for two bloody years, the war—Powhatan's War the settlers came to call it—dragged on. Pocahontas, in the meantime, had been forbidden to traffic with the invaders, and after Smith's departure, she probably had little motive to visit Jamestown in any case. The massacres of 1609 drove a wedge between her and her father, however, and in early 1610 she went to live with the Potomac tribe. There she took under her protection a young English hostage, originally planted among the Potomacs by Smith, and since isolated by the war.

In September of that year, Captain Samuel Argall blundered into the Potomac River after becoming lost in the bay. The peaceful Potomac Indians treated him well, and Argall carried back to Jamestown the story of Pocahontas's most recent service to the colony. Governor La Warr sent the story to England, along with a glowing account of the commercial potential of the Potomac Valley. Since it was the only good news to come out of Virginia that year, the London Company rebroadcast the Pocahontas story in England as part of its efforts to attract new colonists. Though the young Indian woman did not know it at the time, it marked the beginning of a new career for her—that of propagandist for the Virginia colony.

The company sent over more reinforcements in the summer of 1611 and yet another governor, Sir Thomas Dale. A professional soldier, Dale turned the colony into an armed and disciplined camp. When Indians attacked a settlement he retaliated by burning their homes and cornfields. In early 1612 Dale even succeeded in establishing a branch settlement (Henrico) at the falls of the James. It was clear, even to Powhatan, that the invaders could not be controlled, as he had hoped. Yet the fighting went on.

Desperate for peace, the near-bankrupt London Company suggested kidnaping Indian children to use as hostages. The idea lay quietly for some months, fermenting in its own malignancy, and then someone in Virginia thought of seizing Pocahontas. The scheming Captain Argall was sent to carry it out.

Sailing into the Potomac in April, 1613, Argall met secretly with the chief of the Potomac Indians. As Pocahontas's host (and hence responsible to Powhatan for her safety), the chief was understandably leery of the abduction scheme. He was no friend of Powhatan, however, and when Argall promised him help in the event of trouble—and the threat that he would make an enemy of the English if he did not cooperate—the peace-loving chief yielded. With a copper kettle "and some other less valuable toys" Argall bribed two warriors to lure Pocahontas onto his ship. He then sent a messenger to tell Powhatan that his favorite daughter was in English hands.

Her father's response must have disappointed Pocahontas. Governor Dale demanded an end to the war, a return of captives, and a "great quantity" of grain. Powhatan sent instead a few Englishmen that he held captive and a canoe full of corn, and declined any further communication. The fighting, though more and more desultory, went on. Powhatan clearly felt that his daughter was in no real danger. The English could not afford to harm her without losing their bargaining chip. It was a stalemate.

Almost. There was one other factor that neither side had reckoned—the flexible amiability of Pocahontas herself. Governor Dale housed her with the Reverend Alexander Whitaker, a minister of the English church, who had a hundred-acre farm near Henrico. Encouraged by Dale, whose system of discipline for the colony included a strict moral code and compulsory church attendance, Reverend Whitaker acquainted her with the Anglican ritual. Pocahontas already had a small English vocabulary, taught her by Smith. She now memorized the Apostle's Creed, the Lord's Prayer, and the Ten Commandments—with what comprehension we will never know. After versing her in the short question-and-answer series of the Anglican catechism, Whitaker in the spring of 1614 baptized her in the fellowship of the Church of England and renamed her Rebecca.

Pocahontas's conversion to Christianity was the culmination of her nearly life-long effort to bridge the races. Her new commitment shows a remarkable capacity to adapt to a wholly alien culture. The gesture was the more ennobling because it meant she had to abandon forever her father, her friends, and her former life. That it made her more useful to the English as a pawn in the chessgame of colonization she never fully comprehended.

Soon after her conversion, Pocahontas cemented her allegiance to the invading race by marrying John Rolfe, a neighboring planter. A survivor of the Bermuda shipwreck, Rolfe had come to Virginia in 1610. He was of genteel family in England, with modest wealth and apparent West Indies connections. He early developed an interest in tobacco as a marketable crop, and, discovering that the tobacco grown by Virginia Indians was too harsh for English palates, he began experimenting with seeds brought from the West Indies. In June, 1613, he sent the first shipment of his "West Indies" tobacco to London. Its success meant, at long last, an economic foundation for the colony.

A middle-aged widower, Rolfe soon became infatuated with Pocahontas, who was then in her eighteenth year. They met at first in church and then in the fields, where Pocahontas showed him how to cultivate, trim, and deworm tobacco. Rolfe bore all the usual English prejudices against "savages," but he rationalized his desire with the notion that he was aiding in her religious regeneration. After the baptism ceremony Rolfe wrote to Governor Dale for permission to marry, and Dale, recognizing the strategic value of such a match, readily agreed. Pocahontas too was willing. She had been well treated by the English, she told her father in a special message, and she planned to live among them ever after.

Powhatan, to everyone's relief, also gave his approval; he even agreed to make peace. Powhatan may have been searching for just such a face-saving opportunity. His force of warriors, never very numerous, was becoming depleted, and the fighting had disrupted Indian agriculture. By 1614 his people were forced to purchase corn from the Virginians. The turnabout further enhanced the status of the whites, whom the Indians had long scorned for being unable to grow their own food.

The wedding ceremony took place on April 5, 1614, in the Jamestown church, decorated for the occasion with wildflowers. Powhatan himself did not attend, but he sent his brother to give the bride away. Governor Dale, ever alert to strategic advantage, offered to marry Powhatan's other daughter, but the aging monarch declined. It was not brotherly, he said, "to desire to bereave me of two of my children at once." In the same message, however, he promised peace and abandoned any hope of incorporating Jamestown into his realm. "I am now old," he said, "and would gladly end my days in peace, so if the English offer me injury, my country is large enough, I will remove my self farther from you."

The London Company also saw advantage in the marriage. Londoners' image of Virginia as a beleaguered outpost in a hostile wilderness had long hindered the company in its efforts to attract capital and colonists. Pocahontas's conversion and marriage signified not only peace, but the fact that Indians could be converted, tamed, and made into useful citizens of the empire. It promised a new day for Virginia, and the London Company, teetering as ever on the edge of bankruptcy, hastened to make the most of it.

In 1616 the company sponsored a home leave for Rolfe, "his new convert and consort," and their infant son, Thomas. Rebecca, as she was to be known in England, took with her a small entourage of Indian relatives and one of Powhatan's councillors, Tomocomo. Still trying to gain information about the long-range threat to his people, Powhatan gave his agent a long stick and told him to cut a notch in it for each person he saw in England. Tomocomo took a look at one of London's bustling streets and abandoned his census.

Lord De La Warr himself took the Rolfes under his care. They were feasted by the Bishop of London and introduced to the king. Inviting them to attend a play in his company, King James saw that they were seated in a position of honor. Crowds of the curious attended Rebecca everywhere she went. For her, though, the dramatic highpoint of the trip was a meeting with John Smith. Having supposed him long dead, she was taken quite by surprise when they met at Brentford near London. Her first reaction was anger that he had not kept in contact. But she also reminded him that he and the Virginia colonists had not kept their part of the bargain he had made with her father in the death-and-resurrection scene of 1607. It was a severe reprimand, and Smith missed the point as usual. He treasured the encounter to the end of his life. Smith sailed soon after on another voyage to America, and they never met again.

After a few months in England, her health began to fail. Exposed to an alien climate and bacteria for which she had no natural defense, she lost strength and vitality. It was pneumonia, perhaps, or tuberculosis— both would kill thousands of Indians in the centuries to come. In March, 1617, the Rolfes prepared to return to America in hopes that in her native country she might recover. While they waited for their vessel at Gravesend, near the mouth of the Thames, her condition suddenly worsened. Seeking to comfort her grieving husband, she reminded him that "all must die. 'Tis enough that the child liveth." Then, at the age of twenty, she died. Young Thomas Rolfe did live, became a wealthy planter in his own right, and fathered numerous progeny, whose descendants would come to boast of their Indian blood. Her son was Rebecca's ultimate triumph.

Pocahontas (1596?–
1617). This portrait of
1616, rendered during
her brief sojourn in En-
gland, reflects her dream
that the white and red
races coexist in harmony.
Given the Christian name
Rebecca after her conver-
sion, she presented herself
to the artist in the garb of
an English gentlewoman.
(Courtesy of State His-
torical Society of Wisconsin.)

Promoter of Empire

The London Company approved of John Smith's administration of its
Virginia colony. The company followed his advice in devising its future
policy, and it had even placed him in charge of colonial defense. When
he appeared in London, however, in the fall of 1609, accompanied by
complaints of his behavior in Virginia, company officials had second
thoughts. Outspoken to a fault, Smith showered the company with a mixture of advice and criticism. As conditions in Virginia improved under
Governor Dale, the company's directors felt less indebted to Smith, and
they increasingly resented his low-born presumptuousness.

Yet Smith persisted. The Virginia experience had changed his life.
The cause of New World empire fired his imagination. He devoted the
next few years (during which his source of income was as mysterious as
ever) assembling all the available accounts of Virginia (including his own),
its landscape, climate, and native peoples. Published in 1612, *The Description of Virginia* was a geographical and ethnological triumph, and

it was also a priceless piece of propaganda which—together with Pocahontas's conversion and marriage—helped to reverse the common Englishman's view of the New World.

It also brought Smith to the attention of colonial promoters, among them the leaders of the Plymouth Company, which had tried to settle "northern Virginia" (New England) at the same time that Jamestown was founded. With their backing, Smith in 1614 again found himself sailing westward, in command of a fleet of three ships with the ambiguous mission of finding whales and gold. Smith never had much hope for finding gold in North America (if he mentioned the possibility it was probably only to win financial backing), and after an ineffectual attempt to harpoon a whale he settled into the main business at hand—exploring. He sailed along the northern coast, mapping with precise detail every cove and headland. As was his custom, he pinned a name on every physical feature he mapped, but, ironically, none of the names stuck, except the one he gave to the region as a whole—New England. Then he paused to hunt and fish along the shore in order to bring home cargo enough to pay the costs of the voyage.

Because of the treachery of one of his captains, who carried his load of fish to Spain, Smith's cargo did not fully reimburse the Plymouth adventurers. But his enthusiastic description of the New World's potential for fish and furs encouraged the investors to name him Admiral of New England and send him on another cruise.

This voyage turned out less satisfactorily. He was intercepted in mid Atlantic by a fleet of French warships. While Smith was aboard the French flagship showing his credentials (the two nations were not then at war), his pusillanimous crew slipped away and fled for England. Once again Smith was a captive, this time on a French man o' war. He eventually escaped (again with the aid of a mysterious woman who appears only as a name in his account of the affair) and made his way back to England. In the meantime, he made good use of his idle moments in captivity by committing to paper his discoveries of the previous year. His *Description of New England* was published in 1616.

Like his earlier work on Virginia, this piece played a major role in drawing the attention of Englishmen to the New World. Among those who read it was a tiny band of religious exiles in Leyden, Holland. Convinced that New England was the only safe haven for their peculiar form of Puritan faith, the Pilgrims rented a ship (the *Mayflower*) and sailed for the New World in 1620. Hearing of their plans, Smith offered the Pilgrims his services. They chose instead for military adviser Captain Miles

Standish, another professional soldier with experience in the Netherlands. It was a wise choice, for Smith, who had only a perfunctory acquaintance with religion, would not have been sympathetic to the Pilgrims' utopian dreams. Nor was he one to follow the lead of others.

The *Mayflower*, as it turned out, was Smith's last chance for New World adventure. In November, 1620, just as the Pilgrims were coming in sight of the Massachusetts coast, King James granted the northern portion of North America to the newly created Council for New England. This cabal of wealthy merchants and landed grandees had its own plans for the region, and it quickly dismissed the advice of John Smith.

Smith spent most of the next ten years in London, searching for backers of new expeditions, and intermittently putting together his entire life story. An anthology of earlier writings glued together with autobiographical detail, this work appeared in 1624 under the title *The Generall Historie of Virginia, New England, and the Summer Isles.*

As much promotional effort as it was history, the *Generall Historie* stressed the glorious potential of North America; it needed only industrious colonists and wise administration. The book reflected Smith's own considerable experience in the field of colonization, but it was also an implied criticism of the policies of the London Company. It thus added immensely to the difficulties of the company, already staggering under the impact of renewed Indian war. In 1622, Opechancanough, Pocahontas's uncle and Powhatan's successor, staged a coordinated uprising that nearly wiped out the Virginia colony. In 1624, King James I, who had never liked tobacco anyway, dissolved the company and put Virginia under royal control.

The *Generall Historie*, though denounced by nearly all who had participated in the founding of Virginia (no one had escaped Smith's scathing criticism), established at last Smith's reputation as a writer. Characteristically, he entered upon his new career with prodigious energy. Within the next three years he published three more books, variously titled "Grammars" and "Dictionaries," all of them practical handbooks for soldiers and sailors. Then, in 1630, he published his complete autobiography, *The True Travels, Adventures, and Observations of Captain John Smith in Europe, Asia, Africa, and America, from Anno Domini 1593 to 1629*. Here the world learned for the first time how his Turks' heads insignia originated, and of his adventures as Mediterranean pirate and Tartary slave. So incredible was his story that no one was sure what was fact and what fancy. Like his earlier accounts of Virginia, there is much in his life story that is exaggerated, including his own role in history. Yet there is also much that can be verified. Beneath the picturesque fluff of poet-promoter was the hard kernel of an historian.

After the countless adventures and harrowing escapes, Captain John Smith's death was anticlimax. He died peacefully in his bed on June 21, 1631.

SUGGESTIONS FOR FURTHER READING

There are several good biographies of both John Smith and Pocahontas. Bradford Smith, *Captain John Smith* (1953), is noteworthy for its introduction by Laura P. Stryker, the scholar who traced Smith's travels through Europe, locating the placenames, and rehabilitated Smith's reputation as a narrator. Philip L. Barbour, *The Three Worlds of Captain John Smith* (1964), is excellent reading, and Alden T. Vaughn, *American Genesis: Captain John Smith and the Founding of Virginia* (1975), is the most recent study. Students interested in Pocahontas should be wary, for her life has been the subject of much romantic biography. Of the factual details of her life we really know very little. Grace Steele Woodward, a noted authority on American Indians, has done a short sketch entitled *Pocahontas* (1969). Frances Mossiker, *Pocahontas, The Life and Legend* (1976), fleshes the biography with a narrative of the early Virginia colony. J. A. Leo Lemay, *Did Pocahontas Save Captain John Smith?* (1992) provides an historian's recent appraisal of that famous incident. Frederick W. Gleach, an anthropologist, provides fresh insights into Powhatan's thinking and policies in *Powhatan's World and Colonial Virginia: A Conflict of Cultures* (1997).

2

William Bradford: Pilgrim

William Bradford came from the same English yeoman stock as John Smith. He had the same sort of inner drive, the same talent for command. Bradford too was a self-made man. Yet there the similarity between the two ended. Bradford had none of Smith's flamboyance, none of his wanderlust, none of his penchant for violence. In character and personality Bradford and Smith were as different as New England and Virginia.

The Making of a Puritan

England was a troubled land in 1590, the year of Bradford's birth. Queen Elizabeth's military and financial aid to the Netherlands was a drain on England's resources. Angered by the English intervention, Spain declared war in 1588 and sent a naval armada to invade England. The armada was destroyed, but invasion fears lingered. Beggars roamed the countryside; highwaymen stalked the roads. Rapidly rising prices were changing living patterns that had existed for centuries. Profit-minded landlords fenced in their estates, changed crop land into sheep pasture, and sent their surplus workers away. The unemployed drifted into cities, where they often turned to crime.

Not least among the nation's ills was never-ending religious controversy. Under Queen Elizabeth's predecessors, her half-brother Edward and half-sister Mary, England had swung wildly from Protestantism to Catholicism. Elizabeth, though a Protestant herself, sought a compromise when she came to the throne on the death of Mary. Her compromise was essentially a political one, enacted into law by parliament. By law, the Queen was made the head of the church in England, with power to appoint the Archbishops and Bishops who administered it. The Book of Common Prayer—essentially a Roman liturgy translated into English—was established by law as the model for Anglican church services. Every citizen was obliged to attend this state church and to pay taxes for its support.

Some Protestants were not happy with this Elizabethan compromise. To them the Church of England seemed only a variant of the Roman Church, with the Queen, rather than a Pope, at the head. They wanted to make the English Church more Protestant, stripping it of Roman forms and ceremonies. They would eliminate Bishops and Archbishops altogether, deprive the clergy of their colorful vestments, and remove kneeling and the sign of the cross from the Communion service. They desired, in short, a simple church, modeled on the unadorned faith of the earliest Christians; hence they were called Puritans.

Elizabeth rejected all Puritan demands. She would not even let parliament discuss the subject. For the first decade of her reign the Queen kept a tight lid on religious controversy.

Then, in the 1580s, a few years before Bradford was born, a more radical form of Puritanism appeared. Its best-known adherent was Robert Browne. Thus the radicals were called Brownists, or sometimes "Separatists." Influenced by the ideas of the Swiss theologian John Calvin, Brown believed in the doctrine of predestination, the notion that God alone selected the "Saints" and that He did so at the beginning of time. Thus certain individuals were destined, even before they were born, to go to heaven after they completed their earthly existence. And, having been chosen, they would naturally lead upright lives during their brief earthly tenure.

An intense religious experience convinced Browne and his followers that they were among the Chosen, that they were "Visible Saints." And they naturally worried about attending church with sinners. The Church of England, after all, because it embraced everyone in the land, was full of sinners. Indeed, its connection with the state was itself a probable source of pollution. Political appointees pervaded its ranks. The Brownists wanted to withdraw from this worldly institution. They wanted a separate church that was both voluntary and exclusive, confined to Saints.

Elizabeth had spurned her Puritan critics, but the Separatists' ideas were too dangerous to be ignored. They rejected not only the authority of her church, but the authority of her government. Once people began forming voluntary congregations, selecting their own ministers and managing their own affairs, the whole structure of government would crumble. Radical Protestants were already declaring bishops and archbishops superfluous. What might be next—aristocrats? Even a queen?

Elizabeth's government hounded the Separatists relentlessly. Many were jailed, a few were hanged for treason. Browne himself, after months as a fugitive, renounced his faith and returned to the established church. Until Elizabeth's death in 1603, Separatists were few, furtive, and impotent.

Such was the world into which William Bradford was born—insecure and unsafe, held together by force and brutality. His father died when William was a year old. When he was four, his mother, marrying again, sent him to live with his grandfather. That gentleman died two years later, and his mother followed soon after. William spent his adolescence in the care of uncles. These kindly men, though common farmers, saw that he obtained some schooling, though precisely where we do not know. English schools were few and private, the sideline often of some local clergyman. Bradford learned to read and write, but beyond that he had to educate himself. Somewhere, perhaps the clergyman's library, he obtained books. He learned a little Latin, even a bit of Hebrew. He almost certainly read Foxe's *Book of Martyrs*—it was the centerpiece of every English library— that gory recital of Protestant executions in the time of "bloody" Queen Mary. It filled him with a lifelong fear and hatred of the Church of Rome and anything that hinted of popery.

Bradford was twelve when he came into contact with Puritanism. He attended church in a neighboring village, in company with a young friend, and was charmed with the simple Protestant service. The minister, a pleasant, fatherly sort, also filled a personal void in the young man. Every Sunday thereafter, ignoring the protests of his more conventional uncles, Bradford walked twelve miles to attend the Puritan church. At some point he underwent the deeply emotional conversion experience, the miraculous happening that convinced him he was one of the Elect of God. In 1606, when a group of fellow Saints formed a Separate church at Scrooby, a village somewhat nearer his home, Bradford joined them.

The Scrooby congregation, being Separatists, met in secret, usually at the home of William Brewster. Educated at Cambridge, then a hotbed of Puritanism, Brewster was village postmaster, a position that carried considerable prestige. Brewster was in his forties; Bradford attached himself to him, again in a filial sort of way, and the two became lifelong companions. Besides Brewster, the most important member of the Scrooby congregation was John Robinson, another Cambridge graduate. Robinson joined the group as an ordinary member, but before long he became its teacher, a position second to that of minister. When the group moved to Holland, leaving behind its original pastor (who, though a Puritan, was ordained in the Established Church), Robinson was elected minister. Robinson and Brewster, each possessing an extensive library, completed Bradford's education.

The Leyden Exiles

Puritans hoped much from James I when he came to the throne on Elizabeth's death in 1603. As king of the Scots (his accession placed England and Scotland under the same crown) James had gotten along reasonably well with the Presbyterians, a Scottish form of Puritans. On his way south to London, James was intercepted by a group of English Puritans, who presented him with a Millenary Petition, so named because it contained a thousand signatures. The petition asked the king to cleanse the English church of popish manners, such as kneeling and chanting, and to seek a learned clergy that could expound on the Bible. James, seeing where such reforms might lead, flatly refused. "No Bishop, no King," he is said to have replied, meaning that church and state leaned upon one another. James tolerated Puritans, as Elizabeth had, because they at least worked within the framework of the Established Church. But his minions continued to hound the Separatists.

Late in 1606, not long after the Scrooby congregation was organized, government authorities arrested Brewster, fined him for not attending the state church, and deprived him of his postmastership. The punishment was a signal for neighborhood persecution. Separatists, because of their secretive habits, were always objects of suspicion. After Brewster's disgrace, "the prophane multitude" (Bradford's phrase) scorned them on the street by day and spied upon their houses at night.

For some years Separatists had been trickling across the North Sea to Holland, where they received toleration and, because the Dutch Reformed Church was also Calvinist in inspiration, even sympathy. Flight was dangerous, for it was illegal to leave England without permission. But to many it seemed equally dangerous to stay. After all, a person could be jailed for only one crime at a time.

One by one, the Scrooby Separatists sold their property and slipped quietly over to Boston, a nearby port on the North Sea, where they bribed a passage to Holland. Too often unscrupulous ship captains took their money and then betrayed them. Bradford was twice arrested at the gangplank and placed in jail. Not until August, 1608, did he and Brewster, who stayed behind to help the poorest families, make it to Amsterdam.

Toleration greeted the Pilgrims (Bradford's name for the emigrants) in Holland, but so did hunger. They had no skills, except for tilling the soil, and there was no land available in crowded Holland. Eventually they congregated in Leyden, a booming textile center. Clothmaking, at least, was an easily acquired art. Bradford became a weaver of fustian, a cloth made by combining cotton and linen. When he came of age in 1611, he inherited a small bit of property in England. He sold it, bought a small house in Leyden with a loom, and went into business for himself. Two years later he married sixteen-year-old Dorothy May, a fellow exile.

By then the English community in Leyden numbered some 300. Most of its members were well employed, prosperous, and as content as exiles can be. Bradford ascribed the community's happy condition to its pastor, John Robinson. Far more than minister or teacher, Robinson was a born leader, patient and understanding, firm in his principles, yet receptive to new ideas. Influenced in part by the tolerant Dutch, Robinson gradually liberalized Pilgrim church practices.

It was a tenet of Separatist doctrine that the Elect could not take communion with non-Saints, no matter how virtuous they might be, nor could Separatists attend a "false" church, such as the Anglican or Dutch Reformed. This posed some social problems, for there were some in the English community in Leyden who were not Separatists, and the Dutch themselves felt offended by the Separatists' exclusiveness. Robinson eventually ruled that Separatists might, without risking their sanctity, pray or read Scripture with their English and Dutch neighbors, though he held firm on the communion ceremony. Pliability and pragmatism would be the hallmarks of William Bradford's leadership in America. Some of that at least he absorbed from his youthful idol, John Robinson.

The Dutch environment also enriched Bradford's education. Freed from the Spanish yoke, the Netherlands blossomed in the early seventeenth century. Amsterdam became a major commercial and financial center; Dutch painting was the envy of Europe. The Dutch government, republican in form and broadly representative, was a century and a half ahead of the rest of the world. Such an environment could only reinforce the democratic tendencies inherent in the Pilgrims' system of congregational self-government. The whole notion of government by consent of free, responsible citizens, a concept inherent in the Mayflower Compact, owed as much to the Dutch as to the English background of the Pilgrims. And it was a system that Bradford, as governor of the Plymouth Colony in New England, would find comfortable.

The Mayflower Voyage

Life in Holland was not without its difficulties. Not least among them was the problem of maintaining an English identity. The Pilgrim community was shaped in the forge of persecution; amidst the easy tolerance of Holland it began to slip apart. Pilgrim sons went into commerce or the military and never returned. Others, attracted by worldly pleasures, were drawn, as Bradford put it, "by evil examples into extravagant and dangerous courses." Pilgrims worried especially that their children were "in danger to degenerate," as Bradford expressed it. The welfare of the family was central to Puritan thought. The morale welfare of children was a major motive for the Puritan migration to New England. The Pilgrims in bustling, free-wheeling, almost-modern Holland, were the first to feel it.

The outbreak of war in central Europe in 1618 added a new threat. If the fighting widened (it did—into what became known as the Thirty Years' War), the Dutch would almost surely be involved, and there was no guarantee that they could withstand a new assault from their ancient foe, Spain. Neighboring France, newly recovered from a religious civil war, was equally menacing (France did come to dominate the Thirty Years War in its latter stages).

It was time again to move. Not individually, as they had come to Holland, but as a community. The exile had strengthened the religious bonds among them. Gradually the Pilgrim leaders had formed the idea of a model community, a city of the righteous, enjoying God's special favor, showing the way for all humanity. Nowhere in Europe could such an experiment be tried, for it would suffer either ferocious opposition or corrupting assimilation. The lonely wilderness was the proper place, just as it had been for the ancient Jews. The hostile environment would keep the community together and hold it on a righteous course. The thoughts of Bradford, Brewster, and other Pilgrim leaders turned to the New World. In that empty land there was space enough for social experiment.

First, they needed permission. In early 1619 they sounded out the London Company on the possibility of settling in Virginia. The company's treasurer, Edwin Sandys, a London merchant with Puritan sympathies, approved the idea. A batch of well-motivated, industrious colonists was precisely what Virginia needed at that point. Sandys discreetly plumbed the views of the king. James, he learned, would not grant official permission for religious heretics to migrate, but he would not interfere if they made the move quietly and peaceably.

None of this was very reassuring to the exiles. Some (though not Bradford or Brewster) argued that the Virginia colony was a mere extension of England. They would suffer the same religious torment there as they had in Yorkshire. Other fearful souls wondered if the king's half-hearted consent was a "sandie foundation" on which to build a colony. Bradford, who seems to have been willing to take his chances in Virginia, replied that the king's formal approval was no protection in any case, even if it was stamped with a "seal as broad as the house floor," because the king could always revoke it.

Negotiations ate up the better part of a year. Then in early 1620 a London merchant named Thomas Weston turned up in Leyden. Weston was a smooth-talking speculator ever on the lookout for a shilling or a florin. He was longer on promises than on performance, as the Pilgrims were eventually to learn, but at this juncture he had a solution to their dilemma. He advised the Leyden leaders to drop their negotiations with the London Company and form a company of their own. He even offered to organize a consortium of London investors to finance their voyage.

Impressed with Weston's businesslike attitude, the Pilgrims agreed to his proposal. Weston returned to England and began enlisting subscribers to a joint stock company. Most of the seventy-odd "adventurers" were London merchants. None had much interest in the utopian dreams of the Separatists; they looked only for quick and substantial profits. Weston convinced them that the Pilgrims were industrious and frugal enough to exploit and ship home the natural riches of the New World.

In abandoning talks with the London Company the Pilgrims also seem to have abandoned thought of settling in Virginia. New England, isolated and deserted (of Europeans at least) was better suited to their purposes. John Smith's map and *Description* of 1616 was all the guide they needed.

While the Pilgrims sold their houses and packed their belongings, Weston was busy in London. In the spring of 1620 the old Plymouth Company (founded in 1606 along with the London Company for settling Virginia) was reorganized as the Council for New England, and King James confirmed its title to the northern half of North America. Ever the opportunist, Weston appealed to this new council for permission to settle in New England and received a grant. It did not have the status of a patent directly from the king, but it did give the Pilgrims a legal excuse, if not a clear title, for a settlement in New England.

Weston then insisted on renegotiating his agreement with the Pilgrims. Bradford and Brewster grumbled angrily at the new conditions, but they had to accept them or lose their backing. Under Weston's terms the Pilgrims would be mere employees of the joint stock company with no rights of property in New England. Then, if the colony succeeded, after seven years all property would be divided equally between settlers and investors. The arrangement soured relations between the emigrants and the company, but Bradford and his fellows honored the agreement until they found the resources to buy out their canny benefactors.

The new conditions were discouraging, however, and some of the wavering decided not to go after all. Nor did the community have the resources for all to leave at once. So it was decided that the "youngest and strongest part" would pioneer; the rest would come later. Since there was some chance that they would never be reunited, each group was to be an "absolute church" unto itself. John Robinson remained in Leyden with the majority. Ruling Elder William Brewster went with the pioneers. Most of the children were also left behind, among them William Bradford's five-year-old son John. They would be brought over when the American wilderness was at least partly tamed.

Pilgrim leaders then began to worry that the band of emigrants might be too small to survive in the wilderness, so they invited a Puritan congregation in Amsterdam to join them. When this overture failed, the investors panicked and began recruiting in London. The enlistment of "Strangers" to accompany the "Saints" modified considerably the utopian purpose of the voyage and spelled trouble for the future. But again Bradford and his fellows had little choice but to make the best of it.

In the end, the Strangers made up more than half (60 out of 102) of the passenger list on the *Mayflower*. Even many of the Saints were unfamiliar with one another, having been recruited in various parts of Holland. Of the original Scrooby congregation only Bradford, Brewster, and one other person sailed on the *Mayflower*. On the other hand, there were some potentially valuable colonists among the Strangers. One such was Miles Standish, a professional soldier who had signed on as military adviser to the colony. Not one of the ship's passengers, moreover, signed himself "gentleman," a fact that Captain John Smith would have noted with glee. Most were workingmen, artisans, and shopkeepers, the petite bourgeoisie of English society. That in itself saved Plymouth from some of the difficulties that had plagued Jamestown.

The rendezvous for all these groups was Southampton on the English Channel. There the London adventurers had engaged two vessels, the *Speedwell* and the *Mayflower* both veterans of the Atlantic trade. The

Speedwell proved to be hopelessly misnamed; it was slow and leaky. After a couple false starts that wasted much of the summer it was finally abandoned at Plymouth. Some of its passengers went aboard the *Mayflower;* others probably found a convenient excuse to stay home. The *Mayflower* sailed at last on September 6. Good sailing weather had been wasted; it was to be a stormy crossing.

    The *Mayflower* was not a small ship for her day—measuring 113 feet by 26— but she was not built for the load of humanity that jammed her decks. The crew of thirty occupied the forecastle on the main deck; food and drink filled the hold. The only place for 102 passengers to sleep was between decks, and it must have been indescribably crowded. The galley could accommodate only the crew for meals. Passengers had to cook over a small charcoal fire on deck. Most ate their food cold. There was not enough water for bathing and no privacy in any case. Most passengers probably did not change clothes from beginning of the voyage to end. The one blessing was that the *Mayflower*, having previously been involved in the wine trade, was considered a "sweet" ship. Think of the discomfort if its previous cargo had been a load of fish from Norway!

Saints in the Wilderness

On November 9, 1620, the *Mayflower* stood off Cape Cod, its weary throng peering through the evening mists at the clay bluffs of Truro. Two days later, after a hesitant effort to explore the coast, they anchored inside the Cape. No one seems to have had much stomach for further sailing. Since they were outside any known political jurisdiction, they felt it necessary to draw up a governmental agreement among themselves. The resulting Mayflower Compact established a "civil body politic" to pass laws for the general good of the colony, and all signers agreed to obey those laws. Every adult male signed the agreement, including some who were indentured servants (that is, under a contract to work for another for a specified period of years). Thus, the Separatists' democratic method of determining church affairs pointed the way to political democracy in their colony. The male assemblage then elected as governor John Carver, wealthiest of the Leyden emigres. Although the Leyden group was in a minority, it dominated the affairs of the colony from the beginning.

    The next few days were spent repairing a small sailboat (shallop), which they had brought for fishing and trading. It required a good deal of work because, having been stored between decks, it had been used by some as living quarters. While that went on, Miles Standish led a party on foot to explore Cape Cod. Standish came upon a small group of Indians, who promptly ran away. Somewhat farther on he discovered their settlement, a few bark houses and a cornfield. The Pilgrims helped themselves to the Indians' corn, making a mental reservation that they would reimburse the Indians at the first opportunity (they did). They saved the corn for springtime planting.

Within a week the shallop was ready, and they began exploring the coast. Bradford, as one of the "principal men," went on each expedition, though apparently Standish remained in command. By early December they still had not found a site that combined safe anchorage, fresh water, and potential farmland. On December 6 the *Mayflower*'s pilot, who had sailed the coast before, suggested they try a small inlet across the bay from Cape Cod, a spot that John Smith had labeled Plymouth on his map. They sailed the shallop there the next day, braving a wintry storm. The site was not perfect. The soil was as poor and sandy as the Cape, and the harbor was small. Abandoned cornfields nearby suggested that the Indians might already have squeezed from the land what little fertility it had. They decided to take it anyway. Approaching winter had substantially reduced their options.

Bradford returned with the news only to find tragedy on the *Mayflower*. His wife Dorothy had either jumped or fallen from the ship and was drowned. What happened exactly we shall never know, but Bradford's reticence on the subject (a single line in his journal) suggests that it may have been suicide—a fit of depression, perhaps, born of the hard voyage, the desolate landscape, and the lowering winter.

They worked the *Mayflower* across the bay to Plymouth, a job that required several more days because of winter gales, and on Christmas day they began the task of building a village. The Separatists had no compunction about working on Christmas, since they regarded it as a holiday nowhere sanctioned in the Bible. Their more conventional associates may have had some misgivings, but they doubtless recognized the need for hurry.

A row of cottages—crude affairs of sticks and bark and mud—sprang up along a footpath that led away from the harbor. Then they built a storehouse for their food, implements, and other belongings. The captain was eager to unload the *Mayflower* so he could start for home, but the building process was slow. Not until March 21 did the last of the passengers come ashore.

The winter was a mild one, by New England standards, but the Pilgrims suffered much from cold and hunger. More than a quarter of them died that winter. No more than a handful of men were available at any given moment for defense. Indians lurked in the woods and occasionally stole implements, but they never attacked. Plymouth was a fortunate location in that respect. The Indian tribe that originally inhabited the site had been wiped out a few years previously by smallpox, a contagion spread among them by European fishermen. Thus—unlike the Jamestown settlers—the Pilgrims did not offend Indian sensibilities by appropriating someone's turf. Their neighbors were more curious than angry. But the colonists also developed, quite by accident, a very valuable friend.

He turned up about March 16, a tall, handsome Indian wearing nothing but a slim loincloth about his waist. He marched boldly into the settlement just as the Pilgrims were holding a meeting on the subject of defense. "Welcome," he said in passable English, told them his name was Samoset, and asked for beer. When the Pilgrims recovered from their surprise at finding an English-speaking native, they scurried around to find him a drink. The ship's beer was gone by then, but they managed to come up with some "strong water" (probably a rum highball).

Samoset, it developed, lived far to the north (in present-day Maine) where he had frequently encountered English fishermen. In addition to teaching him some English they had obviously treated him kindly, for Samoset adored Europeans. He had walked all the way from Maine just to visit Plymouth, and he obviously planned to stay. When night came he showed no sign of departing, and the Pilgrims hastily made a place for him to sleep (though they prudently posted a guard over him through the night).

Samoset told the colonists of their neighbors, the Wampanoags and of Massasoit, their chief. The next morning the Pilgrims sent Samoset off to find a sample warrior or two, and he returned with five Wampanoags. These were sociable enough. After eating they entertained the English with dances and singing. It being a Sunday, the Pilgrims were embarrassed by such frivolity, but they hid their distress. The Indians then offered to trade some deerskins, but the Pilgrims drew the line at that sort of Sabbath breaking. They sent the Indians off in search of more skins, with an invitation to return on the morrow.

When the Indians failed to come back after several days, Samoset was again sent into the woods. This time he returned with the news that Massasoit himself was coming for a visit. He also had in tow an English-speaking friend whom he introduced as Squanto. This gentleman had had a remarkable career. He was a member of the tribe that had originally occupied the Plymouth site. In 1605 an English exploring party picked him up and carried him off to England. He returned to New England in 1614 with Captain John Smith, but he was no sooner reunited with his family than one of the ship captains in Smith's fleet seized him along with about twenty other men and carried him to Spain to be sold into slavery. Squanto somehow escaped and made his way to England, where he lived for a time in London. He returned to America with another exploring party in 1619. His village by then was gone, dispatched by small-pox, so he went to live with the Wampanoags. Yet he must have been impressed by the comfort and quality of European life, for he settled permanently with the Pilgrims. He and Bradford became good friends, and to the end of his life he served Bradford well as Indian emissary. To Squanto, as much as to Bradford himself, can be ascribed the success of the Plymouth colony.

Shortly thereafter Massasoit himself appeared with a gaudily painted retinue. Cautiously he demanded an exchange of hostages to guarantee his safety. The Pilgrims obliged by sending Edward Winslow to his village. Winslow proved to be an able diplomat himself, and for many months Indian relations remained excellent. Indeed, so friendly were the local natives that they became a nuisance. One by one warriors would drop into the settlement for a chat, and they invariably stayed for dinner. The colonists, ever short on food, were torn between hospitality and self-interest. Eventually they asked Winslow to intercede. He gave Massasoit a red coat by way of introduction and then explained the problem. Indians were welcome when they had beaver pelts to trade, but social visits would have to stop. Massasoit was obliging, though Winslow found his lengthy statement "very tedious." Thus the colony became accepted and the world was at peace as spring gave way to summer. After a "hard and difficult beginning"—as Bradford put it—the settlement seemed likely to succeed.

Governor

The Pilgrims had agreed to hold annual elections, a democratic concept that was entirely original. Neither the English nor the Dutch govern-ments dared to risk their mandates with such frequency. On March 25 (New Year's Day under the calendar then in use) the Plymouth colonists reelected John Carver. A few days later he took sick while working in the common corn field and died. The electorate then chose William Bradford its chief executive. He would be reelected annually—except for five years when he begged a respite—until his own death thirty-six years later.

The new regime was in fact a triumvirate. Winslow became, in effect, foreign affairs adviser, and Miles Standish was secretary of war. All three were in their early thirties, all had recently become widowers. None of them—it should be remembered—was a minister. Plymouth originated as a holy experiment, but it was never controlled by the church. Indeed, at this point it did not even have a minister. Church services, though regular and lengthy, were informal, with various persons offering prayers and supplications. Elder Brewster, the best educated of the colonists, delivered most of the sermons. The church was central to the community, but government, throughout the history of the Plymouth colony, was firmly secular.

Spirits rose with the coming of spring. Squanto showed the English how to plant Indian corn. He grouped seeds in small hills (which aided pollination) and fertilized them with dead fish (herring probably, or inedible alewives). And then he posted guards over the cornfields to keep wolves from digging up the fish before they rotted. Bradford himself saw that the shallop was kept busy. As soon as one batch of fishermen came in with a load another group was sent out. No one was allowed to come in empty-handed; they stayed at sea until they caught something. Even John Smith had never achieved such discipline.

During the summer the mud and branch huts were replaced with houses of plank construction, probably under the supervision of John Alden, a carpenter by trade. Thatch was used for roofing, as it was in England; chimneys were of wood fireproofed with clay. By autumn there were eleven houses, four storage buildings, and a church that doubled as a workshop.

When the corn harvest was in, Bradford decreed a day of Thanksgiving. Harvest festivals are as old as humankind, but Bradford may have been reminded by a more immediate model, the Thanksgiving celebrated every October 23 by the people of Leyden in memory of their liberation from Spanish rule. Thankful also that his people could walk "as peaceably and safely in the woods as in the highways of England," Bradford invited the Indians. Massasoit, evidently realizing that this was a suspension of the rule against dropping in for dinner, showed up with ninety hungry warriors. But he was also aware what his throng might do for the colonists' foodstocks and sent his men into the woods after deer. For three days the Pilgrims and their guests gorged on venison, Canada goose, and shellfish, all of it graced with wild plums and dried berries, and washed down with wine made from wild grapes. Miles Standish held a military review, which no doubt held the secondary purpose of impressing the Indians with the Pilgrims' readiness, and athletic contests were held. It all sounds magnificent until one thinks of the cooks and servers. If, as seems likely, these tasks fell upon the women, their struggles must have been heroic. Counting even the teenagers, there were only ten women in the entire colony! Widower Bradford, however, considered the fete such a success that he staged another the following year.

Bradford was quick to learn the symbolism of Indian diplomacy. In the winter of 1621 a leader of the Narragansetts, who resided to the west and south of Plymouth, sent Bradford a gift of several arrows wrapped in a snakeskin. Bradford realized that it was a bid for Narragansett domination of southern New England, including Plymouth (much as Powhatan had claimed with John Smith), and he turned to Squanto for advice. The governor then sent back to the Narragansetts the snakeskin filled with bullets. It was a standoff—and perhaps just as well, for the governor was soon faced with a threat from another direction.

In the spring of 1622 Massasoit warned Winslow that a neighboring tribe, the Massachusetts, was plotting to attack the settlement. Bradford thought to strike first, but he was reluctant to act without consulting his people. On March 23, the day when the colony customarily assembled to resolve disputes and elect officers, Bradford addressed the meeting, outlining the problem and asking for guidance. After some debate the citizenry authorized him to do whatever he felt was necessary, a clear vote of confidence in his leadership.

The plan that Bradford worked out was both simple and effective, though it ill befit a Saint. He sent Miles Standish with eight men to visit the Massachusetts pretending to trade. When the opportunity arose they were to ambush a few as a warning to others. Standish did just what he was told. He and his men killed five Indians, including one of the tribal chiefs whose head Standish brought back to Plymouth. Bradford posted the head on the town fort in the way criminals' heads were displayed on the London Bridge. The action, barbarous though it was, forestalled the Indian conspiracy—if, indeed, one existed at all.

With peace ensured, Bradford turned his attention to the colony's sickly economy. The harvest that year was not a good one, and the colony scraped through a hungry winter. They survived only by keeping the settlement's lone fishing boat constantly at sea with periodic replacement of crew. The root of the problem was obvious enough. So long as each colonist was an employee of the London adventurers, sharing rations from the common storehouse, there was little incentive to work. The Separatists themselves were sufficiently motivated, but the fortune hunters sent over from London were not. Bradford had no authority to distribute parcels of land, but he took it upon himself. In the spring of 1623, after consulting the "chiefest" among the colonists, he gave land to each family, the size of the holding varying with the size of the household.

Free enterprise, not surprisingly, was an instant success. More corn by far was planted that spring than ever before. It was a good thing, too, for in July the ship Anne stood into Plymouth inlet with more mouths to feed, a human cargo of 32 Saints and 61 Strangers. The new arrivals, misled by glowing accounts of Plymouth published in England, were shocked at the skinny frames and shabby attire of the old colonists. Some wept, others threatened to go back home.

Bradford was no more pleased with the aspect of the newcomers. The London adventurers had seemingly scoured the city for hirelings; some were known criminals, others so shiftless that Bradford expected to have to send them back at public expense. But there were some welcome arrivals as well, among them a bride for Miles Standish, wooed and won by mail. And there was Alice Southworth, a member of the Leyden congregation whom Bradford had invited to come to Plymouth after Dorothy died. They were married a month after her arrival, the ceremony conducted by the deputy governor. Separatists considered marriage a civil rite, not an affair of the church.

The summer months were lean since every grain of corn had been planted in the ground. The colonists subsisted on venison and wild berries. But the autumn harvest provided, for the first time, an ample food supply. After a comfortable winter Bradford decided that his job was done. He had been governor for three years; he had seen the colony through its time of troubles. At the spring meeting of 1624 he announced his retirement. He told the colonists to find another governor and advised them to ease that gentleman's burdens by increasing the number of assistants. The colonists, however, would not let him go. It was a powerful tribute, a measure of the extent to which he had grown into the job. Deeply moved, Bradford accepted reelection, together with an expanded council of five assistants.

Throughout Bradford's tenure the government of Plymouth remained as spartan as its church. In addition to governor and assistants there were a clerk, a treasurer, a constable, and a marshal. All service was voluntary until 1639, when the town court at last gave Bradford a salary of £20, to which the various towns were invited to add "what every man shall think meet." The council, consisting of governor (who had a double vote) and assistants, served as executive, legislature, and judiciary. The town had no jail; the care and feeding of an idle prisoner would have been considered a needless expense. Most offenders were simply fined; those guilty of serious offenses were executed. Bradford's own sense of justice and humanity is evident in every page of the court journal. On one occasion he fined a colonist 6 shillings 8 pence for assaulting another, and then fined the victim 5 shillings for provoking him. Bradford could also be harsh when necessary. One young man was convicted of sodomy with a mare, a cow, two goats, five sheep, two calves, and a turkey. The animals were killed before his eyes and thrown into a pit, and then he was hanged. "A sad spectacle it was," commented Bradford, with as much pity perhaps for the animals as for the man.

So good was the corn harvest in 1624 that the Pilgrims sold their surplus to the Indians for furs. Every ship that stopped in the colony was sent back with a load of furs and lumber. Far from being satisfied, the London investors upbraided the colonists for not sending enough. In addition to being "contentious and intolerant," the adventurers accused their employees of being "negligent, careless, wasteful, and unthrifty."

The Plymouth settlers, seeing the profits of their labors go to others, were equally dissatisfied. Thus in 1625 Bradford instructed Miles Standish, who was apparently returning to London for personal reasons, to open negotiations for a new contract. The arrangement was completed the following year when the colonists bought out the London investors for a sum of £1,800, to be paid in annual installments over a period of nine years. It placed a heavy burden on the colony, but it meant freedom. Bradford promptly decreed a new allotment of lands, with each person receiving twenty acres. Cattle and sheep, previously held in common, were distributed by lottery.

Bradford insisted, however, that trade remain a government monopoly until the colony's debts were paid. He also established a branch settlement on Cape Ann to facilitate trade with the Indians. In the next few years other settlements cropped up in the interior. Plymouth's exports expanded steadily. In the years 1631 to 1638, for which statistics are available, the colony shipped almost 14,000 pounds of beaver pelts to England along with 1156 deerskins. London agents cheated the colony at every turn, but the debt to the proprietors was paid off on time.

In the spring of 1628 the Dutch, who had settled on Manhattan some years earlier, addressed a letter to "the noble, worshipful, wise, and prudent Lords" of Plymouth, offering to trade. Bradford replied in Dutch, though his command of it was a bit rusty after nearly ten years. In friendly tone he acknowledged his debt to Holland for having given him sanctuary in "freedom and good content" for so many years. Plymouth, he informed them, was well provisioned with food, but it might be willing to purchase furs.

That, it turned out, was precisely what the Dutch had to sell. A few weeks later Dutch traders appeared in Plymouth with a boatload of beaver. Since they had corn enough of their own, they swapped the furs for Plymouth tobacco. Tobacco had been grown in Plymouth for some years (presumably ever since food shortages ended). The seed probably came from Virginia, though the leaf was hardly of Virginia quality. It suited the Dutch, however. They also persuaded the Pilgrims to take £50 worth of strung shells, or wampum. The Pilgrims at first thought they had been cheated, but they soon discovered that the Indians viewed the shells as currency. Plymouth soon had its own wampum works, probably at Bradford's direction. It greatly eased the fur trade, for it relieved the Pilgrims of carting around bushels of corn. In fact, as the chief source of wampum in New England, the Pilgrims were able to monopolize the fur trade for some years, even after the founding of the Massachusetts Bay Colony. It was one more favor they owed the Dutch.

Saints and Statecraft

By the end of the 1620s the Plymouth colony seemed secure, its holy experiment a success. It was on good terms with its Indian neighbors, the fur trade was flourishing, and it no longer had to suffer insults from London financiers. Still, Bradford worried, and his concern deepened with his advancing years. The Pilgrims began to experience the same problems they had in Holland. Peace and comfort brought their own distractions. The sacred commitment of the first founders melted away; the second generation was more worldly, more perfunctory in its faith. And there were external threats as well. Trespassers settled on lands claimed by Plymouth; interlopers cut into the fur trade. And then in 1630 came a new and gigantic migration from England to settle at nearby Massachusetts Bay. Although relations between the Bay Colony and Plymouth were cordial, on the whole, tiny Plymouth was from the first the junior partner. It stood in constant danger of being absorbed by the wealthy and powerful Bay Colony—as it was some years after Bradford's death. Plymouth's dimming prospects gave Bradford a melancholy old age.

The difficulties with Thomas Morton were a forecast of the future. In 1625 Morton and a Captain Wollaston, partners in the fur trade, settled about twenty-five miles north of Plymouth (the site of the later village of Quincy). Plymouth considered the site part of its own territory, but with a shaky patent of its own it did not feel up to evicting the trespassers. Morton and Wollaston had brought from England a number of indentured servants to work the trading post, but the operation failed, perhaps because servants did not make enterprising trappers. After two years Wollaston gave up and went to Virginia to sell his servants to tobacco planters. Morton stayed on and freed his, and thereafter the settlement prospered. Morton's agents scoured the woods as far as Maine, offering competitive prices for beaver pelts, and cutting into Plymouth's trade. He even sold guns to the Indians to increase their hunting proficiency. Convivial by nature, Morton turned his outpost into an island of gaiety in the frosty wilderness. He erected an eighty-foot-high maypole as a standing invitation to carouse and frolic, and nailed to it a poetical ode to joy of his own composition. Before long tales of "riotous prodigality" reached the ears of the Saints in Plymouth. Morton named his community Mare Mount ("Mountain by the Sea" in Latin), but the pun was not lost upon the Pilgrims, who referred to it as "Merry Mount."

Convinced that God himself would put an end to "ye beastly practices of ye madd Bacchinalians," Bradford did nothing, for the moment, to interfere. But he knew that Plymouth could not long withstand losses in the fur trade, nor suffer the arming of Indians. In a "friendly & neighborly way" he wrote Morton to warn against selling arms and liquor to Indians. When Morton denied wrongdoing, Bradford reminded him that the king had outlawed selling arms to Indians and that Morton risked "His Majesty's displeasure." "The King is dead," Morton replied, reminding Bradford of the recent demise of James I and the succession of his son Charles, "and his displeasure with him."

Convinced that a continuation of this dialogue would make Morton even more "hautie and insolent," Bradford ordered Captain Standish to go arrest him. More prudent than usual, Standish took nine men with him and lurked in the woods until most of Morton's people went off to trade. Then he moved in on Morton and two of his men. What happened next is not clear since accounts differ quite dramatically. Standish claimed that Morton threatened a fight but was too drunk to lift his gun. Morton recorded that he surrendered voluntarily to "Captain Shrimp" in order to avoid bloodshed. Whatever the case—and reality was very likely something quite different from either account—Standish returned to Plymouth with Morton, and Bradford sent the merrymaker back to England on the next ship. Morton turned up again two years later, but this time Bradford had help in his crusade against "joylity," help from the Puritans of the Bay Colony.

The settlers at Massachusetts Bay were religious dissidents like the Separatists at Plymouth, driven from England by the purges of Charles I and his Archbishop, William Laud. They shared with the Plymouth people the Calvinist doctrines of Grace and Election. They differed from the Separatists principally on the issue of separation; they had remained

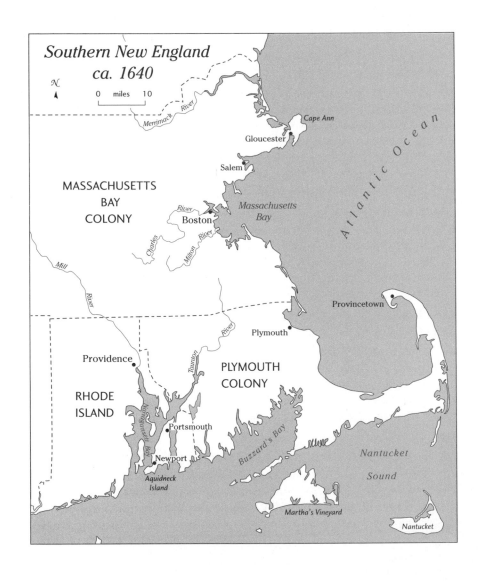

in the Church of England, seeking to purify it from within. Archbishop Laud's purge of Puritan ministers together with growing political opposition to the arbitrary regime of Charles I drove them at last to seek refuge in the New World. But they came with the same utopian dream as the Pilgrims—to set up a "Bible Commonwealth," a godly community that would serve as a model for all humankind.

Bradford did not regard the Bay settlers as trespassers, for their charter of 1629 placed the colony well to the north of any lands claimed by Plymouth. Moreover, since the Bay Colony had obtained its patent directly from the king, it had a better title to its lands than Plymouth did. Bradford was also delighted when the Bay authorities organized their churches on the Congregational model. Actually the Bay Puritans had little choice. They were fleeing the authority of bishops and archbishops; it was logical to let each congregation govern its own affairs. Plymouth leaders, however, took it as an encouraging imitation of their system.

Relations between Bradford and John Winthrop, governor of the Massachusetts Bay Colony, were occasionally strained, but they made a strong effort to cooperate. Though they came from roughly the same part of England, the two men had little else in common. Winthrop was a Cambridge-educated country squire, Bradford a self-made yeoman. Yet Winthrop was quick to recognize Bradford's qualities of character—"discreet and grave" he described him.

In 1634 a murder occurred in one of Plymouth's fur outposts on the Kennebec River. Some time later, when John Alden stopped in Boston on business, Bay Colony authorities arrested him as a suspect, even though the Bay Colony had no jurisdiction in the matter. Bradford promptly sent Miles Standish up to obtain his release, a mistake since Standish was not known for diplomatic skill. Governor Winthrop listened to Standish bluff and bluster for awhile, then released Alden and arrested Standish. Bradford himself finally had to journey up to Boston to smooth things over.

Plymouth profited substantially from the founding of the Bay Colony. It supplied the early settlers with corn and cattle, and the stream of migration to Massachusetts kept farm prices high throughout the 1630s. But the rapid growth of the Bay Colony also created problems for Plymouth and for Bradford. In the middle of the decade several Massachusetts congregations moved west to the Connecticut River, settling on lands that Plymouth considered its own. The westward movement also antagonized the Indians, and by the end of the decade Plymouth found itself for the first time involved in a major Indian War.

The fighting was ghastly, and Bradford joined in without a tweak of

Christian conscience. In 1637 a combined Bay-Plymouth army marched to the main Pequot village on the Mystic River, surrounded it, and put the houses to the torch. As the Pequots fled the fire, the English cut them down. "Those that scaped the fire," wrote Bradford, "were slaine with the sword." The Plymouth governor admitted it was "a fearful sight to see them thus frying in the fryer, and the streams of blood quenching the same, and horrible was the stinck & sente thereof," but he felt nevertheless that the victory was "a sweete sacrifice." The incident may reveal more of European attitudes toward the Native Americans than it does of Bradford's character. It nevertheless can hardly be regarded as his finest hour.

During the 1630s Bradford obtained periodic relief from the burdens of office, but after a vacation of a year or two the voters always restored him to power. After 1640 he no longer resisted, accepting the electorate's annual bestowal as a duty. He may even have come to regard it as a right, as chronic officeholders sometimes do. He worried continually, however, about the future of Plymouth. Hemmed on all sides by more wealthy and populous neighbors, the future of the colony seemed bleak. In 1642 the long-simmering hostility between King Charles and Parliament exploded into civil war. The war, which lasted until Charles was captured and executed in 1649, halted emigration and caused economic distress throughout New England.

Worse than political weakness and commercial distress was Bradford's perception that the second generation of Plymouth colonists did not share the pride, the mystique that had bound the first settlers to one another. In 1648 he set out to remind the young generation of its heritage with "A Dialogue, or the Sum of a Conference between some Young Men, born in New England, and sundry Ancient-men, that came out of Holland and Old England." In a breezy, anecdotal style, designed to appeal to the young, Bradford recounted the story of the Scrooby congregation, the persecution it suffered, and its pilgrimage to Holland and America.

It was an eloquent plea, but it had no discernable effect, if indeed it was read at all by the young. Nor could Bradford derive much comfort from the knowledge that he was not alone in his crusade. To the north the ruling elders of the Bay Colony were also striving to recover the purity and sanctity of the founders. And they were no more successful than Bradford.

As early as 1630 Bradford began writing his monumental *Historie of Plimouth Plantation*, and the project filled his later years. It was both good history and a sermon to the young. It was a candid description of the founding of the colony, but it also sought to place Plymouth, dwindling in political importance, at the center of the worldwide regeneration of mankind. "As one small candle may light a thousand," he wrote, "so the light here kindled here shone unto many, yea in some sort to our whole [English] nation." Although Bradford's *Historie* is one of the finest pieces of literature to come out of colonial America, he himself seems to have felt that it failed in its primary mission—the reformation of the younger generation. He never bothered to have it published, nor took much care to see that it was preserved. After his death it was handed around among various families, and finally became buried and forgotten in a library in England. Not until 1856, two centuries after his death, was it discovered and put into print by the Massachusetts Historical Society.

Bradford worked on his *Historie*, recording events as they happened, until 1648 when he suddenly stopped. The final entries are simply *"Anno 1647. And Anno 1648."* It was a confession of failure, the end of a utopian dream. By then his old companions were gone. Edward Winslow had been attracted back to England by the Puritan revolution against King Charles, and he never returned. Brewster died in 1643, and with him went the communion of Saints that had given Plymouth special meaning. Bradford followed him in 1657, and in 1691 Plymouth itself ceased to exist, absorbed in the royal colony of Massachusetts. Only the Pilgrim tradition—democratic government and religious freedom—lived on.

SUGGESTIONS FOR FURTHER READING

For those with leisure and patience the most rewarding study of Bradford and the Plymouth Colony is Bradford's own history, *Of Plymouth Plantation, 1620–1647*, in any of several editions. The importance of Bradford's history is discussed by Peter Gay in *A Loss of Mastery: Puritan Historians in Colonial America* (1966) and by Andrew Delbanco, *The Puritan Ordeal* (1989). Bradford Smith's *Bradford of Plymouth* (1951), is the best biography. George F. Willison's *Saints and Strangers* (1945) is an entertaining as well as authoritative history of the Plymouth Colony. John Demos' *A Little Commonwealth: Family Life in Plymouth Colony* (1970) presents another side of the story. Collin G. Calloway, *New Worlds for All: Indians, Europeans, and the Remaking of Early America* (1997) provides new insights on Bradford's relations with the Indians.

3

Anne Hutchinson:
The Saint as Critic

Outside the church the air was warm and damp with spring. Daffodils bobbed in the breeze in the churchyard. In the distance sheep munched on the freshening grass of Lincolnshire's hills. The church, named for St. Botolph, was built at the end of the fourteenth century when its parish, the village of Boston, was England's second largest port. And it was a magnificent structure, thought to be the largest in England "which has always been a parish church." Inside the church the minister stood in a massive pulpit (installed especially for him) under a vault that rose to nearly 150 feet. St. Botolph's boasted the highest steeple in Europe.

Despite the magnificent setting, the atmosphere in the church was tense and expectant. From the pulpit, high under the arched ceiling, Vicar John Cotton stood in dark gray robe, preaching without the white, wide-sleeved surplice worn by clergy of the Church of England. He had decided to cast off such Romish trappings, the young vicar was saying, and he would likewise do away with the sign of the cross at baptism and kneeling at communion. It was a daring move, as his congregation well knew, for it risked the displeasure of the princes of the church, the bishops. Indeed, it placed the congregation itself in some danger, for the village of Boston was a notorious center of Puritanism. Was that not the North Sea port from which Separatists had escaped to Holland some seven years before?

The parishioners of St. Botolph's were doubtless willing to accept the risk, for they had invited Cotton to their parish in full knowledge of his growing disenchantment with the Established Church. Cotton had previously been a lecturer in Emmanuel College, Cambridge, a well-known hotbed of Puritanism. Upon making his appointment, the city fathers of Boston felt obliged to soften up the Bishop of Lincoln with an appropriate gift. Even so, the bishop's court kept a close eye on the young maverick. Thus there was danger in his formal announcement of nonconformity, but his conscience required it. Henceforth he would sniff out and expose every trace of Rome that lingered in his faith. Cotton had no wish to separate from the Church of England, as others had done in Lincolnshire and neighboring counties; cleansing it of error he felt was lifework enough for anyone.

Sitting in John Cotton's congregation that May Sunday in 1615 was Anne Hutchinson, twenty-four years old and mother of two. Anne and her husband William had ridden twenty-four miles the previous day from their home village of Alford just to attend the young vicar's service. A woman of finely toned religious scruples, Anne had traveled widely and listened to numerous clerics before she discovered one that suited her. Many were attracted by John Cotton's silken voice and rhythmic discourse, but Anne found in him a kindred spirit, a mind as penetrating and a will as persevering as her own. As Cotton drifted from bearing to bearing through the tortuous logic of Calvinist theology, Anne followed him, and when he drew back from the final abyss, she pressed on. Her questions (she never pretended to have answers) did more than trouble the clergy. They struck at the very heart of society and government as it then existed. In a corrupt and compromising world a saint can be a troublesome citizen.

Path to Salvation

She was brought up in a rectory, the Bible her chief intellectual nourishment, religious disputation her principal exercise. Her father, Francis Marbury, was a minister of the gospel with a soulful of principles and a tongue to match. After a brief tenure in Marshalsea prison—cast there by an episcopal court for daring to question the qualifications of its clergy—he found a living in the Parish of Alford, a small market town nestled between the Lincolnshire hills and the fens, or marshes, that bordered the North Sea. There in 1591 was born Anne, the second of his thirteen children. Shortly thereafter the bishops' court swooped down upon him once again and dismissed him from his post. He secured a place in a London church a few years later, which he held until his death in 1611.

How much her father helped to shape Anne's life can only be guessed, but she certainly emerged from adolescence with many of his headstrong qualities. In the rectory she also received a better than average education for a female, as well as a talent for public disputation. And from her father's frequent brushes with the ecclesiastical law, she probably imbibed a healthy disrespect for earthly authority.

In such a household, however, obedience to spiritual authority was unquestioned. The Bible was Anne Marbury's intellectual compass, as it was for most English people of the day. One of the principal aims of Protestantism had been to place a Bible in the hands of everyone and supply a learned clergy to explain its meaning. During the Reformation the Scriptures went through several English translations, culminating in the literary classic sculpted by the savants of King James in 1611. So exquisite was the new version that the flowing language took on a spiritual meaning of its own. Anne Marbury absorbed every passage, pondered it, and stored it away in her mental recesses for future reference. The Bible was her beacon, her means of ordering and resolving the conflicts and tensions of daily existence.

In 1612, a year after her father died, William Hutchinson, an old friend from Alford, journeyed to London to ask her hand in marriage. Anne consented, and the couple returned to Alford to live. William was a cloth merchant of considerable intelligence and ample means. Mild of temper and unswerving in his affection, William Hutchinson was in many respects an ideal mate for a strong-willed woman. He followed her unquestioningly through every twist and turn that religious zeal brought to their lives.

For twenty-two years William and Anne Hutchinson lived comfortably in Alford. William's business prospered enough to maintain a growing family. Children came with almost annual regularity, fifteen in all. All but one survived the perils of childhood, testimony itself to Anne's care and competence as nurse and mother. Maternal duties never distracted her from her religious devotions, however. Not long after she was married— just when she never specified—she suffered the exhilarating experience that was the core of Calvinist faith. She was reading the Song of Solomon, Bible in one hand and perhaps a nursing infant in the other, when suddenly her entire being was suffused with warmth. She felt visited personally by God.

She turned naturally to the Bible for explanation. What did it mean to be one of the Elect? Wherein did Saints differ from common mortals? She found a partial answer in the writings of the great mystic Paul. "I am crucified with Christ," Paul had said. "Nevertheless I live; yet not I, but Christ liveth in me." Such answers, of course, only raised new questions. Did Christ actually dwell in the body of every Saint? If so, did not this make the Saint more than human, a fraction of the Divine? Her parish minister failed even to address himself to such questions in his Sunday services. It was then she discovered John Cotton, vicar of St. Botolph's. The journey to Boston was long and the Hutchinsons could not afford to make it every Sunday. But they went as often as they could.

Anne absorbed every luscious word, treating Cotton's sermons with the same loving reverence she accorded the Scriptures.

John Cotton's reference point was the Genevan divine, John Calvin. "I have read the fathers," he once said, "and the schoolmen and Calvin too, but I find that he that has Calvin has them all." Calvin projected a God of infinite power who had exclusive authority over salvation and the entry of Saints into heaven. When He created Adam and Eve, God placed them in a paradise of Eden on the understanding that they would merit such treatment by good behavior (Puritans called this bargain a "Covenant of Works.") However Adam and Eve broke the Covenant and were expelled from paradise, and after the "fall" all of their descendents—i.e., all mankind—deserved only damnation.

God thereafter—so runs the Calvinist reasoning—revealed His infinite mercy by saving a few select individuals. God made this selection at the beginning of time and through His own unfathomable Grace. In the course of time He would send his son, Jesus Christ, a blend of divine and human nature, "to make intercession and peace between God offended, and man offending." Christ's death satisfied God's justice and laid the basis for the salvation of the Elect. When those persons whom God had selected chanced to be born, He informed ("called") them of their destiny. This summons, in the minds of Puritan theologians, took the form of a contract between God and His Saint, or Covenant of Grace, as it was called. As part of the covenant, God remitted all sins and instilled a faith (called "justification") that hardened the Saint and enabled him or her to cope with the sins of the world (the position of being inured to daily temptations was called "sanctification"). Thus, the Saint would lead an upright life that merits, but does not earn, salvation. No one could earn salvation by good deeds, for to do so would infringe upon the absolute authority of God.

Calvin's theology, logical though it seems, had some pitfalls. The principal one was the lack of ethics in the system. If God controlled everything, how could people be credited for doing good or blamed for evil? Since the Elect were a tiny minority of the world's population, it meant that the vast majority were condemned to hell. What reason had they to behave properly? One who felt condemned to suffer in the hereafter might well decide to lead a riotous, pleasure-filled existence in this life.

Puritan ministers avoided this sort of fatalism by modifying Calvin's thought in several important ways. Although few were destined to salvation, it was the duty of all human beings, they argued, to make the effort, to prepare themselves for God's grace. And it was the function of the ministry, as physicians of the soul, to show the way. Preparation itself was an arduous process, involving faith, commitment, and responsible behavior. Good conduct (or Covenant of Works) was thus implicit in the Covenant of Grace. God might not reward all welldoers (He was still the arbiter of heaven), but, said the Puritans, he was certain to punish the sinners. Some were even prepared to argue that God was not totally arbitrary, that He stood ready to offer His grace to any who would receive it. All He required was a voluntary commitment, a willingness to open one's heart to Christ.

Such reasoning would have appalled Calvin, for it gave people a freedom of choice as well as a role in their own salvation. It also troubled a logician such as John Cotton, for it weakened the authority of God. A God who offered grace to all believers was little more than a traffic director at the gates of heaven. The gift of God's grace, Cotton contended, must be free and absolute; in fact, it even preceded faith. It was implanted in the human soul by means of an intimate union with Christ, and from that union flowed not only faith but rectitude and all the other marks of a Saint. The soul, in turn, is assured of its election by an inward witness, a conversion experience so overpowering that it left no doubt. The regenerate individual then proceeded to do God's holy work, but his or her actions stemmed from the Holy Spirit within and not from any fear of earthly law or authority.

John Cotton's logic also had some pitfalls. How close was this union between the soul and Christ? How physical was the presence of the Holy Spirit? Cotton at times gave his listeners the impression that the regenerate individual was totally captive to the Holy Spirit, without will or means of his or her own. To the unwary or untrained listener that might imply that the living Saint was a sort of demigod, not obliged to defer to earthly laws and customs. If very many people reached this condition, society itself would dissolve. The dangers inherent in this line of reasoning had long since been recognized by Puritans and others. They had even given the heresy a name, antinomianism (from the Greek *nomos,* meaning law).

Cotton drew back from the abyss of antinomianism by leaving the role of Christ ambiguous. Christ did not actually dwell in the regenerate soul, he stated in one sermon, rather He served as a model on which converts fashioned their lives. Cotton's sermons differed from those of other Puritan ministers largely in point of emphasis. He stressed God's love and mercy and deemphasized the efficacy of human works. But Anne

Hutchinson saw in what direction his thoughts led. Fearlessly she pressed on to the murky ends of Calvinist logic. The Bible, as always, helped light her way. Reverend Cotton seemed to be saying nothing more than Saint Paul had said fifteen hundred years before. The Holy Ghost, she concluded, had come to reside in her, and the gift she possessed came from God alone. Those who talked of works were mere hypocrites, more dangerous than common sinners because they were more devious in their methods.

There was a point in all this where logic itself failed. God's gift of grace, as Anne conceived it, was so immediate and overwhelming that it amounted to a minor miracle. In fact, every time God called one of His Elect it involved some intervention in the material world. It followed, then, that revelation did not end with the Biblical age (as Puritan ministers professed); instead God revealed Himself and His works continually. And His Saints could see this just as the ancient prophets of Israel had. At this point Anne's chain of belief verged on mysticism, and that would ultimately be her downfall.

The Puritan clergy, being nearly all university men trained in the ministry, insisted upon a rational approach to religion. Their theology was a carefully formulated set of postulates, and when logic failed them they drew back, compromised, and then camouflaged the compromise with ambiguities. As a result, they instantly dismissed as deluded fanatics all who claimed to have an "inner light" or boasted of prophetic powers. Anne Hutchinson never went quite that far, but in proceeding as far as she did she ultimately aroused suspicion.

Passage to New England

The precise details of Anne Hutchinson's intellectual odyssey cannot be known. Her beliefs did not attract attention in Alford, a small place where any sort of deviant behavior would have been instantly recorded. Her conversations even with John Cotton were few in number and confined to generalities (at least so Cotton said some time later when he was trying to disassociate himself from her). Yet there are glimmers of her progress. In 1623 the Reverend John Wheelwright came from Cambridge to assume a vicarate in the nearby village of Bilsby. Wheelwright was a radical Puritan who had been constantly in trouble with the authorities while at the university. He soon became close friends with the Hutchinsons and later married William's sister Mary. Wheelwright was also attracted to Anne Hutchinson's ideas, and sometimes after a lengthy session with her he reshaped her thoughts into a Sunday sermon. When the Hutchinsons moved to New England, Wheelwright followed soon after.

About the same time a woman preacher appeared in the Isle of Ely, in neighboring Cambridgeshire. Ely was notorious for its radical sects, and the female preacher was apparently a mystic with a sizable following. Mrs. Hutchinson never met the woman of Ely nor heard her preach, but she seems to have approved the woman's doctrines. The model of a female lay preacher may also have caught her fancy. The role of women was narrowly circumscribed in seventeenth century England. They had few legal rights, and custom confined their activities to the household. For an intelligent woman longing to break free of social constraints, antinomianism provided considerable opportunity. It freed the regenerate human of earthly authority; it made her a law unto herself. Kept in the heart such beliefs released inner tensions; promoted publicly they opened the gates to feminist revolution. The woman of Ely had taken the public stage with no visible penalty. Why not others?

As already noted, it cannot be ascertained with precision just when Mrs. Hutchinson reached the final stage of her intellectual travels. But the year 1630 is a fair guess; that is to say, shortly before she removed to New England. Had her ideas matured much before that she would have attracted more attention in old England. Two of her daughters died in that year, probably of bubonic plague. They were the first children to be taken from her by the implacable God in which she believed. Emotional shock is commonly associated with mystical revelation, though whether this happened in Anne Hutchinson's case we cannot be sure. In a later account of herself she described what amounted to a second conversion experience, and it seems to have come about this time. Whatever the cause, she was brimming with the zeal of a new convert when she at last took ship for New England.

In 1633 John Cotton's sermons came to the attention of church authorities in London. Archbishop William Laud's Court of High Commission ordered him to appear before it on charges of failing to conform to the practices of the Church of England. Cotton instead fled to the seacoast, in company with another nonconforming cleric, Thomas Hooker (who was later to found Connecticut), and took ship for Massachusetts. Anne Hutchinson was determined to follow him. He was her guide and teacher; she knew of no other minister who could take his place. William agreed. If he had misgivings about leaving a comfortable living for the uncertain fortunes of the New World, he swallowed them silently. In the fall of 1633 their oldest son Edward and William's younger brother sailed for Massachusetts to prepare the way. The rest of the family followed in the spring.

Boston, Massachusetts Bay Colony, was only four years old when the Hutchinsons arrived, but already it was a thriving seaport. The founders of the Bay Colony, profiting by the experiences of Jamestown and Plymouth, had come well equipped for planting a community in the wilderness. The initial migration of 1630 included over a thousand people, together with livestock, farm tools, and household goods. Every year thereafter came new waves of migrants, pushed out of England by the political and religious persecution of King Charles. Wilderness quickly yielded to farmland, and Massachusetts was soon feeding herself, with even a tiny surplus for export. Many of the immigrants were people of means, like the Hutchinsons, and Boston hummed with tradesmen willing to fill their needs. For some years immigration was the colony's chief source of income.

In tacit recognition of the Hutchinsons' wealth and social standing, the town selectmen of Boston granted them a half-acre lot on the corner of Sentry Lane and High Street, a neighborhood where some of "the very best people" lived. Across the way was the imposing residence of John Winthrop, governor of the colony until replaced in an election just four months before the Hutchinsons arrived. Next door to the Hutchinsons were John and Mary Coggeshall, themselves new arrivals, having moved into Boston from nearby Roxbury. Coggeshall was a prosperous silk merchant, an occupation which itself bespoke the growing sophistication of the city's economy. In deference to his status (Massachusetts Bay never had the democratic inclinations of Plymouth) the voters had made him one of the town's selectmen and a deputy to the General Court. Coggeshall's religious views were a matter of some question, however; the clergy had examined him closely before admitting him to the Boston congregation. He would in time become one of Anne Hutchinson's most loyal adherents.

The Hutchinsons blended smoothly into Boston's social elite. William resumed his cloth trade and received capable help from his sons Edward and Richard, both now in their twenties. From the General Court he obtained a grant of 600 acres to the south of Boston, and he soon added farm produce to his wares. Within a year of his arrival the freemen elected him to the General Court, and in 1636 they made him one of the town selectmen. William's religious views were sufficiently conventional that he was admitted to the Boston church without difficulty, but Anne had more trouble. On shipboard during the Atlantic crossing she had criticized the sermons of a minister who was among the passengers, accusing him of

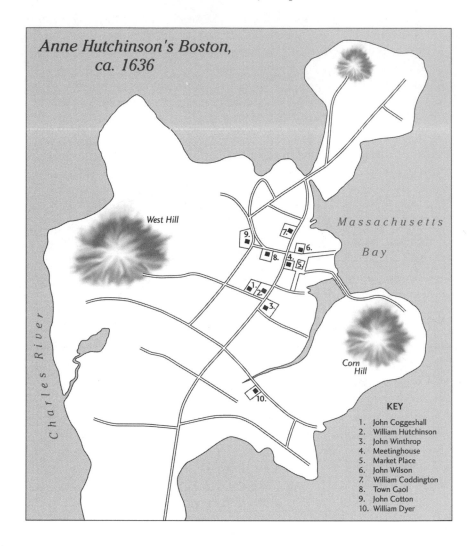

Anne Hutchinson's Boston, ca. 1636

West Hill

Massachusetts Bay

Charles River

Corn Hill

KEY

1. John Coggeshall
2. William Hutchinson
3. John Winthrop
4. Meetinghouse
5. Market Place
6. John Wilson
7. William Coddington
8. Town Gaol
9. John Cotton
10. William Dyer

relying too heavily on good works as a sign of justification. That worthy made a point of attending her church interview, and at his instance the clergy questioned her rather closely. John Cotton came to her defense, however, and after some discussion she was given full membership in the Boston congregation.

Despite an enormous household (eleven children, Anne's sister, Katherine Marbury, and two spinster cousins of William's), Anne found time for a profession of her own. She had practiced nursing part-time in England, and she brought her various herbs and medicines across the sea with her. Booming Boston was in desperate need of medical practitioners; there were only three physicians in the entire town in 1634. The sole nurse prior to Anne's arrival was Jane Hawkins, a midwife who dealt in various nostrums for the poor. Anne was soon engaged in a daily round of visits, winning an acceptance by Boston's elite that must have given her considerable pride and satisfaction. Thus the Hutchinsons transplanted themselves from old England to new with scarcely a broken root. But the reason for their move had been religious, and religion would bring them trouble.

Saints and "Opinionists"

Massachusetts, like Plymouth, was born of an utopian dream, a dream of a modern Zion for God's Chosen People, a commonwealth of Saints planted in the American wilderness. But unlike Plymouth, Massachusetts, never pretended to democracy. Although elections were held annually, voting and officeholding were confined to members of the church. Governor Winthrop, moreover, ruled with a firm hand. Civil regulations and rules of conduct emanated from the governor and his circle of assistants; not until 1634 did the General Court undertake to legislate on its own. The Bay Colony's government was as firmly secular as Plymouth's—no minister ever held political office. But religion was in its every fiber. The magistrates who enforced the law dealt equally with civil crimes, such as theft, and religious deviance, such as heresy or failure to attend church. The clergy managed the news (the Sunday sermon was often a commentary on current events), they monitored public discourse, and they controlled the education system. When Roger Williams, minister of the Salem congregation, proclaimed the Separatist doctrine that civil officials had no authority over the church, governor and assistants banished him from the colony. The Bay Colony let each congregation manage its own affairs, but that was as far as they would slip toward Separatism. The idea of separating church and state was inconsistent with the dream of a Bible commonwealth.

Yet, like all utopian schemes, Winthrop's Zion was modified in practice. Boston was a worldly community that lived on trade. Merchants were its natural leaders. They dominated the town's board of selectmen and its delegation at the General Court. They were upright men, for the most part, but they were also men of affairs. It was just this atmosphere of worldliness that disturbed Anne Hutchinson. To her it seemed the natural result of the ministerial compromise that accepted good works and social rectitude as evidence of justification. Carried to extremes, it meant that any hypocrite could buy his or her way into heaven with some deathbed philanthropy.

A few weeks after the Hutchinsons landed, John Wilson, minister of the Boston church, returned to England to settle some family affairs. John Cotton, who had since his arrival been serving as an assistant in the large Boston congregation, took Wilson's place. For the next twelve months Cotton had the ear of the Boston citizenry, expounding his misty concepts of grace and love. The Bostonians were delighted with him, though it is unclear whether it was his doctrine or his sonorous voice that appealed most. Church membership, virtually static for some years past, doubled in one year. Cotton fomented, in fact, a minor religious revival.

Anne Hutchinson, of course, was in earthly paradise. She began holding informal meetings in her own house on the day following church service in order to repeat the substance of Cotton's sermons to housewives whose duties had prevented them from attending church. The women themselves were eager learners, frequently interrupting her with questions and demands for further explanation—violating rules of conduct enjoined upon women in more formal circumstances. Anne, who felt she knew Reverend Cotton's mind better than anyone, began to expound upon his ideas, simplifying them for the benefit of her poorly educated congregation. And in doing so she lost the delicate but nonetheless crucial distinction between Cotton's doctrines and her own.

Anne's discourses became quite popular. The circle expanded; a few husbands turned up. Several couples even came from out of town. Before long Anne had to set up two meetings, one for women alone, and one for both men and women. It was an interesting cross section of Boston society. There was the usual assortment of tradesmen and artisans, ill-educated people of the sort often attracted to odd religious exercises. But the majority were wealthy merchants, such as William Coddington. Mrs. Hutchinson's appeal to merchants and their well-dressed wives was curious but scarcely surprising. Her emphasis on the Covenant of Grace made religion something internal. Assurance of salvation, as she described it, was a mystical experience witnessed Only by the spirit. It had nothing to do with a person's daily behavior. For persons whose livelihood depended on some occasional sharp trading and who were too busy to compensate with good deeds, Anne Hutchinson's concept of inner witness could be quite comforting. If this was hypocrisy, it was a subtler form of it than the hypocrisy of works that Anne combatted. Too subtle, at least, for her; she simply welcomed all comers into her parlor.

Deputies and selectmen also came to hear Mrs. Hutchinson, but there was one conspicuous absence, John Winthrop. For the moment, even that did not matter, for Winthrop was no longer governor. In the spring of 1636 the colony's freemen, rebelling at his heavy-handed rule, had replaced him with young, twenty-three-year-old Harry Vane. A recent arrival in the Bay Colony, Vane was a rare species, an aristocrat turned Puritan. His father was a member of the king's Privy Council and Comptroller of the King's Household (in effect, treasurer of England). Young Harry became enthralled with Calvinism while on a diplomatic embassy to Geneva and ruined thereby a promising political career. When Sir Harry proposed a trip to New England, Archbishop Laud himself sought to dissuade him, but the king gave his consent. The king may have worked on the subtle notion that a residence among the Saints would bring the lad to his senses, but more likely he was simply ridding the court of a nuisance. Subtlety was not King Charles' strong suit.

A man with influence at court was precisely what the Saints of Massachusetts needed, and Vane soon found himself elevated to the governorship. With almost equal speed he became a devotee of Anne Hutchinson. Having been exposed to Calvinism in its birthplace, he was no doubt confused by the doctrinal niceties worked out by the English Puritans. Mrs. Hutchinson offered him a simpler, even in fact a purer form of Calvinism, and he drank up her sermons, seated side by side with rough-handed housewives and brass-buttoned businessmen. Governor Vane's presence gave the Hutchinson circle a certain status and legitimacy.

Suspicious but powerless to interfere, John Winthrop could only grumble to his diary about Mistress Hutchinson and the "opinionists" she inspired. Significantly, he did not at this point call them antinomians, for Mrs. Hutchinson had not gone that far. She never denied the authority of government or the necessity of civil law. His concerns were more subtle, and more theologically based. Winthrop believed—as did a majority of Puritans—that the realization of God's grace was not the end of an individual's torment. The Visible Saint worked his or her way to Heaven and the Hereafter through a wilderness of temptations and could be expected to yield occasionally. Winthrop's own diary over a period of twenty-five years in England and America is a confession of constant backsliding, suffered humiliation, submission to Christ, and rededication to virtue. The images employed by Winthrop—and, indeed, most of the Puritan clergy— were masculine images of wrestling, self-bruising, and horse-taming; the preservation of virtue was a physical triumph over evil. Anne Hutchinson, on the other hand, seemed to have a more feminine concept of grace—

once apprehended, it was always present, a guiding light for a lifetime of virtue. Well before he came to view her as a threat to law and order, Winthop disparaged her followers as slackers looking for an easy door to Heaven.

The Tangled Web of Doctrine

By the time the Reverend John Wilson returned from England, a majority of the Boston congregation was infected, though in varying degrees, with Hutchinsonian tenets. This circumstance did not trouble the Reverend Cotton, who was flattered that his sermons and lectures aroused so much attention. But John Wilson was a more dogmatic pastoral leader and a more compromising intellect. He had long since subscribed to the comfortable formula that a person who *does* good *is* good, and he left to God the wearisome task of discriminating between true Saints and glib hypocrites. At the same time he was not one to tolerate a variety of opinions in his congregation, especially by untrained laymen and outspoken females.

Wilson was not long in discovering divisions within his congregation, for Anne Hutchinson made no effort to conceal her views. One sermon was enough to convince her that the good pastor subscribed to the Covenant of Works, and she promptly announced the fact to her parlor coterie. Curious to determine whether such views were common among the clergy, she traveled to other towns for Sunday services and discovered to her horror that not a single minister—save Cotton, of course, and her recently arrived brother-in-law John Wheelwright—was fit to serve.

Emboldened by her audacity and secure in their own social and economic position, the Hutchinsonians took the offensive. They openly courted support with public appearances in Boston and other towns. Inevitably their ideas, already a simplified distillation of Calvinism, became simpler still on the public stage. And there were the inevitable distortions by poorly informed enthusiasts. One visitor to Boston was shocked to encounter a woman on a street who offered to take him to another female "who preaches better Gospel than any of your black-coats that have been at the Ninniversity, a woman of another kind of spirit, who hath many revelations of things to come."

Amidst the hubbub, the clergy, long troubled by rumors of heterodoxy in the Hutchinson household, decided to act. On December 12, 1636, nine of them convened at John Cotton's house to interview Anne Hutchinson. What, they asked her, did she perceive to be the difference between their sermons and those of Reverend Cotton? He preached a covenant of grace, she told them bluntly, and they dwelt on works. What's more, she added, warming to her subject, she did not consider any of them properly sealed in the spirit of Christ, and until they were sealed—that is, until they had full assurance of salvation and that Christ dwelt within them—they could not be useful ministers. The concept of sealing was new to the clerics, and they argued at length about its meaning. They succeeded only in confusing themselves, and after some time they agreed to adjourn. Later that evening or the next morning a smaller group met and drew up sixteen queries for John Cotton to answer. For Mrs. Hutchinson, if it was not a victory, it was at least a standoff. And with odds of nine to one against her that was not bad.

Two weeks later the Hutchinsonians retaliated with an effort to censure and remove their pastor, John Wilson. They mustered a clear majority of the congregation, but Cotton intervened to save his colleague. Since the congregation was not unanimous, he pointed out, a motion of censure was, under the rules, out of order. The procedural move saved Wilson (and perhaps Cotton's reputation among his peers, as well), but the bitterness lingered. Amid the rancor, applications for church membership declined, and in January the church rolls were closed to new members altogether. The verbal battle between grace and works had so confused things that the church elders were not even sure they could tell a Saint from a sinner.

In its fall session the General Court had declared Thursday, January 19, 1636–37, to be a day of fasting and prayer with services in every church in the colony. The Boston congregation that day was given a double treat—a sermon by John Cotton and then a lengthy prophecy from John Wheelwright. Obviously the Hutchinsonians were still in control, though it is not exactly clear who was masterminding their strategy. The elders of the Boston church were nearly all adherents of Mrs. Hutchinson's doctrines, but it is unlikely that they would have allowed her to play much of a role in church politics. They probably acted as a committee with William (himself an elder) acting as intermediary between church and the Hutchinson parlor.

Wheelwright's oration was nothing less than a Hutchinsonian call to arms. Implying that most of the clergy in the colony were under a covenant of works, he urged the Bostonians to fight for their ideals, even if it meant causing "a combustion in the Church and Commonwealth." This bellicose summons was too much for John Winthrop. He had long since had misgivings about some of brother Wheelwright's notions. A month earlier the two had tangled publicly over the question (central to antinomianism) of whether Christ actually entered the soul of the regenerate human. But prior to the Fast Day sermon there was little Winthrop could do about this incautious clergyman. The Puritans never claimed the power to control ideas; they left heretics, like sinners, to be punished by God. Thus their objection to heresy was not theological but civil—heretical ideas disrupted the community.

The Bay Colony, as conceived by Winthrop and other leaders, was an organic community of Saints that lived and behaved as a unit. They envisioned themselves, like the Hebraic tribes of the Old Testament, as God's chosen people living in a model community under His special care. Since church and state were mutually dependent, disruptive religious ideas were a civil offense. Thus Reverend Wheelwright offended doubly. He not only uttered dubious theological notions, but he called his followers to defend them with physical violence. That was sedition!

When the deputies of the General Court assembled in March for their spring session, it quickly became clear that Winthrop had been at work. The legislators, sitting in their judicial capacity as magistrates, summoned Wheelwright to answer questions about his sermon. Wheelwright's responses were mild and conciliatory, but the court convicted him anyway of sedition and contempt. Throughout the proceedings Governor Vane did his best to obstruct and delay, but Winthrop's forces were too well organized. Having carried his point, Winthrop tactfully agreed to delay sentencing of Wheelwright until the fall session. The real test of strength between Hutchinsonians and the orthodox would be the spring election of deputies.

The Boston congregation was outraged at the treatment accorded Wheelwright. Just before the deputies adjourned the Bostonians handed them a petition and remonstrance, signed by seventy-four persons, pointing out that Wheelwright's sermon had not in fact produced any civil commotion, and they denounced the deputies for interfering in the affairs of the church. The court naturally rejected the petition, but Winthrop carefully filed it away for future use. Because it criticized the judicial authority, the petition itself was evidence of sedition.

The May elections doomed the Hutchinsonians. The Boston delegation was still firmly in their camp, but that was all. Every other town returned deputies committed to Winthrop and orthodoxy. On May 17 the new court met at Newtown (pointedly avoiding tumultuous Boston) and there restored Winthrop to the governorship. Then, in order to isolate the Hutchinsonians and prevent them from receiving reinforcements, the court adopted an alien act, stating that no immigrant could remain more than three weeks in the colony without the express consent of a member of the governor's council or two of the magistrates. Having isolated his foes, Winthrop offered them an olive branch—Wheelwright's sentence was once again postponed in order to give him a chance to recant. Wheelwright remained defiant, but it served only to isolate him further.

In August, 1637, Sir Harry Vane returned to England to join the mounting Puritan uprising against King Charles. He had been a petulant and unreliable ally, but his adherence had clothed Anne's doctrines in legitimacy. His departure left her at the mercy of the triumphant Winthrop.

Trial and Banishment

John Winthrop prepared for the final denouement of Anne Hutchinson with the same care he had used to turn the political tide in his favor. In September, 1637, he convened a synod of ministers to restore some doctrinal order to the church. The clerics resurrected the queries they had put to John Cotton some nine months before and secured his assent to the most important ones. With Cotton returned to the fold of orthodoxy, Wheelwright was left standing alone, shorn of influence. He too was at Winthrop's mercy. The synod then adopted a resolution denouncing private meetings of church members as "disorderly and without rule," and it forbade lay members to question ministers about the content of their sermons. Though it did not single her out by name, the synod effectively deprived Anne Hutchinson of any association with the church.

Even God seemed to turn away from Anne Hutchinson that autumn. In October she and Jane Hawkins delivered a baby of Mary Dyer, one of Anne's earliest and most devoted followers. The baby was premature, monstrously deformed, and, fortunately, dead. They buried it in secret in order to protect the mother, but a physician let out the word. Rumor magnified the horror of the event and fomented the suspicion, already current, that the Hutchinsonian women were tainted with witchcraft. Anne herself was unwell that autumn, suffering perhaps the first symptoms of menopause. She was pregnant and was shortly to be delivered of a stillbirth. It seems quite likely that the tactical blunders she committed at her subsequent trial can be traced to her poor physical and emotional condition.

On November 2 the General Court met at Newtown for its fall session. Sensing the drift of public opinion away from the Hutchinsonians, Winthrop had taken the trouble to dissolve the old assembly and ordered new elections. About half the towns elected new men who had never served before. That the novices would cooperate with the wishes of the governor was to be taken for granted. The political tenor of the new court was evident on opening day when the deputies refused to seat two of the delegates from Boston, one, John Coggeshall, who had signed the March petition and one who admitted favoring it. The court then summoned Reverend Wheelwright, listened patiently while that contumacious gentleman denied his guilt, and then sentenced him to banishment. Wheelwright spent several years in the lonely foothills of New Hampshire before returning, contrite and forgiven, to the Bay Colony.

The court then summoned back the recently expelled Coggeshall, who had been the most outspoken of the Hutchinsonians. He was accused of signing the Boston petition and making public statements that brought the court into disrepute. The court disfranchised him and ordered him not to disturb the public peace again "upon pain of banishment." With his decks cleared for battle, Winthrop summoned before the court "the breeder and nourisher of all these distempers." The final contest would have been a total mismatch had it not been for Mrs. Hutchinson's ready wit, prodigious memory, and indomitable will.

Anne Hutchinson appeared before the court on November 7, 1637. She was given no attorney, nor apparently did she ask for one. The magistrates sat as judges and jury. Winthrop opened the interrogation by asking her about the meetings in her parlor. She blandly reminded him that such meetings were common in Boston before her arrival and there was no regulation against them until the synod of 1637. Winthrop replied that the earlier meetings were simply Bible classes for the explication of Scripture; her sessions involved analysis and criticism of sermons. Since Winthrop had never attended one of her meetings, Anne knew he relied on hearsay. She answered by demanding that he produce the exact phrases in which she had criticized anyone.

After some more verbal sparring the subject shifted to the question of covenants. Did she not declare publicly that the clergy of the colony preached only a covenant of works? No—she had said only that they did not preach a covenant of grace as clearly as Mr. Cotton did. Did she deny the value of good works? No—ethical behavior was a civic duty, but it was not a road to salvation. So it went: thrust and parry. And so far a standoff.

It soon became clear, however, that the magistrates had inside information about her religious views. Some of the clergy must have relayed the substance of their December interview with her, even though she had been given the impression that her statements there were privileged and confidential. Sensing that the clergy were being drawn in whether they willed or no, Reverend Hugh Peter offered to testify. Summoned by Winthrop, he declared that in the meeting at John Cotton's home in December, 1636, Mrs. Hutchinson had called them all, save Mr. Cotton, unfit to minister the testaments—a statement that was an exaggeration, if not altogether untrue. One by one the other ministers came forth to substantiate Reverend Peter's testimony. Nightfall mercifully ended that first session with Mrs. Hutchinson clearly on the defensive.

She returned to the offense the next morning, however. After consulting her own notes of the December meeting and concluding that the ministers had distorted her meaning, she demanded in court that they be made to testify on oath. This placed the clergy in a dilemma, for to agree to an oath was to imply that their veracity was otherwise in doubt. While the court ruminated on this proposal, John Coggeshall offered to testify. The court refused on grounds he had not been present at the meeting. Anne then called John Cotton to the stand. That worthy's recollection of the event disagreed substantially with the testimony of Hugh Peter. Mrs. Hutchinson, he recalled, had not described the clergy as unfit, but rather as "not sealed." And the meaning of that had occupied the rest of the interview.

Cotton's testimony confounded the court. The magistrates could not pursue the issue further without damaging the reputations of the clergy. The prosecution had simply fallen apart. A competent defense counsel— had Anne possessed one—would have moved for a dismissal at this point, and the court would have had little choice but to grant it.

Even had Anne remained silent she might have won, but she did not. At this critical juncture she chose to speak, even though Winthrop motioned to her to be still. Perhaps the psychic tensions of her pregnancy (her stillbirth was yet some weeks off) clouded her judgment; or perhaps, conscious of her rectitude, she simply felt the need to be vindicated. In any case, she launched into a lengthy description of her conversion experience and her decision to come to the New World. The nub of it was revelation. God had personally revealed Himself to her and implanted His spirit in her soul. Moreover, it was God who told her to follow John Cotton to Massachusetts, and God who would redeem her in the end, regardless of what civil authorities might do. Revelation, the implanting of the Holy Spirit, the threat of a curse if the Bay Colony harmed her— this was rank antinomianism, as well as sedition, and it brought the magistrates to rigid attention. Did she actually expect God to intervene and rescue her? asked one. Hastily John Cotton interceded, explaining that

Mrs. Hutchinson meant only that providence was on her side, as it was with all Saints, but she did not really expect a miracle. Seeing her peril, Anne too tried to backpedal, but Winthrop quickly called a halt. She stood condemned, he announced. There followed an effort by several of the more bloodthirsty magistrates to condemn Cotton as well, until Winthrop reminded them that the clergyman was not on trial.

Winthrop then asked for a show of hands, and all but three of the deputies voted for conviction. Without further consultation Winthrop pronounced sentence. She was to be banished from the colony, the banishment to take effect in the spring, and in the meantime she was to be held in confinement.

As soon as the trial ended William Hutchinson sailed with a few friends to find a new residence for his family and their theological allies. He originally intended to examine Long Island and Delaware Bay, the one a Dutch settlement, the other Swedish, and both safely out of the reach of Massachusetts Bay, but on a stopover in Providence, Roger Williams persuaded him to settle in Rhode Island. They could have Aquidneck Island in Narragansett Bay, Williams suggested; he even offered to purchase the site from the Indians. Hutchinson agreed, and in March, 1638, he and eighteen cohorts became the owners of Aquidneck (later renamed Rhode Island) for the sum of forty strings of wampum.

At that very moment Anne Hutchinson was again on trial. This time it was a church trial on twenty-nine charges of doctrinal error. Clergy and ruling elders served as prosecution; the Boston congregation itself was the jury. The hostility of the scene showed how mercurial her Boston following had been. Few Bostonians truly understood what she had been saying. They thought she had been expounding the doctrines of John Cotton; when they discovered her tenets were largely her own, they quickly turned against her. By March only a tiny coterie of friends and neighbors remained.

The church trial was an incredible performance. The ministers allowed themselves to be drawn into an argument over Biblical authority, and there Mrs. Hutchinson was on home ground. She nimbly skipped through the Testaments, matching them passage for passage, countering one authority with a quote from another. It proved nothing except that the Scriptures could be used to prove almost anything, and the congregation sat utterly bewildered. It was soon clear that the clergy themselves were on trial, for she began asking them questions that probed the fundamental mysteries of life, death, and eternity. Groping to defend the elaborate structure of their faith, the clerics answered with evasive metaphors and ambiguous allegories. They simply could not, or would not, peer into the murky theological depths into which Anne plunged in her single-minded search for answers.

All of this occupied two long days, at the end of which Mrs. Hutchinson was exhausted and on the verge of collapse. John Cotton took her into his home and let her rest for a week, while he pounded away at her mind and heart. At length he persuaded her to return to the congregation with a written recantation. This she did on Thursday, March 22, reading her confession of errors in a voice so low that Cotton had to repeat much of what she said. As she drew to a close she could not resist a final flash of self-respect. "My judgment is not altered," she cried out, "though my expression alters." Her errors were in language, she was saying, not in doctrine. Instantly, the prosecutors were on her like a wolf pack. She had been lying all along!, one of them shrieked. That only added to her crimes! From the congregation a friendly voice interceded. Since she had confessed her errors, she ought to be shown mercy, it suggested. But the clergy would have none of it. The vote was taken, and it was unanimous as the Hutchinsonians sat in terrified silence. Reverend John Wilson, savoring his revenge, pronounced the excommunication: "I command you . . . as a Leper to withdraw yourself out of this Congregation."

As she started down the aisle, Mary Dyer rose from her seat, locked her arm in Anne's, and walked with her. Gone was the mask of humility. A man standing by the door whispered, "The Lord sanctify this unto you." And Anne replied in sturdy voice: "The Lord judgeth not as man judgeth. Better to be cast out of the Church than to deny Christ."

From Rhode Island to New Netherland: The Ending

At the end of March, 1638, Anne Hutchinson departed for Rhode Island, accompanied by her still-loyal followers—John Coggeshall, the Coddingtons, and a couple dozen more. The settlement at Aquidneck grew, nurtured by the generosity of Roger Williams and fed by a stream of dissidents from Massachusetts. A government similar to that of Massachusetts was organized on the island, and William Coddington was elected governor. With all this Anne Hutchinson had nothing to do. She lay abed for many months, exhausted by her ordeal and desperately ill.

The lengthy illness nevertheless gave her considerable time for reflection, and it was a much different woman who stepped out onto the street of Pocasset (as the settlement was called) some time in the fall of 1638. The judicial ordeals had severely shaken her doctrinal commitment. Could any human being ever expect to know absolute truth? Lacking it, did anyone—clergy included—have a right to impose his or her beliefs upon another? Perhaps the most important commitment of all was the commitment to free inquiry, the courageous pursuit of truth wherever the path might lead. Freedom of conscience suddenly seemed to her more important than the Covenant of Grace. Since there was no need for persuasion or proselyting, there was no need for a trained ministry. The Congregational Church, she came to see, was just as clogged with needless forms and ceremonies as the Church of Rome. A simple piety, practiced, perhaps, in informal association with like-minded friends, was all that God required.

Separated from Anne Hutchinson by a few years and 3000 miles of ocean, a young Englishman named George Fox was coming to the same conclusion. The society he founded (it refused even the term "church"), the Society of Friends, or Quakers, embraced nearly all of Mrs. Hutchinson's views. It centered upon the concept of inner witness, the spark of divinity that comes from union with Christ, and the Friends carried the notion—as Mrs. Hutchinson surely would have—to the end of human equality, racial as well as sexual equality. Anne Hutchinson died before the Quakers reached America, but her followers were among their first adherents. Mary Dyer was in fact one of the first Quaker martyrs, hanged by the Bay Colony magistrates for spreading the gospel of simple piety.

Anne Hutchinson's new faith preempted any further religious crusades, but it did not prevent her from taking an active role in the social and political life of her new home. And when she emerged from her sickbed she did not like what she saw. William Coddington was a man of Winthrop's ilk—domineering, single-minded, doctrinaire. Why he had come to Rhode Island at all is a mystery, for he set up a union of church and state nearly identical to that of Massachusetts. While Mrs. Hutchinson pondered this new crisis some visitors from Plymouth showed her an alternative. The government of Plymouth, they explained, was totally secular and controlled by the people. Church and state were separate realms; neither had authority over the other.

Impressed with this revolutionary idea, she took it to her husband. William, as usual, agreed with her. Coddington, however, dug in his heels when confronted with the proposition that he share power with others. He did agree to give the freemen a veto over his actions but countered that by appointing a constable to monitor "civil disturbances," that is, political opposition. The Hutchinsons, growing more circumspect with age and experience, retired quietly to await the spring elections. Annual elections were the law throughout New England; whether they would become customary on Aquidneck remained to be seen. Coddington, having received his popular mandate, did not, given the miniscule size of the community, expect to have to stand another in the foreseeable future.

In April, 1639, Coddington made the mistake of visiting Boston for a few days on business, and the Hutchinsons used the time to organize support. A town meeting of April 28 surprised Coddington with a demand for an election. Coddington objected; the freemen held one anyway, choosing William Hutchinson. Coddington and his handful of supporters withdrew and ultimately left Pocasset to found their own village, Newport, on the southern tip of Rhode Island.

With the overthrow of Coddington the Hutchinsons at last had an opportunity to devise a governmental compact of their own, and a remarkable document it was. It came as close to modern democracy as any framework could in the seventeenth century. All adult males had the vote, and majority ruled in the town meeting. The executive consisted of a governor and eight assistants, and there was separate provision for courts, so that executive and judicial functions were clearly separated. Trial by jury was guaranteed. The courts would follow precedents and procedures of the English common law. Nowhere in the compact was there a hint of religious influence. Separation of church and state was made explicit two years later when the settlement passed an act stating simply: "It is ordered that none shall be accounted a delinquent for doctrine." Not only is this the first statute for religious freedom in America, it is breathtaking in its scope. It protected every form of belief—even the right of disbelief.

Coddington soon recovered from his pique, and relations between Pocasset (soon renamed Portsmouth) and Newport were remarkably good. In 1640 the towns united to form a single government for Aquidneck Island. Under the agreement, in which Anne seems to have played a major role, Coddington accepted the Hutchinsonian form of democracy and in return received the governorship. William Hutchinson, obliging as ever, took the humbler position of magistrate.

Their internal problems resolved, the Aquidneck Islanders turned to problems of foreign policy. The chief threat to their safety, ironically, was Massachusetts Bay. Having expelled the Hutchinson crowd, Massachusetts now seemed to want them back, or more particularly, it wanted their island. Winthrop, still governor, was the main force behind this expansionism. Possession of Aquidneck would give Massachusetts a port on the south coast of New England close to the fur trade, and it would give the

Bay Colony a base of operations against the Indians of southern New England. The annexation threat produced some anxious consultations between the islanders and Roger Williams in Providence. It was decided to unite all the Rhode Island settlements in a new colony, and in the spring of 1642 Williams journeyed back to England to seek a charter. He ultimately obtained one, but it was too late to help Anne Hutchinson.

William Hutchinson died in the summer of 1642. Although Anne had been the stronger half of the partnership, the loss left her lonely and afraid. She brooded about the Massachusetts threat, and her fears deepened when two of her sons traveled to Boston on business and were clapped in jail. She decided to move to New Netherland, where she would be forever beyond the reach of Bay Colony magistrates. She left in the fall of 1642, taking her four youngest children with her. Thirty-five families from Aquidneck decided to accompany her, former disciples no doubt, who also lived in terror of Massachusetts.

Dutch authorities, ever in need of farm population, welcomed the refugees, and some Dutch land jobbers found a place for her at Pelham Bay on land they had recently acquired from the Indians, or so they said. Actually they had never paid the Indians for the land, and the Indians deeply resented Mrs. Hutchinson's arrival. For a time they hid their resentment, and even accepted her invitations to dinner. But in the spring of 1643, when the Indians retaliated against the sharp-trading Dutch with a general war, they began by wreaking vengeance on the innocent who never knew she had transgressed. Anne and her four children were tomahawked to death.

SUGGESTIONS FOR FURTHER READING

The tricentennial of the founding of the Massachusetts Bay Colony (1630) occasioned the appearance of three biographies of Anne Hutchinson, written by Helen Augur, Edith Curtis, and R. K. Rugg. None of them is very satisfactory. The best study of the theological controversy is Emery Battis, *Saints and Sectaries: Anne Hutchinson and the Antinomian Controversy in the Massachusetts Bay Colony* (1962), although it is marred by condescension (he explains much of Anne Hutchinson's behavior, for instance, in terms of her need for male guidance). Lyle Koehler, "The Case of the American Jezebels: Anne Hutchinson and Female Agitation During the Years of Antinomian Turmoil, 1636–1640," *William and Mary Quarterly*, 3rd ser., XXXI (January, 1974), 55–78, makes a determined but not very successful effort to demonstrate that the Antinomian controversy was in reality a seventeenth century version of Women's Liberation. Two recent accounts, which clarify orthodox Puritan thinking and Winthrop's attitude toward Anne Hutchinson are Charles L. Cohen, *God's Caress: The Psychology of Puritan Religious Experience* (1986), and Andrew Delbanco, *The Puritan Ordeal* (1989).

4

Nathaniel Bacon:
Empire and Frontier,
The Clash of Cultures

It was a deeply troubled band of Virginians that trooped by ones and twos into the assembly hall at Jamestown that sultry late-summer day in 1674. Some had ridden all the way from the Potomac falls—the frontier now extended that far—down the pine-shrouded footpath that led across the Rappahannock, the York, and a dozen lesser streams to the seat of empire on the James. Others had less far to travel, but the trail was just as lonely. South of Jamestown tidy tobacco lands marched boldly off toward the horizon, but within a few miles they hesitated, gave way to patches of pine and honeysuckle, and then halted altogether. In the valley of the Roanoke River, not more than 100 miles from Jamestown, the long-leaf pine still ruled the landscape. The frontier was not a line of demarcation, but a few spots of sunlight in the canopy of green where red men and white had put in their patches of corn while keeping a wary eye on one another.

Royal interference was the most immediate concern to the burgesses gathering in the colonial capital. Delegates from the Potomac valley had known for some time that the king had given their lands away to a royal favorite, Lord Thomas Culpeper. The fragment of Virginia that lay between the Potomac River and the Rappahannock had become the personal fief of one man, and Virginia pioneers, who had carved their farms from the thickets of oak and ash, now found themselves the lowly tenants of a distant landlord. Indeed, rumor had it that Lord Culpeper planned to reward his friends with manorial estates in the Northern Neck. Such grants normally included the privilege of creating a manorial court, with the right to collect fines, escheats, and other emoluments of justice. Thus money that normally went to the maintenance of county government would be diverted to the ermine pockets of some English aristocrat. Now it was learned that King Charles had granted the rest of Virginia to two other cronies, together "with all rights appurtenances . . . jurisdictions . . . and royalties whatsoever." It was this ominous news that had brought members of the House of Burgesses trooping into Jamestown.

The Virginians felt betrayed and bitter. The king's insensitive attitude was a poor reward for the years of loyalty they had given him. When the Puritans executed the king's father, Charles I, and made England into a Bible Commonwealth, Virginians had stuck by the crown. Young Charles II, in exile in Holland, admiringly referred to the colony as his "ancient dominion." Yet even in exile he had made a preliminary grant of the Northern Neck to Lord Culpeper; he merely confirmed it when he recovered the throne. It was a poor way to treat a friend, or even a "dominion."

Financial woes further darkened the mood of the assembling burgesses. For some years the price of tobacco had been falling, due to the simple economic fact that Virginians grew more of the fragrant weed than the English could smoke or chew. For a time the Virginians sold their surplus to the Dutch, but then the Puritan regime of Oliver Cromwell adopted a Navigation Act that excluded Dutch ships from the English colonies. After the restoration of the king, parliament reenacted Cromwell's navigation system and tightened it further. An act of 1662 specified that tobacco, along with other "enumerated" colonial products, could be shipped only to Britain. That left Virginians with no market for their staple but British merchants, who paid as little for it as possible and then tacked on insurance and freight charges.

The Virginians tried to diversify, but finding a suitable substitute for tobacco was difficult. Their land was not marshy enough for rice, the climate not warm enough to grow cotton or sugar. Grain and livestock the English already had in abundance. The king, moreover, drew a tidy revenue from the tax on tobacco; he viewed with suspicion the Virginians' efforts to displace it. The governor of the colony was equally resistant to change, for the tax on tobacco exports paid his salary as well. The Virginians were trapped.

The planters adjusted as best they could. Most farms, except for the very smallest, were nearly self-sufficient. Planters produced their own food and clothing; they needed cash only for tools, kitchen utensils, and perhaps some imported bits of finery. A share of the crop was usually sufficient to procure the services of a miller, wagoner, or boatman. They would have fared tolerably well in a barter economy but for the government. The colonial government demanded that taxes be paid in coin, and it levied taxes by the head or poll. Although slaves were counted as polls, for whom taxes had to be paid by the owners, the capitation tax nevertheless seemed to fall disproportionately on those least able to pay. At least the poor thought so.

Thus the annual assessment brought an annual scramble for the little coin that existed, and tight money further weakened the price of tobacco. Nor did the government, for all the demands it put on Virginia's suffering taxpayers, appear to spend its money wisely. Sir William Berkeley, governor of the colony for the past forty-two years (except for a brief interval under the Cromwell regime), used the revenue principally, it seemed, to further his own authority. He secured the cooperation of the most powerful men in Virginia by giving them offices and favors. Having found a docile assembly, he called it back year after year to enact laws and levy taxes. Virginia had not had an election since 1660. Local government echoed the tight-knit comradery of the colonial regime. In each county a small group of justices of the peace, selected by the governor, allocated the local assessments. Too often, it seemed, the chief beneficiaries of their largesse were themselves.

The forts ordered by Governor Berkeley during the Anglo-Dutch war early in the 1670s were a case in point. Nearly everyone agreed that the fortifications were necessary; Virginia with its many rivers was very vulnerable to naval attack. But the work was undertaken, as usual, by political favorites, and the costs were far higher than the results seemed to justify. So dilapidated were the forts that in 1673 a Dutch squadron paraded right up the James River, seizing and burning tobacco ships. So nasty was the mood of the citizenry in that year that the governor's circle expressed private relief that the yeomanry had not made common cause with the Dutch. Tax collections in the spring of 1674 brought an armed and angry mob to the court house in New Kent county. Only the exertions of local leaders prevented an uprising on the spot.

Thus the burgesses faced trouble on two fronts as they assembled in Jamestown in September, 1674. A grumbling populace associated them with the governor and suspected them of corruption, while an indifferent king frittered away their estates and status. Nor was the governor much help. A popular figure in Virginia in his youth, Berkeley had grown into a stiff and crotchety old man. The king was already making plans to replace him. Rumors circulated through the royal court that the new governor would be Lord Culpeper.

Since there was little the burgesses could do about the popular discontent without relinquishing their own authority, they turned to the threat from abroad. After some discussion they decided to send three agents to London to negotiate with court officials. Their mission was to buy out the proprietors to whom Charles had given Virginia and then establish the rights of Virginians on a more secure foundation. The primary difficulty, as both burgesses and their agents saw it, was that Virginia had no charter. The original charter granted to the London Company had been revoked by King James in 1624; ever since that moment the Virginia government rested on nothing more official than the periodic instructions sent to the governor by the privy council. Shorn of a chartered identity, Virginia had become, in the view of the burgesses, the king's plaything.

The colonial agents arrived in London with some "heads" of proposals that amounted to a blueprint for a new charter. The draft would have allowed Virginians to incorporate for the purpose of buying out the recently named proprietors, and by guaranteeing Virginians title to their lands it would have prevented the king from pulling a similar stunt in the future. It granted broad powers of legislation to the Virginia assembly and left to the Crown only a power of review over its laws. It specifically guaranteed that no taxes would be levied on Virginians except by the "common consent" of the governor and assembly.

Underlying these proposals was a rather firm notion of Virginia's place in the empire. Englishmen who moved to America, the burgesses were clearly saying, did not lose any of the rights and privileges they enjoyed at home. Colonists were the equal of any other Englishmen, so far as government was concerned. It was an interesting statement, one of the earliest shots in the long contest over the meaning of empire. King Charles would have done well to give it his earnest attention. Instead, he rejected the charter in May, 1676, a hundred years almost to the day before another Virginian, Richard Henry Lee, presented the Continental Congress with a resolution for American independence.

At the moment that King Charles disposed of the assembly's charter proposal, Virginia was enveloped in the flames of revolution. The king's rejection had nothing to do with it. The common people, as it turned out, had little interest in a charter. Such a document would only have confirmed the position of the corrupt and stodgy elite. The grievances of the small farmers could be resolved only by overthrowing the elite, either by arms or ballots. Revolution or political upheaval, either one required a leader. Ironically, just such a man stepped off the boat onto the soil of Virginia in the summer of 1674, just a few days before the burgesses gathered themselves in Jamestown. His name was Nathaniel Bacon.

The Making of an Indian Fighter

Nathaniel Bacon's family background was not the sort that commonly breeds revolutionaries. His long and lustrous pedigree boasted wealthy grandees, statesmen, and philosopher-scientists. His father was an English country gentleman, possessor of half a dozen manorial estates. A cousin had become one of the wealthiest men in Virginia, related by marriage to the governor himself. Born in 1647 at Friston Hall, Suffolk, Nathaniel Bacon was brought up in an atmosphere of polished plate and deferential servants. Dancing and fencing masters instilled in him some of the social graces expected of a gentleman, and at the age of thirteen he entered St. Catherine's Hall, Cambridge. It was customary for the son of a landed gentleman to be escorted through college by a tutor, who supervised his studies, managed his finances, and guided his conduct—in short, a blend of friend, father, and factotum. The young aristocrat was excused from attending classes and given only the most perfunctory examinations, when he suffered any at all.

Such a system, of course, had little to offer either a young man's mind or his character, and Bacon emerged from the experience as idle and improvident as he entered. After a year his father pulled him out of the college, set him up with a private tutor at home, and then financed a tour of the continent. Somewhat broadened, if not exactly educated, Nathaniel returned to Cambridge and earned a Master of Arts degree. He then put in a year or so at Gray's Inn, London, to absorb a dash of law. It was not intended that he would make law a career; rather it was part of the training of a squire-to-be. He would need it when serving as a justice on the county court.

In 1670 he married Elizabeth Duke, daughter of a neighboring gentleman with pedigree as lengthy if not quite as illustrious as Bacon's. It is perhaps a measure of Nathaniel's reputation in the Suffolk countryside that her father rejected the match and disinherited his daughter when she ignored his command. The marriage failed to settle Bacon into the genteel routine expected of his station. He became involved in a variety of shady schemes, among them one to defraud a young friend of his inheritance. It almost seemed an act of desperation when his father sent Nathaniel to Virginia in the summer of 1674 to make a new start in life. Elizabeth loyally accompanied him.

Nathaniel Bacon received a warm welcome in Virginia. He was, after all, of that class of gentry that the Virginians themselves flattered by emulating. His cousin, also by name of Nathaniel, had a seat on the governor's council, and through him the young arrival was related to the governor by marriage. Bacon, moreover, arrived with capital enough to place himself well in a society where money was the principal measure of station. His father had generously endowed him with £1800 to make his new start. Bacon bought an established plantation in the Curles, where the James River writhed through the gently sloping tidal landscape before entering the broad estuary of Chesapeake Bay, and he purchased an additional farm (to be managed by an overseer) above the falls. Settlement was then just reaching the rolling piedmont of central Virginia, and the overseer's chief task was to push back the hardwood forest and turn the red clay soil into productive tobacco land.

Governor Berkeley's reception of the newcomer bordered on the enthusiastic. He promptly granted Bacon's request for a license to trade with the Indians, even though he had previously limited such licenses to a few favorites. And on March 3, 1675, he named Bacon to the Governor's Council, the body that served as advisers to the executive while simultaneously functioning as upper house of the legislature and final court of appeals. Why Berkeley should have so signally honored an untested young man, resident in the colony less than a year, remains a mystery. Some have suggested that it was a form of bribe, a means of preventing Bacon from giving voice to popular grievances. Yet there is no evidence that Bacon at this point regarded himself as a tribune of the people. More likely the appointment was due to the influence of Bacon's cousin and Berkeley's own respect for noble blood.

Though flattered no doubt by the governor's bounty, Bacon evinced no great interest in politics. In the course of the next year he attended only three sessions of the council and failed to leave any mark on its record. Tobacco culture, an art in itself, seems to have consumed his attention. But he could scarcely have missed hearing the murmurs of his neighbors' discontent, nor escaped the disappointment of receiving a pittance for his own crop from some imperious ship captain. Indian depredations would bring him, angry and belligerent, into the political arena.

Ever since 1644, when Powhatan's bellicose brother Opechancanough made his final effort to wipe out the Virginia colony, the border had been at peace. Remnants of Powhatan's once-powerful confederacy—Pamunkies, Mattaponies, Chickahominies, and Rappahannocks—lived on reservations scattered among the white settlements. They provided guides and warriors to flesh out Virginia armies when raiding parties (usually Iroquois) appeared from the north or west. Racial tension was never far from the surface, however, especially as the frontier marched onto the piedmont and displaced tribes hitherto unmarked. The Iroquois of New York, who displayed through these years an aggressive expansionism that would have been envied by any Bourbon king or Hapsburg emperor, were an additional source of instability. In 1674 they chased their ancient enemies, the Susquehannas, south into Maryland where that tribe—itself untamed by white standards—settled in uncomfortable proximity to Potomac plantations.

Trouble erupted in July, 1675, when a petty argument between a Potomac planter and some Doeg Indians who lived across the river led to the murder of the planter's servant. A party of white vigilantes promptly set out after the Doegs, killed ten of them, and, through carelessness in identification, killed fourteen Susquehannas as well. The Susquehannas naturally retaliated, and that brought forth an even larger force of frontier militia, which laid siege to the Susquehannas' encampment, slaughtered four chiefs who came out to negotiate, and then adjourned without achieving victory. The outraged Susquehannas took to the warpath, and their raiding parties penetrated deep into Virginia, killing dozens of settlers and forcing many others to flee for their lives. Among the victims was the overseer on Bacon's inland farm. Even after the raids ceased in January, 1675/6, hysteria among whites continued to mount as news trickled in of King Phillip's war in New England. That uprising, when tied to the activities of Iroquois and Susquehannas, seemed to indicate a continental Indian conspiracy aimed at pushing the Europeans into the sea once and for all.

Governor Berkeley, experienced executive that he was, remained calm amidst the panic. During the autumn he ordered the arrest of the whites who had started the fighting, and he rejected the suggestion that an army be sent into the field for fear that it might assault friendly Indians. The frontier militia had already evidenced a distressing inability to distinguish varieties of natives.

Summoning the assembly into session on March 7, Berkeley proposed instead the construction of forts for defense. The assembly, ever obedient to the governor's wishes, promptly voted the funds. The forts did nothing to ease popular fears. They were no barrier to Indians, who easily slipped in between, and settlers who hid in them could not tend their crops. The cost, moreover, only added to the heavy tax burden, and there were still rancorous memories of the corruption that had attended the coastal forts built to fend off the Dutch.

Later that spring rumors spread that the Indians were massing for a new attack. A new group of vigilantes—a curious mixture of landed gentlemen (including the first William Byrd) and buckskin-clad farmers—gathered at the falls of the James. Bacon, incensed over the murder of his overseer, joined the band and was promptly elected its leader. Friends, including Byrd, seem to have had a hand in the election, and it is true that the selection of a member of the governor's council did confer a certain element of legitimacy to the hot-tempered throng. But there was also an element of charisma in Bacon's personality. One observer described him as dark of hair and countenance, of only medium height and build, and given to fits of melancholy. Yet he must have been an impressive speaker, because his voice invariably stirred men to action. He had the commanding presence of an aristocrat and the speech mannerisms of a commoner. By turns eloquent and profane, he could lead men through the jaws of hell or—what was equally terrifying—the dark and sinister paths of the wilderness. Bacon wrote Berkeley for permission to march, received an unsatisfactory reply, and impulsively plunged into the woods with his army of a hundred or so frontiersmen. He would punish the Indians himself and do it without cost to the colony.

Bacon headed south to the Roanoke River, where a band of Susquehannas was rumored to be camped. His route followed an old trading path that wound southwest toward Tennessee. The trail crossed the Roanoke at Occaneechee Island, where the Occaneechee tribe had built a fort. Depending on the mood of the Occaneechees, the fort was at times a refuge and at times a nuisance to white traders. Bacon's ill-equipped farmers were footsore and hungry by the time they reached the island. The Occaneechees took them in and even agreed to slaughter for them the Susquehannas who were camped nearby.

With that dirty work finished, Bacon prepared to return home. In need of food for the journey, he offered to purchase some, but the chief of the Occaneechees, whose own stocks may have been low after a particularly harsh winter, resisted. In the midst of the discussion the chief massed his warriors along the river bank opposite the island, a show of strength probably designed to improve his bargaining leverage. Sensing himself in danger, Bacon turned suddenly on the Indians in the fort, ordering his men to fire through the peepholes in the stockade. He slaughtered the entire lot, men, women, and children. He then returned home to a hero's welcome. Virginia frontiersmen cared not a bit that the only Indians he had killed were friendly ones.

Bacon's Laws

Frontiersmen worshipped Bacon not simply because he was an Indian killer. They liked him because he was a man of action, willing to cut through the briar patch of official policy, willing even to defy the governor. Bacon's impulsive sortie set ablaze the smoldering popular dissatisfaction with Governor Berkeley, his crony-ridden regime, and his flaccid defense policy. The monthly meetings of the county courts, usually festive occasions when law mingled with horsetrading, became scenes of angry discussion and ugly threats.

Governor Berkeley had journeyed to the falls of the James to intercept Bacon, but he arrived too late. Keeping his temper, albeit with some difficulty, Berkeley issued a proclamation denouncing the band as "unlawful, mutinous, and rebellious," but offering to pardon them if they would but return to their homes. Bacon was deprived of his seat on the council and exempted from pardon. Then, aware of his slipping prestige, Berkeley called for elections to a new assembly, the first to be held in sixteen years. To appease the populace further he announced that all adult white males might participate in the election (an act of 1670 had confined the vote to property owners).

When they returned from Occaneechee Island to find that they had been branded as mutineers and rebels, Bacon's men were furious. They felt they had only been defending their homes. Others in the western counties were inclined to agree. Finding his first proclamation ignored, Governor Berkeley on May 29 issued another, reiterating the charge that Bacon was a rebel and ordering him to Jamestown to answer for his actions.

A few days later the voters of Henrico County met at Varina Court House and elected Bacon to the new House of Burgesses, together with his friend and staunch ally Captain James Crews. Taking forty armed men for protection, Bacon set sail down the river to Jamestown. Reaching the colonial capital, Bacon asked for permission to land, and was greeted instead with a volley from the fort. Prudently he retired back up river a few miles and anchored for the night. Under cover of darkness Bacon slipped back into Jamestown for a conference with William Drummond and Richard Lawrence at the latter's house. Drummond was a Scot who had earlier served as governor of North Carolina. Lawrence was an Oxford graduate and probably an attorney, for there were few other occupations in that tiny seat of government. One chronicler who knew Lawrence well described him as one of the governor's earliest and most vocal critics. Berkeley himself, when the whole affair was over, described Drummond as "the original cause of the whole rebellion." Thus Bacon's clandestine meeting with these two political activists is of enormous significance. It shows that he was not simply an impetuous Indian-hater unconcerned with politics (as some have described him). He was clearly trying to broaden the base of his dispute with the governor. Since both Drummond and Lawrence were members of the newly elected assembly, the three may well have been drawing up plans for political reform.

Bacon returned to his ship and prepared to head home the next morning. The governor meanwhile had sent armed vessels after him, and after a brief chase they captured him. Bacon and his men were carried to Jamestown as prisoners. Taken before the governor, he seemed silent and downcast. Gone was the brazen bushwhacker of Occaneechee. Perhaps Lawrence and Drummond had calmed his militancy in the hopes of trimming the governor in a more substantial way, through the assembly. Rather than punish Bacon, the governor wisely offered to take his parole, his word as a gentleman that he would behave peacefully in the future. After a short conference with his namesake cousin, Bacon submitted. Obviously pleased, the governor restored him to his seat on the council and promised that he would give him a military commission. Since one person could not sit in both Houses at the same time, the action had the effect of depriving him of his seat in the House of Burgesses, where his fiery oratory and gifts of persuasion might have proved troublesome. Berkeley at least was no amateur.

The wide franchise and combative popular mood produced an electoral revolution that spring. "The giddy people," reported one analyst, returned only eight supporters of the governor. The rest were demanding change. The governor opened the assembly with a pointed warning that the delegates not be misled by the "two rogues," Lawrence and Drummond, but the burgesses ignored him. There were immediate demands for an investigation of the way the colony's revenues were handled and accounts kept. After several days' discussion of this proposal, the governor sent word that Indian affairs must take precedence over all other legislative affairs. To this he appended a request that two members of the Governor's Council be allowed to sit with the lower house. The notion of spies in their midst produced "many discontented faces," but no one had the will to object. They turned dutifully to the Indian question.

The Queen of the Pamunkies was brought before the house to explain why her tribe had not assisted the whites in their struggle against the Susquehannas. She replied that the last time they offered assistance they lost most of their warriors, among them her husband. Asked how many warriors she could provide in the present emergency, she suggested two. After further browbeating she raised the ante to twelve and stalked out. Governor Berkeley's policy of employing Indians against Indians was not working out.

Through all of this Bacon became increasingly restless. Nothing, it seemed, had changed. The Susquehannas, abetted, it was rumored, by "friendly" reservation Indians, struck deeper into the settlements. Bacon's wife Elizabeth wrote him that one raiding party had appeared within three miles of his own plantation. The governor kept delaying his commission. The House of Burgesses was thoroughly cowed. Friends told Bacon that the governor was plotting to have him killed. Disgusted with the political situation and apprehensive for his own safety, Bacon asked Berkeley for permission to return home. His wife, he said, was sick. The governor reluctantly granted the request. Changing his mind, the governor sent a patrol after him. The posse ransacked Lawrence's house, where Bacon had stayed, but failed to catch him.

Bacon's return to Henrico signaled another spontaneous uprising. From all over the patchwork of clearings that marked the frontier, angry farmers dropped their hoes, picked up their guns, and trooped off to Bacon's home at the Curles. If the governor could not stop the Indian raids, they would do it themselves. The governor had broken his promise, Bacon told them, by denying him his commission. He no longer felt bound by his parole. The mob fed on itself. Bold talk by one shored up the courage of another. It was decided to march on Jamestown to secure a commission at gunpoint. Then they could summon the entire colony to arms against the Indians.

With his "army" of a hundred or so Bacon started off down the high road that led through Middle Plantation (later Williamsburg) to Jamestown. It was a curious assortment of rebels, for marching side by side with untutored farmers in homespun shirts were men of wealth and education, such as William Byrd and James Crews. Bacon himself later insisted that they had no intention of "leveling" Virginia society. The contest was a matter of rights, including the right of self-defense.

Learning of the commotion at Henrico, Governor Berkeley summoned the militia to defend Jamestown, but they straggled in too late to help. Bacon paraded into Jamestown unopposed on the afternoon of Friday, June 23. His men, foot soldiers and horse, lined up smartly on the green next to the capitol. A drumbeat called the assembly into session; Bacon stationed a guard outside the council chamber and demanded his commission. The governor, ever alert to good theater, bared his breast, and cried: "Here, shoot me, fore God, fair mark, shoot!" Bacon declined, protesting that he had no intention of hurting a hair on the governor's head. He wanted only the commission promised him. The governor wheeled and left the council chamber. Bacon followed, gesticulating, and shouting: "God damn my blood, I came for a commission, and a commission I will have before I go!"

Once again out on the green, Bacon spotted the burgesses staring at the scene from the windows of their chamber. He ordered his men to point their guns at them and exploded with some more "new coined oaths." He then stomped into the House of Burgesses to appeal to that body for a commission. Although the House was sympathetic, it had to remind Bacon that only the governor had authority to issue military commissions. Bacon then launched into a lengthy and rather revealing address. He explained that his men had taken up arms only to defend themselves, and they objected to paying high taxes to a government from which they derived no benefit. There was urgent need, he explained, for an investigation of governmental corruption and a reform of the colony's revenue system.

Bacon's defiant call to action broke the legislative logjam. Lawrence, Drummond, and other reformers had statutes already drafted; some may even have been presented to the House before Bacon arrived. Bacon's appearance gave the burgesses the courage to act. By the time they adjourned two days later they had passed a dozen pieces of legislation aimed at revamping the colony's government. Several of the laws were directed at grasping and inattentive officials. The office of county sheriff was to be rotated annually among the justices of the peace, and no person was allowed to hold two county offices at the same time. Another statute imposed fines for excessive fees and unauthorized charges by county officials.

Another set of statutes was directed at expanding the role of the people in government. The parish vestries, which had become self-perpetuating bodies, were thenceforth to be popularly elected. The act of 1670, restricting the suffrage to property owners in assembly elections, was repealed. Another act provided for the election of representatives in each county, equal in number to the justices named by the governor, to share in the levying of taxes and the passage of county regulations. Members of the Governor's Council were no longer to be exempt from taxes, and no Councillor was allowed to sit on a county court.

These were truly "Bacon's Laws," for his uprising had given the burgesses courage to pass them and cowed the governor and council into approving them. When they were repealed a year later, the chief excuse was that they were passed under duress. It is a shame that they were repealed, for it would be more than a century (well after the American Revolution) before the common Virginian had another chance to share so fully in the government.

On Saturday, June 24, while the burgesses labored over their legislative agenda, Berkeley yielded to "solicitation and importunity" from all sides and granted the commissions to Bacon and his men. The next day the burgesses presented governor and council with their enactments; Berkeley approved the laws and dissolved the assembly. On Monday Bacon departed for the West to hunt Indians anew.

Bacon's Rebellion

On July 1, 1676, Governor Berkeley wrote a friend: "How miserable that man is that governs a people where six parts of seven at least are poor, indebted, discontented, and armed." The last was the significant point, for Bacon's army was growing rapidly. By the end of July he could count a force of seven hundred horsemen and six hundred foot. The governor meanwhile had lost whatever support he had. When some loyalists of Gloucester County petitioned grievously that Bacon's men had carried off their horses, arms, and powder, Berkeley dashed across the York River to seek their support. Mustering the county militia, he told them that he intended to march against the rebel Bacon, whereupon the militia turned their backs and strode off the field chanting "Bacon Bacon Bacon." Mortified, the governor fainted and fell from his horse.

On July 29, Bacon changed his mind, abandoned the Indian campaign, and headed back to Jamestown. In view of the governor's weakness, he might have done better to pursue the Indian campaign. Given the fears of the frontiersmen and his penchant for killing any Indian in sight, it almost certainly would have added to his laurels. But he also knew that the governor, though presently weak, would strike whenever he picked up some support. Perhaps Bacon decided to eliminate the menace once and for all.

So Bacon retraced his steps down the road to Middle Plantation, while a special detachment swept through restive Gloucester. Berkeley fled across the bay to the Eastern Shore, and Bacon found himself in control of the colony. On August 3 he issued a "Declaration of the People," drafted, apparently, with the help of Lawrence and Drummond. This document, a bid for broad popular support, summarized the grievances against the governor, both in his domestic administration and in his Indian policy. Denying that he was a rebel, Bacon stated that his followers desired only to present their "sad and heavy grievances" to His Majesty, the King. He signed the Declaration, "Nathaniel Bacon, General by Consent of the People."

To be a gadfly without responsibility had been a fairly easy role; to be a rebel come to power, Bacon discovered, was much more difficult.

It was now his turn to fret about discontent—and he could be sure that the still-wealthy and still-influential elite were that, at least. And what to do if the king sent ships and men to Virginia? It was known that Berkeley had written London of his troubles, and a royal army of 2000 was rumored to be on the way. (The king did send an army, though it had not yet departed.)

To resolve these problems Bacon summoned to his headquarters at Middle Plantation a convention of the "prime gentlemen" in the area, among them several Councillors. He demanded a loyalty oath of them, and they agreed not to aid Berkeley in any way. Then he exacted another promise—that they would also resist any force the king sent to Virginia until the king could be made acquainted with the situation. The "prime gentlemen" objected to this, knowing full well where it might lead. Throughout a long afternoon and evening Bacon worked on them, mixing threat with reason. Late in the evening a messenger appeared with word of a new Indian raid, this time in neighboring Gloucester County across the York River. (Since it is unlikely the Susquehannas would bother to penetrate so far into the white settlements, it might seem that Bacon was right in his feeling that "friendly" Indians were not always friendly.) The messenger also reported that the planters were defenseless because Governor Berkeley, on his way to the Eastern Shore, had cleaned out their fort of arms and powder. That seems to have done it, and the assembled gentlemen subscribed to Bacon's oath.

Bacon was still broadening his objectives. In a candid conversation with a fellow Indian-fighter from Henrico (who preferred killing red men to Red Coats), Bacon suggested that his army could defeat anything the king sent over. How so, his incredulous captain asked, and Bacon replied that both Maryland and North Carolina were ripe for rebellion. This was intelligence, not a dream. William Drummond had no doubt given him the particulars of North Carolina politics; one John Culpeper, who was in Jamestown in May, 1676, led a rebellion there the following year. Maryland, groaning under an administrative system similar to Virginia's, experienced its own rebellion a few years later. That Bacon was aware of this discontent and willing to utilize it for his own ends suggests that his political ideas had matured substantially. He was grappling with the possibility of throwing off the imperial yoke altogether.

Having neutralized the civilian population, at least in the arm of Virginia that lay between the James and the York rivers, Bacon moved to secure his military defenses. He ordered the seizure of all vessels in the lower bay area, fitted them with loyal crews, and put them to guarding the coast against counterattack from the Eastern Shore. He then turned back to the Indian problem. The raids in Gloucester were particularly worrisome because, even if the Susquehannas were responsible—and no one could be certain—they must have acted with the knowledge, perhaps even the support, of the Pamunkies, whose village lay astride the trail into the county. The antagonistic behavior of the Pamunkies' queen before the assembly had already rendered that tribe suspect.

So Bacon set off for Gloucester. The Pamunkies, always well posted on the movements of white armies, fled into the woods. Bacon gave chase, caught up with one band, killed a few, and captured forty-five. Back at the Middle Plantation with his captives in tow, he learned that Berkeley had struck in his absence. With a small force recruited on the Eastern Shore and some ships supplied by Eastern Shore planters, Berkeley captured Bacon's guard vessels one by one, using a variety of ruses. He also commandeered every tobacco ship that hove into the bay. By early September his flotilla numbered nineteen, mostly sloops of various sizes, and he felt strong enough to move against Jamestown. Overawed by Berkeley's fleet, and unaware that the governor's army was inconsiderable, Bacon's sentries fled the town. On September 7, 1676, the governor stepped ashore and fell upon his knees to thank God for returning his capital.

A week later Bacon's army moved down from Middle Plantation and camped at Green Spring, the governor's home plantation a few miles from Jamestown. They were exhausted from days of forced marches, and Bacon himself was wracked with fever. That evening they moved to the narrow neck connecting Jamestown "island" with the mainland, and began building breastworks. Unsure of the strength of Berkeley's force and in need of time to complete his fortifications, Bacon sent horsemen out in search of hostages. They returned with women from nearby plantations, several of them wives of members of the Governor's Council. These he placed on his earthworks and sent a warning into Jamestown not to attack. This ungallant action (for which historians have taken him sharply to task, although they are often willing to condone his unconscionable treatment of Indians) gave Bacon time to finish his fortifications.

When the women were removed, the governor ordered his men to attack. The assault force edged forward cautiously, and when Bacon's men opened fire they turned and ran. As one observer put it: "Like scholars going to school, they went out with heavy hearts, but returned home with light heels." Realizing that his Eastern Shore recruits had neither the numbers nor the morale to hold the city, Berkeley returned to his ships on September 19, and sailed down the James to the roadstead where the river joined the bay. Gazing back upriver that evening, he could see the flickering light of his burning capital.

Military necessity dictated the burning of Jamestown. Just the day

Bacon's Entry into Jamestown and the burning. As imagined by 19th-century artist Howard Pyle. (Picture Collection, The Branch Libraries, The New York Public Library.)

before Bacon had received word that Captain Giles Brent, military commander of the Northern Neck and a former friend, had gone over to the governor's side and was marching south with a thousand men. Brent, like many another loyal Virginian, may well have decided that Bacon had gone too far in the overthrow of established authority. With this new threat from the northwest, Bacon could not risk another surprise move in his rear. To prevent the governor from reoccupying Jamestown, he burned it.

Lawrence and Drummond, revolutionaries to the end, led the way, each setting the torch to his own house. The village then consisted of twelve brick houses and a number of frame ones, most of which doubled as inns or taverns. Nothing was spared, not even the assembly hall, although Drummond was considerate enough to remove the colony's records to a safe place.

The threat from the north evaporated as quickly as it had arisen. Learning of Berkeley's defeat at Jamestown, Brent's men deserted their leader and returned to their homes. Organized resistance to the rebellion had collapsed; Bacon was the de facto governor of Virginia. Though he was growing sicker by the day, he made a strong effort to bring peace and order to the distracted colony. He named three committees: one to govern the area south of the James, where there were rumors of lawless plundering, even though the area had not been involved in the fighting. A second was to accompany the army to see that its procurements were made with fairness and civility. The third was to handle the Indian problem.

Whether he might have summoned the assembly and attempted to obtain some sort of popular mandate for his regime we shall never know. For at that critical moment in the rebellion—October 26, 1676—he died. His last illness was described as a "bloody flux," a fever accompanied by dysentery that usually connoted a water-borne disease such as typhus or typhoid. For weeks at a time, during the late summer months, he had lived and fought in the swamps, enduring incessant rains and autumn chills. His body, not yet fully acclimated to the American environment, broke under the strain. Friends gave him a secret burial so that Governor Berkeley could not make a trophy of him. His grave has never been found.

Rebellion's Aftermath

Nathaniel Bacon's was not simply a one-man rebellion, an Indian fighter gone berserk. It was the tip of an iceberg of popular grievances, only a few of which had anything to do with Governor Berkeley's Indian policy.

Nor did the rebellion die out suddenly upon Bacon's death. His army remained in the field, and Virginians remained quiescent under the rule of his subordinates. Berkeley's initial effort to make a landing on the western shore was easily repulsed; not until January, 1677, was Berkeley able to make good his return. Bacon's successor, Captain Joseph Ingram, unfortunately lacked Bacon's charisma, and he found Virginia impossible to defend against a force with naval superiority (Berkeley was still commandeering incoming tobacco ships)—a problem that Governor Thomas Jefferson would again encounter during the American Revolution.

The arrival of a British army in early 1677, together with commissioners to investigate the uprising, likewise confounded the Baconians. Few if any of them had any notion of overthrowing the king's authority. Lawrence escaped to the frontier and was never seen again; Drummond was captured and hanged. A handful of other leaders made their way to Boston, but most of Bacon's followers simply returned to their plantations. They had reason enough to be peaceful. Governor Berkeley so alienated the royal commissioners by his complaints and pitiful pleas of self-justification that the commissioners displayed open sympathy for the rebels. Their report was an objective assessment of the grievances of Virginians. Bacon's laws were repealed by a new assembly in 1677, but Berkeley was replaced and no governor thereafter dared to rule with his high-handed contempt for popular opinion. Indeed, the political history of Virginia for the next century is essentially the story of the growing power of the popularly elected House of Burgesses, as it whittled away at the authority of the governor and the empire that he represented.

King Charles II did grant Virginia a new charter in 1676, but it was not at all what Virginians had wanted. It did confirm their land titles, with the exception of the Northern Neck, but it made no mention of their rights. This was not a reaction to Bacon's rebellion; rather it reflected a growing desire in London to exert greater royal authority over the empire. The empire, in the view of Charles II and his ministers, was made up of superiors and inferiors. Colonists did not have all the rights of Englishmen; they were subordinate beings who possessed only those rights that the king chose to give them. This concept of empire would be a source of tension between colonies and the mother country for the next century, and it would ultimately provoke revolution and independence. Nathaniel Bacon lived and rebelled in vain—but only because he was ahead of his time.

SUGGESTIONS FOR FURTHER READING

The classic description of Bacon as a precursor of the American Revolution is Thomas Jefferson Wertenbaker, *Torchhearer of the Revolution* (1940). Wilcomb Washburn, *The Governor and the Rebel* (1957), portrays Bacon as a renegade Indian fighter whose "rebellion" had no long-range significance. David S. Lovejoy, *The Glorious Revolution in America* (1972), is a balanced account with fresh insights of its own. Edmund S. Morgan, in contrast to Washburn, feels that the rebellion was a social upheaval of major importance: *American Slavery, American Freedom: the Ordeal of Colonial Virginia* (1975). Frederic W. Gleach, *Powhatan's World and Colonial Virginia: A Conflict of Cultures* (1997), summarizes the impact of the rebellion on Virginia's Indians. For a study of the rise of self-government in the Southern colonies after Bacon's rebellion, see Jack P. Greene, *The Quest for Power: The Lower Houses of Assembly in the Southern Royal Colonies, 1689–1776* (1963).

5

William Penn:
The Aristocrat as Democrat

It has become commonplace among historians to describe America as a contrapuntal civilization. In a study that has become a classic, *People of Paradox*, Michael Kammen suggests that biformity, the joining of two forces without losing their individual identity, is the central dynamic of American society. This paradoxical coupling of opposites, suggests Kammen, originated in our colonial experience, in the duality of the imperial situation. Every society experiences the rivalry between freedom and authority, but the colonial situation, with its endless tension between imperial law and home rule, renders the conflict especially poignant.

Independence severed the paradoxical knot of empire, but it ushered in biformity of its own, a duality of federal government and state, each demanding loyalty and service. Nor were the paradoxes confined to American politics. The vastness of the landscape made us a nation of land rovers,

William Penn (1644–1718). The plain clothing and natural hair are clearly that of a Quaker. Yet one would be pressed to find much else in his countenance, whether of piety, purity, or power.

a people seeking to better itself socially and financially by changing its physical surroundings. The fact of change itself became a constant in the American equation; novelty perpetually challenged custom. Unfettered enterprise resulted in "creative destruction," as one scholar phrased it, that altered and still alters the land and its people. The conquest of the wilderness offered symbolic juxtapositions of its own primeval nature contrasted with civilization, hardy Westerner and effete Easterner, pristine countryside versus debauched city.

Each of the colonial Americans we have examined thus far represents this curious counterpoint in different ways. Pocahontas, the cosmopolitan primitive, illustrated the ambiguous position of the American Indian. White attitudes toward the Indian, which oscillated between "noble savage" and "red varmint," also reflected the ambiguity. A character in *The Sot Weed Factor*, a fictional account of early Maryland, expressed the paradox of the Indian thus: "Does essential savagery lurk beneath the skin of civilization, or does essential civilization lurk beneath the skin of savagery?" Captain John Smith, whose coat of arms was three Turks' heads, was no better equipped to answer that question than was Pocahontas.

William Bradford and Anne Hutchinson exemplify the many paradoxes in Puritan New England. Bradford, the practical idealist, crossed the Atlantic to form a wilderness utopia and wound up superintending a bustling commercial center. Unable to reconcile the two, he ended his days in despondency. Anne Hutchinson was an otherworldly saint who was forced to live by laws created for sinners. The injustice of her trial and banishment prompted her to reexamine the ancient question of liberty and authority, and she finally concluded, along with Roger Williams, that the most elementary right of all was the right to be wrong.

Nathaniel Bacon, the conservative revolutionary, who upheld the system while overthrowing its guardians, is the most mysterious one of all. His entire life, from foppish college boy to bloodstained Indian fighter to political visionary, is a paradox. He is the precursor of the American vigilante, the civilian under arms, the violent upholder of law and order.

William Penn, whose life story rounds out this group of imperial pathfinders, draws together these various themes. He was the archetype of the uprooted Englishman, split between imperial restraint and colonial experimentation. He too planned a godly utopia, delicately balanced between democracy and deference, deeply religious yet utterly tolerant, and like Bradford, he lived to see his "holy experiment" vanish in a quarrelsome, commercial metropolis. The tension between reverence and commercialism was inherent in the faiths of both Bradford and Penn.

The godly person was expected to pursue his or her calling energetically. And hard work, especially in the opportunity-filled New World environment, usually produced material success. Yet the church warned its God-fearing adherents not to indulge in worldly luxuries or let excess profits accumulate. Two centuries later John D. Rockefeller resolved the conundrum with the simple explanation "God gave me the money and how could I withhold it from the University of Chicago?" William Penn, by turns aristocrat and democrat, regulator and innovator, saint and land jobber, never found life quite that simple.

The Making of a Friend

Few men have owed so much to their father; few have done so little to acknowledge the debt. William Penn Senior provided his son with his fortune, his social connections, and, indirectly, his American colony, but the son rarely regarded his father as friend and confidante, and never as a behavioral model. The two rarely quarreled; they simply coexisted. The senior Penn and his father, Giles Penn, were seafarers involved for a time in the Mediterranean wine trade. When Spain interrupted their operation and confiscated their property, William Senior forsook business for the public service. He took a commission in the royal navy, and before long received a captaincy. In the English army commissions were usually obtained by purchase; in the navy political influence was the key. In neither service was merit of much account, although a sort of natural selection principle weeded out the truly incompetent. Whenever a naval officer lost a battle, he was usually court-martialed and sometimes executed.

Captain Penn's competence was never at issue, though some grumbled at his rapid rise in the service. Penn received his commission in 1642, the year in which the English civil war began. The victory of Puritans and parliament over the royalist forces of King Charles I placed Penn in a dilemma. He, like most of his fellow officers, was a royalist by habit and a conventional Anglican by faith. Some naval commanders resigned rather than serve under Puritans, but Penn elected to stay. He would serve his country regardless of the party in power. It was a fortunate decision, for within two years opportunity and influence made him an admiral. He was then only twenty-six years old and had never been tested in battle!

In the fall of 1644 Admiral Penn joined a squadron destined for Ireland to suppress an uprising against the new regime. While the crew worked his vessel down the Thames from London, the admiral took a hasty shore leave to superintend the birth of his first child. It was a boy, blessed with his father's name, born on October 14, 1644. The admiral lingered on for a fortnight, ensuring the recovery of Lady Margaret Penn and the baptism of his son, and then sailed off to war.

For the next seven years young William saw almost nothing of his father, who spent his time patrolling the Irish coast. He lived with his mother in a community of navy wives who lived by rigid rules of etiquette. In this atmosphere of social decorum he grew into a somber lad much given to reading. The child being father to the man, he grew from thence into a sober, introspective adult. In the long record of his fully reported life there are only two instances when anyone saw him laugh.

In 1652 the admiral returned home fresh from a raid on the Spanish Main, in which he captured the island of Jamaica. Protector of the realm Oliver Cromwell (the Puritans' republican experiment had degenerated into a dictatorship), instead of offering the usual commendations, clapped him in jail. The ostensible reason was that the admiral had returned home without receiving orders to do so, but the underlying fact was that Penn had refused to make Cromwell's nephew second-in-command even though the Protector had recommended the appointment. The jail term was brief, but for the next few years the admiral lived in forced retirement without pay or the Irish lands he had been promised for his earlier service. The effect of this shore leave on his son, emerging into teen age and un-accustomed to a male presence, especially one with quarterdeck manners, can only be imagined.

In the year 1656 or perhaps 1657, Penn later recalled, he became intensely interested in religion. He was then boarding out at a grammar school run by two "poets . . . of grave behavior." He became acquainted there with the Puritan critique of Anglican ritual and took to reading the Bible with such intensity that, as he later said, he frequently "was ravished by joy and dissolved into tears." Revelations followed, and he became convinced that he was destined to lead a holy life. Such feelings, however, he carefully concealed in the presence of his religiously un-committed and socially conformist parents.

Protector Cromwell eventually restored the admiral to active duty and made up the arrears in back pay, including even the Irish land grant, but the Admiral never forgave his humiliation. He became involved actively, though secretly, in the scheme to restore the monarchy. His exact role is unclear, but when Charles II returned to England in 1660, two years after the Protector's death, he promptly made the admiral a knight and appointed him a navy commissioner at £500 a year.

That same year, young William, aged seventeen, entered Christ Church College, Oxford, as a gentleman scholar. His obligations as a student were essentially those expected of Nathaniel Bacon at Cambridge—aristocratic bearing and no more than an occasional brush with the law. Penn confounded everyone by actually spending a good deal of time in the library. He was nonetheless unhappy in such an environment and dropped out after only a year. His father, still hoping to give him the attributes of a gentleman, then sent him on a continental tour. In 1662 Penn crossed over to France in company with "several persons of rank." To please his parents, so Penn later said, he led the gay life in Paris, wore fine clothes, and took lessons in dancing and swordsmanship.

But this again proved unsatisfying, and before long he enrolled himself in a small Protestant seminary in the Loire valley, about 150 miles from Paris. His best-known teacher there was a man of antinomian views who held that God lived in people's hearts and conscience was the only dictate of behavior.

When William returned from the continent, gilded with French mannerisms without and seething with religious turmoil within, the admiral sent him to Lincoln's Inn, London. The object was twofold: to complete the polish of a gentleman and to establish social contacts for future referral. If he acquired a little law on the way, so much the better, though too much could do harm. The admiral need not have worried on that score, for only the most devoted pedant could have learned anything in that playboy fraternity. Attendance at classes was never checked and students were allowed to hire proxies to perform the work for them. Penn's studies were interrupted, moreover, by periodic vacations at sea in company with his father. Despite his rather despondent childhood, he seems at this point to have come to terms with the aging admiral.

In 1664 a new Anglo-Dutch war broke out, triggered by England's seizure of the Dutch colony of New Netherland. In charge of the seizure was the king's brother, James, Duke of York, to whom Charles had given the colony (with the proviso that he capture it) as a personal proprietary. Although James had limited experience at sea, he was given the office of Lord High Admiral, and the following year he assumed command of England's sea defenses. In June, 1665, off Lowestoft in the English channel, James and Admiral Penn defeated a larger Dutch force. The victory came under subsequent criticism, however, when it was learned that James had failed to pursue the retreating Dutch and annihilate them. The Admiral stepped in to shoulder the blame, and critics, leery of offending the king's brother, were glad to oblige. The barrage, most of it unfair, ended his active career; he retired to a desk job in the naval office. For years thereafter James of York repaid the admiral with secret favors, both to himself and to his son. King Charles too seems to have understood the obligation. When, many years later, the king granted William his American province, he cited among the reasons his gratitude for the Admiral's aid and understanding.

Quaker Martyr

In 1667, while on a mission to Ireland to oversee his father's estates, William Penn became a Quaker. For the better part of his twenty-three years he had been preoccupied with religion, moving to ever more extreme forms of Puritanism. The Society of Friends was the end of the theological line. Its tenets, moreover, blended nicely with Penn's sober personality.

The Society of Friends (derisively named Quakers because they allegedly shook in fear of the Lord) was founded in the 1640s by George Fox. An itinerant preacher who traveled for years in search of a true church, Fox ultimately came to reject nearly all outward forms of worship. The core of his belief was that people's souls communed directly with God, who revealed Himself to the faithful through an inner light—a tenet that Anne Hutchinson would have found quite acceptable. Fox drove on—as Anne might have had she been given the chance—to the conclusion that trained ministers and religious ceremonies were unnecessary; in fact, they interfered with the direct communion of the human soul and God. He proclaimed instead the "priesthood of all believers." His church would not even call itself that; it would be instead a society of the faithful meeting in informal and unpretentious circumstances. Quakers simply grouped together in silence, seeking God through inner harmony, until the inner light moved someone to speak. A service, consisting of long periods of silence interspersed with brief fits of testimony, usually lasted for several hours. When no one felt further compelled to speak (or perhaps discomfort got the upper hand) the meeting simply broke up.

The close relationship between the human soul and the divine being in the Quaker creed downplayed the role, not only of the clergy, but of Christ himself. The Quakers professed themselves to be Christians, but they were not much concerned with the concepts of original sin and salvation through Christ. Christ was a living symbol of salvation, but not a necessary agent, and certainly did not rank on a Trinitarian par with God. This notion led more orthodox Puritans to accuse Quakers of being unitarians, though the charge is not exactly true. Puritans—Congregationalists and Presbyterians alike—also objected to the anti-intellectual bias in Quakerism. Without a learned clergy, they felt, the untutored halt were leading the intellectually blind. The church itself would collapse as each Saint went off on a theological tangent. George Fox, of course, did not care. An institution that required conformity was precisely what he was trying to avoid.

Fox also believed that the Friends ought to practice religion in their daily lives. Humble sobriety was not for Sunday alone; it ought to be part of daily regimen along with plain dress and archaic forms of speech ("thee" and "thou"), which harked back to a simpler past. The injunctions of the Bible, moreover, were to be taken literally. Christ had preached the brotherhood of man, so Quakers refused to carry arms or make war. God had warned against false swearing, so Quakers refused to take oaths. An honest man's word, they said, was as good as his oath anyway. In a society that perceived all Europe to be a potential military threat and which regarded all dissidents as subversives, a group that refused military service and rejected loyalty oaths was naturally suspect.

Fox and the Friends, with the same logical consistency that led to the priesthood of believers, accepted the democratic implications of their faith. The concept of inner light meant that all men, and indeed women too, were equal before God. Thus they refused to doff their hats to aristocrats, as custom demanded, on the grounds that only God warranted such deference. Such behavior, of course, only reinforced suspicion that they were dangerous radicals intent upon subverting the social order.

Had the Quakers been content to practice their faith in quiet they might have been tolerated, although their refusal to swear oaths automatically excluded them from government service, politics, and the universities. But they could not remain quiet. True evangelists, they felt called upon to do God's work by spreading the word. Even so, they might have become lost among the mob of religious exhorters that roamed the English countryside but for their peculiar mannerisms, which drew attention and aroused suspicion. Thus Quaker itinerants by the hundreds were placed in stocks, whipped, or locked in jail, depending on the facilities available. Among the American colonies, Virginia and Maryland tried to ignore them, Rhode Island sheltered them, and Massachusetts expelled them. Their democratic and anticlerical tenets particularly alarmed the Bay Colony authorities. Three Quakers who persisted in returning after being banished were finally put to death, among them Anne Hutchinson's friend Mary Dyer.

One such itinerant showed the light to William Penn at a meeting in Ireland, and the young convert in turn immediately embarked on a missionary tour of England. Since most Quakers were of the middle class at most, Penn's status as a gentleman gave him an early authority in the movement, and as the son of a war hero he was a marked man in public. Authorities could not afford to ignore him as a harmless fanatic. When, toward the end of 1668, he published a pamphlet expounding the tenets of Quakerism, he was summarily thrown into the Tower of London. For seven months he languished there without ever being formally charged of a crime (authorities apparently wavered between sedition and blasphemy). He passed the time defiantly scratching out with prison quill another Quaker broadside. (An inveterate pamphleteer, he ultimately produced 150 books and essays.)

Admiral Penn's position in all this is much to be pitied. A man who had done so much for his son in his own view (and so little, in retrospect), he was doubtless mortified by this latest gaucherie. He was also in poor health, though only in his mid-forties, suffering from gout and incipient alcoholism. Yet, with parental loyalty, he worked the one trump he had, James of York, in trying to secure his son's release. William himself cooperated by writing a counterpoint to the essay that had gotten him in trouble. He titled it An *Apology*, which could mean either apologia (explication) or apology (retraction). The double entendre saved the ministry's face, as well as his own, and he was released in July, 1669.

In Search of a Refuge

It is one of the curiosities of seventeenth-century England that government was cruel precisely because it was weak. The regime of Charles II, newborn and unsure of its support, was haunted by fears of Puritan subversion, Jesuit plots, and foreign spies. Lacking anything resembling a modern police force, the government had only limited means of preserving itself. It did have a professional army, one of the legacies of Oliver Cromwell, and it deliberately quartered the troops in the more unruly villages. Otherwise, authorities relied on professional informers, arbitrary courts, and hanging judges to keep the populace in line. In such an atmosphere of conspiracy, secret meetings, even for placid religious purposes, were objects of suspicion. Early in the Restoration period parliament passed a Conventicle Act designed to limit the religious services of any but the established Church of England. In 1670 the act was tightened so as to make virtually any assemblage unlawful. Quakers thereafter found themselves subject to arrest simply for practicing their faith. Not surprisingly, they began to cast about for a place of refuge. In 1671 George Fox journeyed to America in search of new converts. After two years' wandering through the mid-Atlantic settlements—a region that reminded him of the English west country—he returned fired with the idea of a Quaker colony where the Friends could live in peace.

Opportunity for such an experiment was soon at hand. At the outset of the second Dutch war, England had captured the Dutch colony of New Netherland. The king had offered it to his brother as his personal estate, and the province was accordingly renamed New York. The king's grant, known as a proprietary, was designed to ensure greater royal supervision of the empire while leaving the headaches and expense of colonization to others. The proprietary grant was made to a trusted individual (in this case the king's brother), who was expected to govern in close accordance with the king's wishes (thus avoiding the quasi-independence manifested by the New England colonies). A 1632 grant of Maryland to Lord Baltimore was the first proprietary, and it worked well enough to furnish a model for all later grants. In 1663, the year before the grant to his brother, Charles presented the region from Virginia south to Spanish Florida (named Carolina, after the king) to a consortium of eight proprietors. All were prominent figures in the Restoration government to whom Charles was obligated for political or financial services.

James's New York proprietary extended from the Hudson River to the Delaware River on the South, and from the Hudson to Lake Erie on the West. In 1665 he subdivided this unwieldy tract, conveying the stretch between the Hudson and the Delaware Rivers (New Jersey) to two sub-proprietors, Lord John Berkeley (brother of Virginia's governor) and Sir George Carteret, both of whom were also proprietors of Carolina. The grant did not include the right to govern; it was simply a land conveyance. Interested in quick profits from land sales, Berkeley and Carteret offered attractive terms to prospective settlers—religious toleration and no quitrents. To make things simpler yet, Berkeley and Carteret divided their tract, drawing a diagonal line from the Delaware River to the seacoast. Berkeley took possession of the western half, Carteret took the eastern.

Individual Quakers had already begun purchasing lands in New Jersey when Fox returned in 1673 with his glowing report on the colony's healthy climate and fertile soil. The following year Berkeley suddenly offered his entire holding for sale, and two Quakers, Edward Byllinge and John Fenwick, snapped it up. The sale price for West Jersey was £1000, and since Byllinge and Fenwick were men of modest means, it seems likely that they were simply front men for a consortium of Quakers. Fenwick, in any case, soon transferred his interest to three Quaker trustees, among them Penn. The trustees thereupon named Byllinge governor of West Jersey (though in fact none of these conveyances had carried the right to govern—New Jersey was technically under the supervision of the governor of New York). The first shipload of Quakers headed for West Jersey in 1675, and by 1680 there were some 6000 Friends in the colony.

New Jersey proved an unsatisfactory refuge, however. The devious methods by which they had gained control of the colony left much confusion as to who owned what. Disputes over land titles distracted the colony throughout its history. Quakers were also dismayed to learn that they were subject to the authority of the governor of New York. It was not only alien rule, it was autocratic. Duke James, who shared the Stewart aversion to popular rule, made no provision for an assembly in his province. His governor ruled by executive edict. Thus the Quakers' freedom of worship remained dependent on the whim of a staunchly Anglican autocrat living in far-off Manhattan.

William Penn was especially interested in a refuge that might also serve as a laboratory for political experimentation. Ever since his religious conversion Penn had toyed with radical political ideas. Among his earliest and most influential friends was John Locke, thirteen years older than he, and one of the leading proponents of a limited monarchy. Locke had drafted a frame of government for the Carolina proprietors that included strong guarantees of popular rights. A more recent and more radical acquaintance of Penn's was Algernon Sidney, perhaps the leading republican theorist of the day. Sydney's political career dated back to the early contests between Charles I and parliament, and he remained an unreconstructed republican even after the Restoration. His radical notions would eventually earn him a martyr's death. Prodded by such theorists, Penn dreamed of a New World utopia where the people would have not just religious freedom, but a role in their own government.

In between his periodic stints in jail Penn frequented the royal court. His acceptance there was testimony to his early training. He knew all the arts of the courtier, when he chose to use them, and he had important contacts among the ministerial elite as a result of his sojourns at Oxford and Lincoln's Inn. Both King Charles and James of York singled him out for special attention whenever he appeared at Whitehall. They doubtless still felt under obligation to Penn's father, who died in 1669, but there were probably other factors as well. They may have seen that Penn's plea for toleration of Quakers and other nonconformists would benefit Roman

Catholics as well. James was a practicing Catholic, and Charles was at least sympathetic to the Church of Rome. Papal splendor and Quaker simplicity were ecclesiastical opposites, but they had mutual interests in the fearridden world of Restoration England. It seems likely, moreover, that both of the royal brethren found Penn a more interesting companion than the mindless, fawning sycophants that usually surrounded them.

Penn was also rich enough to play the role of courtier. His father had left him a nice estate in England and extensive holdings in Ireland. In 1672 Penn married Gulielma Maria Springett, a Quaker maid of excellent family, who had an income of £10,000 a year and huge estates in southern England. She proved to be a loving and bountiful wife (eleven children, of whom four died in infancy), who generously allowed Penn to apply her fortune to his New World projects.

On June 1, 1680, William Penn formally appealed to the king and council for a grant of land west of the Delaware River between the Baltimore proprietary in Maryland and the Duke's proprietary of New York. Coming from a known dissident, an ex-convict, the audacity of the request was breathtaking. Imperial authorities, moreover, were just undertaking a move to deprive Massachusetts of its charter and bring that obstreperous colony under control. That they would let yet another religious visionary set up a social experiment in the American wilderness seemed highly unlikely.

Even so, King Charles was not unsympathetic. In his application Penn mentioned a debt of £16,000, which the king owed his father for having financed the royal navy out of his own pocket during the Civil War. Charles, always cavalier with creditors, did not allude to the debt in his discussion of Penn's request, but he did mention the Admiral's "discretion with our dearest brother James," an obvious reference to the battle of Lowestoft. There may have been other considerations, which the king could not afford to mention. James was coming under increasing attack for his Catholicism; one of the newly formed political parties, the Whigs, had vowed to exclude him from the throne (Charles had no legitimate children). A generous concession to an ultra-Protestant group such as the Quakers would demonstrate at least that the Stuarts were not popish bigots.

Though Charles did not mention it, the most important point of all may have been strategic. The tract that Penn requested was inland from the coast. It embraced lands once held by the troublesome Susquehannas, and it stood athwart the ancient Iroquois warpath to the south. The new colony would thus be in a position to help New York with frontier defense, and it would act as a buffer for the Maryland-Virginia frontier.

Thus the king gave Penn's request his blessing, and the councilar machinery entered into a serious, if rather begrudging, investigation of it. When finally approved in April, 1681, Penn's charter had a number of strings attached to it, which reflected the rising concern in London for a tidier, more obedient empire. Penn and his descendants were to be sole proprietors and governors of Pennsylvania (named, by the king, in honor of the Admiral), but any deputy governor Penn appointed would have to have royal approval. The colony was specifically directed to obey imperial trade regulations, which New Englanders were notorious for evading, and every five years it had to submit the laws of its assembly for royal inspection and approval. To ensure that the colony fulfilled its strategic objectives, Penn was required to maintain an army for defense against "pirates, thieves, or invading barbarians."

Penn tactfully accepted all suggestions. When the Bishop of London, who had evidently missed the point on religious toleration, demanded that Penn allow Anglicans to worship in their own church, the proprietor quickly agreed. The good bishop also suggested that Penn ought to purchase the lands he planned to settle from the Indians. That too was redundant, since Penn and other Quakers had scrupulously observed Indian titles in New Jersey, but Penn thanked the bishop and publicly gave him credit for Pennsylvania's Indian policy.

Penn's political skill, in short, disarmed his foes, and the Privy Council's Committee on Trade and Plantations gave its approval. In May, 1681, King Charles declared Penn the "True and Absolute Proprietor" and asked the inhabitants of the colony to render him total obedience. Penn was now the ruler of an empire of 45,000 square miles, more land than any private citizen had ever possessed before. It remained to be seen how much of his power he would turn over to his people.

The "Holy Experiment"

While his charter wound its way through the labyrinth of imperial bureaucracy, Penn gathered a council of advisers to help him draw up a "Frame of Government" for the new colony. Among them were old friends John Locke and Algernon Sidney. The latter is sometimes credited with drafting the Frame, but Penn himself had read so widely among the republican theorists of the Cromwellian age that he most certainly played an active role in the discussions.

The document, published in the fall of 1681, was certainly remarkable for its time. The governor, or his deputy when Penn was not in the province, was to rule in conjunction with an elected council containing seventy-two members. Together they would appoint all officials, including judges, and draft the laws. The council was also to serve as the upper house of a bicameral assembly. The lower house, containing 500 members, had power only to approve or reject laws proposed by governor and council. This limitation in an otherwise democratic structure may have been an oversight on Penn's part, but he also might reasonably have argued that the elected council was a sufficient guardian of popular liberties. The lower house, moreover, was so large as to be unwieldy; some sort of steering mechanism was essential.

Although it was expected that members of the council would be citizens "of most note for their wisdom, virtue, and ability," wealth was not specifically required. Nor was there a property qualification for voting. All taxpayers had the vote, including, presumably, women, though there is no record that any females tried to exercise the right. Women were expressly mentioned, however, in the laws preserving freedom of conscience. Quakers felt that women had the same spiritual gifts as men. Nowhere in the world did there exist a government in which the citizens had so large a voice. Coming, as it would, from a godly, peace-loving people, Penn naturally assumed that the voice would be a harmonious one.

The "Holy Experiment," as Penn called it, was an experiment in religious toleration. The government would make no effort to dictate matters of conscience. This was not, however, even in Penn's mind, an experiment in total religious freedom (in the spirit, a century later, of Thomas Jefferson). It was simply permission to worship, or not to worship, as one pleased. Penn made no objection when the assembly, at its first meeting, restricted voting and officeholding to Christians. The Frame also included a Puritanical moral code for the guidance of Pennsylvanians. "Offenses against God," such as swearing, cursing, Lying, as well as such "other violences" as stage plays, card playing, dice, "may-games, masques, revels, bull-battings, cockfightings, bear-battings, and the like, which excite the people to rudeness, cruelty, looseness, and unreligion shall be respectively discouraged and severely punished."

Although there was no legal church establishment, it was clear that the Friends would dominate the government, frame the laws, and set the tone of Pennsylvania society. Others would be welcome, but they would have to submit to Quaker principles. Working this out in practice proved to be most difficult—for Penn and for his colony.

Settling the Wilderness

Profit was not part of Penn's purpose, but he did expect to be reimbursed for colonization expenses out of land sales. Indeed, he began selling tracts to wealthy friends—several of them speculators who never intended to move to Pennsylvania—as soon as his charter cleared the Privy Council. He also wrote a land sales brochure, aimed not only at Friends but all Englishmen interested in freedom and opportunity. Using information gleaned from George Fox and other travelers, Penn described the climate and topography of his province in glowing terms; it was a figurative Garden of Eden in which no one could fail.

Penn then set up a sales organization. Several agents canvassed Quaker communities in the British Isles, and Francis Daniel Pastorius, a German pietist, spread the word on the continent. The initial response— £6380 in sales in the first two years—was not very encouraging. Penn may have set his price too high: he charged more than West Jersey proprietors did for comparable lands. And the threat of quitrents (Penn would promise no more than to delay collections until 1684) may have been a deterrent. His advertising eventually paid off, however; within a few years a swarm of religious and political refugees from all over western Europe was heading for Delaware Bay.

Having set up his advertising and sales staff, Penn prepared to depart for his colony. There was, however, one final item of business. To prosper, Pennsylvania had to have access to the sea. It was agreed that the boundary between Pennsylvania and Maryland was to be the 40th parallel of latitude, but no one knew precisely where that lay. If that should lie to the north of Delaware Bay (it does, by some distance), Pennsylvania's commerce might be at the none-too-tender mercy of Lord Baltimore. The solution lay in gaining title to the western shore of Delaware Bay, to which Maryland had a rather dubious claim. Since there was a Dutch settlement on that shore at New Amstel (New Castle), the land was probably part of the Duke of York's conquered province. Penn accordingly went to his old friend, who obliged him with a grant of the region, extending from the mouth of the bay inland to a radius of twelve miles north of New Amstel (hence Delaware's curvilinear boundary with Pennsylvania). The new proprietary, consisting of three counties, was referred to as the Lower Counties until the American Revolution. Penn governed them as part of Pennsylvania until 1704 when they obtained an assembly of their own.

A week after receiving the deed to his new possession, Penn set sail for America. His wife, Guli, who was then expecting their seventh child, decided at the last minute not to go. Living conditions on a ship were too primitive to care for an infant. As it turned out, Guli contracted erysipelas, St. Anthony's Fire, toward the end of her pregnancy. She recovered, but the baby became infected and died within three weeks. The infant was probably doomed, in any case, for smallpox swept through the ship in midAtlantic. Penn, who had contracted the disease in childhood, was one of the few survivors.

Pennsylvania was a year old when its proprietor sailed into Delaware Bay, and Penn's deputy, William Markham, had things well in hand. He had established good relations with the earlier inhabitants, Dutch and Swedes, he had set up a ruling council (though, perhaps for lack of numbers, not yet an assembly), and he had selected a site for the provincial capital. Markham's own headquarters were at New Castle, but he wanted to place the permanent seat of government a hundred miles farther up river where the Schuykill River entered the Delaware. The new location would be secure from naval attack, and the rivers gave it access to the hinterland.

With customary care, Penn had sent over plans for his capital, together with a name, Philadelphia. He envisioned a model city with a rational gridiron street plan, riverside parks, and landscaped homes. The one flaw in it was that he forgot to provide for the poor, the artisan class that provided the services on which a city lived. The addition of "backward streets," as Penn called them, with homes and shops for these people, cluttered his green vistas. Commercial necessity soon filled up his riverside parks with wharves and warehouses. Except for its broad avenues and rectangular blocks, Philadelphia came to look much like any crowded and filthy English seaport.

In November, 1682, Penn had a highly successful meeting with Tammamend, chief of the powerful Lenni Lenape tribe (immortalized a century later as Tammany, patron saint of New York democracy). The two leaders agreed to live in peace and mutual respect for each other's lands and rights. A formal treaty was signed the following June in a ceremony depicted, somewhat fancifully, by the "historical" painter Benjamin West in 1770.

Then, in December, Penn summoned his first assembly at New Castle. He had brought over a set of laws, some forty in all, which he and his circle of friends had drafted in England. He wanted the assembly to approve them. The delegates naturally demanded the right to read and discuss them. Penn was dubious. The council, he felt, certainly had the right to debate legislation, but if the huge, inexperienced lower house

"Penn's Treaty with the Indians" (1772), oil painting by Benjamin West. West started the "historical school" of American painting, which used events of American history for its subjects, rather than stories from the Bible or Greek and Roman gods, as European painters had so often done. The painting hangs in Independence Hall, Philadelphia. (Picture Collection, The Branch Libraries, The New York Public Library.)

undertook to do so as well, his proposals would become drowned in a cacophony of opinions. Penn clearly envisioned the assembly as a regularized referendum, with power only to vote "yes" or "no," not "maybe." Yet herein lay the paradox between liberty and authority. In England, Penn had long championed parliament's right to free debate. Was not the principle the same in Pennsylvania? It was, he agreed. Having won their point, the delegates proceeded to rubber-stamp Penn's laws without further discussion. It was, after all, a Quaker assembly, and Penn's was a Quaker code, as liberal and humane as any in the world at the time. There was only one capital offense (murder), while English law listed more than two hundred. Drunkenness, swearing, and sex crimes were to be punished by hard labor or whipping. All offenses were to be tried in civil courts (domestic relations and morals offenses were tried by church courts in England), and trial by jury was guaranteed. The sale of liquor to Indians was prohibited. Finally, to ensure that the assembly would be called into session regularly, the code stipulated that taxes must be levied on an annual basis.

For one who had entered upon colonization with a utopian vision, Penn proved surprisingly flexible. When he summoned a second assembly in the spring of 1683 he suggested that each of the six counties choose only nine delegates. The three in each county with the most votes would serve in the council, the other six in the lower house. He obviously recognized that a 72-man council and 500-man assembly (roughly one-tenth of the adult male population) were too unwieldy to function properly. When the assembly met on March 12, Penn yielded (with his customary misgivings) to the lower house the right not only to discuss but to initiate legislation. The main thing they wanted to initiate, as it turned out, was a new Frame of Government. Penn gave way on this point too. This instrument confirmed the assembly's right to initiate legislation, and it restricted the power of the governor by requiring Penn to obtain the advice and consent of the council for every official act.

Religious toleration and political democracy bred prosperity, just as Penn had anticipated. Ships, jammed with immigrants, arrived at the rate of one a week. Some of the newcomers were Quakers, but by no means all. A group of enterprising Welshmen purchased a tract of several square miles near Philadelphia, intending to establish a barony modeled on their homeland. But the leapfrogging patchwork of settlement touched, surrounded, and ultimately absorbed them before they could institute their Old World scheme. The non-English too began to arrive. Francis Daniel Pastorius, an old acquaintance of Penn's, arrived with his flock from the Rhineland. A wealthy, university-educated German blue-blood, Pastorius was a natural leader. The surname he had adopted (his family name was actually Schaefer) bespoke the authority he commanded over German pietists, who believed, much as Quakers did, in practicing religion in their daily lives. Their community northwest of Philadelphia became known as Germantown.

From the beginning Penn had relied on an inner circle of Quaker leaders for advice. The most prominent of these was Nicholas More, a physician who had been Penn's first customer in Pennsylvania lands. Shortly after arriving in America Penn brought into the group Lasse Cock, acknowledged leader of the Swedish settlement and an expert on Indian languages. Pastorius was admitted to the group when he arrived, as was Thomas Lloyd, spokesman for the Welsh element. The circle thus represented every important ethnic and commercial interest in the colony. Penn increasingly relied on this group for counsel, and the practical advice he received sometimes forced further modification of his utopian dreams.

Penn's flexibility and pragmatism nevertheless calmed political disputes and softened ethnic rivalries. By 1684 the province seemed well on the way to becoming the garden of contentment that Penn's sales brochures had forecast. The imperial connection continued to trouble him, however. In that year the royal Privy Council revoked the charter of Massachusetts Bay and began investigating the other New England colonies. Aware that the imperial bureaucracy had resisted his own grant, Penn worried that he might be next on the council's list. He thus decided to return to England in the hope of deflecting the blow. He expected only a short stay; it stretched out to fifteen years. Indeed, of the thirty-four years that remained to him, only two were spent in Pennsylvania.

Troubles of an Absentee Governor

It is tempting to speculate on what might have happened if Penn had remained in America. During his two-year stay he revealed both ideological flexibility and political aptitude. He might well have developed into a competent administrator and shrewd politician. Instead, he lost touch with his province. As Pennsylvania matured, the assembly naturally demanded greater authority. When Penn resisted, the demand hardened into an antiproprietary movement. When he returned at last in 1699, he faced a well-organized opposition party determined to curb his executive powers. In English isolation Penn also grew more rigid and tactless. He became quarrelsome, vindictive, and given to self-pity. Strife and recrimination clouded his remaining years as proprietor.

Not all of this, it must be said, was Penn's fault. Pennsylvania's demand for autonomy ran contrary to the royal drive for greater administrative control of the empire. Caught between the two, Penn felt he had to side with the empire in order to preserve his charter. He may have been right, but he also might have been a more effective go-between had he remained in Philadelphia. True, he weathered the immediate crisis caused by the revocation of the Bay Colony's charter, but his activities thereafter lacked both polish and good sense. He would have been better off in Philadelphia.

In London Penn renewed his friendship with the king's brother, James, and the association opened for him the doors of English officialdom. Penn disliked being a courtier; it was contrary to all his beliefs. But he played the role as well as anyone in London. He fawned upon the mighty, distributed judicious gifts among the less powerful, and pulled strings when all else failed. Such was his reputation that hundreds of petitioners camped at his door daily to beg his intercession with the court. His most spectacular success was in winning freedom for some 1300 Quakers jailed for practicing their faith.

When Charles II died in 1685 and James became king, Penn's influence reached its zenith. He spent long hours in company with the new monarch, who obviously enjoyed his conversation. Indeed, the friendship was close enough to inspire rumors that Penn was a secret Jesuit ministering to the king. The notion was preposterous, but in those troubled times people were prepared to believe anything. The association, in fact, was too close for Penn's own well-being, for James was rapidly alienating everyone in England. He irritated the Anglican Church by openly avowing his Catholicism, and he incensed the aristocracy by suspending laws and prematurely dissolving parliament. When William of Orange and his wife Mary (James's Protestant daughter) landed in England and James fled to Paris in November, 1688, Penn was ruined. He was arrested a month later, released for lack of evidence, then rearrested when he witlessly blurted out at a dinner party the news that he had been in contact with the ex-king. He was again released, but only on condition that he avoid politics or public appearances. Penn willingly went into seclusion, but he could not escape trouble. His absence from the court itself aroused suspicion. Rumors circulated that he was secretly plotting a Stuart restoration, and he was twice more jailed in the early 1690s.

King William was as anxious to recover royal control of the empire as any of his predecessors. In 1691 he issued a new charter to Massachusetts, making it a royal colony with governor appointed by the king, and the following year he took Pennsylvania into his own hands. The principal reason for revoking Penn's charter was to improve colonial defense. William had declared war on France shortly after taking the throne; the war (called War of the League of Augsburg in Europe, King William's War in America) caused some fighting on the American frontier. A combination of faith and thrift kept Pennsylvania from abetting the war effort, and the antiproprietary party was no more willing to obey the king's orders than Penn's. David Lloyd (a distant relative of Thomas Lloyd), Speaker of the House and leader of the antiproprietary cause, pushed a tax levy through the assembly as a sop to royal commands, but the money was never collected.

In 1694 Penn recovered his colony after convincing the Lords of Trade and Plantations that he would personally see to it that Pennsylvania levied taxes and raised armies. It was a misleading impression, for Penn had no more influence in Philadelphia than the Lords had. Even so, he might have recovered some of his authority had he sailed immediately for the Delaware, but he dawdled another five years in London while carrying on an increasingly irascible correspondence with his deputies in the colony.

End of the Holy Experiment

In 1694 Guli Penn died; "the best of wives and women," Penn called her. Her illness and death had delayed his return to Pennsylvania, but even after she was gone he lingered on in London. Within a year he was in love again. His choice, a good one, was Hannah Hollister, thirty years his junior and daughter of a wealthy Quaker merchant. For some years Penn's estate had been dwindling as he sold off assets to maintain his social station. He might have drawn a salary as governor of Pennsylvania, but he had never asked for one, and the penurious assembly avoided the subject. Hannah's handsome dowry, which she put at his disposal, mended his fortune. Hannah also proved to be a fruitful and successful mother. Of Guli's eleven children, only two survived to maturity. Hannah had seven, of whom five reached adulthood.

In 1699 Penn at last embarked for America, taking with him this time both wife and children. He had hoped to share some of his administrative duties in Pennsylvania with his oldest son Billy, aged nineteen, but that lad proved too unreliable. So instead Penn hired a young school teacher named James Logan as his secretary. It was the best selection he ever made, for Logan became a capable and trustworthy adviser. Billy, whose young wife was pregnant, was left behind.

Philadelphia, a bustling seaport whose commercial tentacles stretched from London to the West Indies, was too crowded, crime-ridden, and noisy for Penn. A decade earlier he had ordered the construction of a mansion on proprietary lands a few miles farther up the Delaware. Pennsbury, he called the place, and it was an English transplant, a stately manor with poplar-lined walkways, formal gardens, and manicured lawns. He originally intended to build and staff it with slave labor, but rising opposition to slavery among both German Pietists and Quakers induced him to use white servants instead. He freed what slaves he had in 1701. Penn commuted between his suburban home and the state house in Philadelphia in a six-oared barge. When politics got rough, Pennsbury was his refuge.

Pennsylvania politics was always rough. The assembly, under the firm command of David Lloyd, considered itself the equal of both governor and council. It felt free to initiate laws of which Penn disapproved and to reject proposals that he earnestly desired. No assembly anywhere in the colonies in 1700 wielded as much power as Pennsylvania's. The European war, and hence the frontier skirmishing, had ended in 1697, but London still wanted the colony's defenses put in order. Penn tried sincerely to obey the wishes of imperial officials, though they ran contrary to his own conscience, but the assembly deliberately frustrated his every request. When it grudgingly appropriated funds, it neglected to levy a tax to obtain the revenue. When it did impose a tax it almost always failed to set up means for collection.

In 1701 Penn perceived a new threat to his charter, as the government of William III began the process of making neighboring New Jersey into a royal colony. He resolved on another trip to London, but before he departed, Lloyd and the assembly demanded a new Frame of Government. Penn, always more flexible when superintending his colony in person, agreed. The Frame of 1701, which lasted until the Revolution, confirmed the powers of the assembly to propose, amend, or repeal legislation. But it also strengthened the hand of the executive. The governor would appoint members of the council and set their terms in office, and the council, though no longer elective, would continue to function as upper house of the legislature. The suffrage was confined to rural landholders and urban taxpayers, a narrower base than first envisioned by Penn but still broader than any other colony.

The "Holy Experiment," Penn's dream of a brotherhood of the godly, had long since fallen victim to party rancor and imperial tension. The Frame of 1701, by formally separating executive from legislature, simply confirmed its demise. Conflict, rather than harmony, was the essence of the new plan. Yet, because it recognized and even balanced the diverse interests of proprietor and assembly, empire and colony, the Frame of 1701 was infinitely more workable than the once-dreamed utopia.

When the Frame was completed, Penn prepared for another Atlantic crossing. He planned only a brief visit, and wanted to leave Hannah and the children at Pennsbury. Hannah, who found suburban life dull, insisted upon accompanying him, however. It was just as well, for he never returned.

The threat to his charter, if one existed, ended in 1702 with the death of William, the accession of Queen Anne (James's other Protestant daughter), and the renewal of war with France. The war placed new stress on his relations with his colony. Indian war blazed on the New England-New York frontier, and pirates roamed the seacoast. The

Pennsylvania assembly made no provision for defense, and Philadelphia merchants openly trafficked with the pirates.

Penn, now past sixty, went from quarrelsome to vindictive. Through James Logan, the only ally he had in the colony, he sent a stream of angry complaints to Philadelphia. He also began demanding what before he had only hinted, a salary as chief executive, even though he was of little use to the colony in London. The salary request was prompted by a renewal of his financial difficulties. Twenty-five years earlier he had incurred a debt to one Philip Ford, who had served as his business agent. Preoccupied with his colony, Penn had delayed payment, while agreeing in writing to a ruinous interest that swelled the sum year by year. In 1707 Philip Ford died, and his widow sued Penn for the astronomical sum of £30,000. That was more than his entire colony was worth (Penn had earlier offered it to Queen Anne for that sum and had been turned down). Penn suffered the humiliation of debtor's prison.

At that juncture, as so often in the past, a friend in high office came to Penn's rescue. This time it was the hero of Queen Anne's war, John Churchill, Duke of Marlborough. The friendship between Penn and Marlborough began when Penn accepted one of Marlborough's captains, Charles Gookin, as deputy governor. Gookin proved a success as an administrator, partly, one suspects, because Pennsylvania had lowered its expectations. The colony had recently suffered the brief but turbulent rule of Billy Penn, which ended when the deputy governor got in a barroom brawl in Philadelphia and fled the colony. Marlborough interceded in Penn's behalf, secured a judicial compromise that scaled the debt to £7600, and sprang the old pacifist-warhorse from prison.

That experience seemed to mellow Penn. He ceased his caustic exchanges with the Pennsylvania assembly and took up preaching once more. He even recovered some of his early liberalism. When the Quaker women of Reading, where William and Hannah now resided, began to agitate for equal rights, Penn took up their cause. Unhappy because they were denied an equal role in society affairs, the women began holding separate meetings. The men thereupon locked them out of the meetinghouse altogether. With Penn among their number, the women set up their own place of worship (probably in a private home), and they held separate services for the next five years.

A stroke in 1712 slowed Penn further. He had great difficulty concentrating thereafter and sometimes had difficulty speaking. Hannah took over his business affairs, and devoted much of her time trying to sell Pennsylvania. The crown was willing, though it balked at giving her a West Indies sugar island in return, as she requested. The opposition of her sons delayed the sale, and then the death of Queen Anne threw everything into confusion. In July, 1718, Penn came down with chills and fever, probably some form of influenza, and died.

By prior family agreement Pennsylvania was divided among Hannah's sons. John, "the American," the only one born in the province, received half; the remainder was divided among his three younger brothers. Pennsylvania and Delaware, which had won a separate identity in 1704, remained in the Penn family until the Revolution. Pennsylvania's Indians, aware that they had lost a good, if unfamiliar, friend, sent Hannah a message of condolence together with a gift of furs in which to array herself for the passage through the tangled wilderness of widowhood. A primitive civility—the paradox lived on.

SUGGESTIONS FOR FURTHER READING

Biformity as an explanation for the American character is one of the many insights of Michael Kammen in his Pulitzer Prize-winning book, *People of Paradox: An Inquiry Concerning the Origins of American Civilization* (1973). The most recent and detailed biography is Harry Emerson Wildes, *William Penn* (1974). Joseph E. Illick, *William Penn the Politician* (1965), focuses on Penn's relations with imperial authorities; and Edwin B. Bronner, *William Penn's Holy Experiment* (1962), concentrates on the founding of Pennsylvania. Mary Maples Dunn, *William Penn, Politics and Conscience* (1967), explores the biformity within Penn himself. J. William Frost, *A Perfect Freedom: Religious Liberty in Pennsylvania* (1990) traces the history of Penn's "Holy Experiment."

PART 2

Swords of Empire

"On that day, the realm of France received on parchment a stupendous accession. The fertile plains of Texas; the vast basin of the Mississippi, from its frozen northern springs to the sultry borders of the Gulf; from the woody ridges of the Alleghenies to the bare peaks of the Rocky Mountains—a region of savannahs and forests, sun-cracked deserts, and grassy prairies, watered by a thousand rivers, ranged by a thousand warlike tribes, passed beneath the sceptre of the Sultan of Versailles; and all by virtue of a feeble human voice, inaudible at half a mile."

—Francis Parkman, *La Salle and the Discovery of the Great West*, describing LaSalle's claim to the Mississippi (April 9,1682)

6

Pierre Esprit Radisson:
The Pathfinder

In the vanguard of empire were the fortune hunters. Not the kings and princes; they were preoccupied with politicians and diplomats. Not the politicians; they were preoccupied with kings and constituents. Not the soldiers; they had neither the imagination nor the enterprise. Once an empire was established, kings and politicians and diplomats and soldiers took a hand in shaping its destiny. But in the beginning was the fortune hunter! Columbus and John Smith, Robert Clive and Warren Hastings, Daniel Boone and La Verendrye, Cecil Rhodes and Sir George Goldie, Stephen F. Austin and Collis P. Huntington. And behind each was a syndicate of investors, silent fortune seekers, sometimes organized as a stock company—a London Company, an East India Company, a Royal Nigeria Company, or a Southern Pacific Railroad. These were the vanguard of empire, the profit seekers, tough-minded and amoral, patriotic only when it served their interests; it was they who spread European languages, customs, and technology around the globe.

The contest between Britain and France for control of North America called forth a full measure of these imperial trailblazers, some of whom are examined in the following section. Perhaps the least-known is the most enterprising of them all—Pierre Esprit Radisson, citizen of no country, who betrayed his native France twice and his adopted England once, who crossed the Atlantic twenty-four times, traversed Hudson Bay seven times, and paddled the length of the Great Lakes twice. Here was the dreamer-realist who spent his life searching for the Northwest Passage and found not the imaginary gateway to the Pacific, but the only passages the continent afforded: the Lake Superior-St. Croix-Mississippi passage to the Gulf of Mexico and the Lake Superior-Lake Winnipeg-Nelson River waterway to Hudson Bay. And he performed these feats at a time when New England and Virginia were little more than agricultural beachheads, and Pennsylvania was not even a dream.

Bred to the Forest

Radisson's memoirs tell us much about North America and little about the man. His travel accounts were written not for posterity, but for patrons; that is, politicians and promoters whom Radisson hoped to involve in some enterprise. And, like all promotional literature, they reveal little about the author except that the sheer immensity of his achievements suggests a man of resource, wit, courage, and imagination. His casual fickleness, whether with wife or with country, also suggests a man of excessive self-concern. But beyond that we know little.

We do not even know where or when he was born, except that it was somewhere in France and sometime around 1640. A Canadian census of 1681 listed his age as 41; Radisson himself claimed in old age that he was born in 1636. Radisson placed the date of his arrival in Canada as May 24, 1651 (it is one of the few dates he ever provided). He landed in company with his parents and three sisters, one of whom, Marguerite, was a halfsister by his mother's earlier marriage. We know nothing of his father's occupation, nor why they came to Canada. The bringing of wife and daughters was in itself unusual. New France, at least in its early years, was populated by soldiers, priests, and fur traders, not women.

The family settled in Three Rivers, a fast-growing community at the mouth of the St. Maurice River, which confusingly forks into a three-pronged delta as it enters the St. Lawrence. Quebec, strategically located at the narrows where the long estuary of the St. Lawrence became a river, was the administrative capital of New France. Montreal, situated at the junction of the Ottawa River and the St. Lawrence, and future capital of the fur trade, was still a beleaguered outpost in 1651. The Iroquois, armed and abetted by the Dutch in Albany, kept the Ottawa passage under warlike surveillance. Thus Three Rivers, which offered a comparatively safe, "backstairs" route into the interior, was flourishing, at least for the moment.

Radisson's adventures began almost as soon as he stepped off the ship. A few months after his arrival he was hunting with some companions, became separated in the chase, and spent most of the day hunting by himself. Toward sunset he came upon the bodies of his companions, who had been killed by Indians. Instantly he found himself surrounded and taken prisoner. His youth probably saved him from death. Fortune was always mixed in her blessings whenever she peered at Radisson, but always she kept him alive to chance new perils.

The raiding party turned out to be Mohawks, a nation of the dreaded Iroquois confederacy, and the next day the band headed for its village on the Mohawk River in present-day New York. Radisson was initiated into the tribe and adopted by an Indian family. He quickly absorbed the language, as well as an understanding of Indian psychology that he used many times over in later years. Given weapons and a certain amount of freedom, he escaped in company with a Canadian Indian who had also been held captive. The pair managed to get within sight of Three Rivers, but the pursuing Mohawks caught up with them just as they were crossing the St. Lawrence to the village. Radisson's companion was killed, and he was taken back to the Mohawk. His Indian "family" welcomed him back, but they could not save him from the gruesome torture that the tribe no doubt considered just punishment. He was strapped to a table for sixty hours, exposed to sun and mosquitoes, while various members of the tribe wreaked their aggressions upon him. Warriors pulled out four of his fingernails. A young child attempted to cut off one of his fingers with a piece of flint. An old man jammed his thumb into a lit pipe and held it there while he went through three pipefuls. Eventually his "family" interceded, he was cut down, and nursed back to health.

Once again a trusted member of the tribe, Radisson accompanied a raiding party into the Ohio country. For some years the Iroquois had been extending their power westward, terrorizing the Algonquian-speaking tribes south of the Great Lakes and forcing them to pay tribute. Their motives were those found in any imperial urge—a natural aggressiveness, national pride, and profit. The profits came from the fur trade. After they trapped out their own lands south of Lake Ontario they pushed westward into the Ohio country, and they soon discovered what many a people has before and since: a middleman makes more money with less work than a producer. Thus they acquired furs from the Ohio tribes, by theft and tribute, or, when truly desperate, by purchase, and they sold the furs to the Dutch (and later the English). Radisson was at this point quite ignorant of the international ramifications of the "Wars of the Iroquois," but he joined lustily in the stalking and killing of an unknown foe.

In October, 1653, he accompanied the Mohawks on a visit to Fort Orange (later Albany). The Dutch governor recognized him as a Frenchman and offered to purchase his freedom. Radisson rejected the offer, so completely had he come to identify with his red brethren, but he later reconsidered. He escaped from the Mohawks, made his way to Albany, was sent on to New Amsterdam, and from there sailed on a Dutch ship for Holland. He moved on to France in the spring of 1654 and then back to Canada. Where he found the money for such travels is not at all clear, though he may have borrowed from old family friends.

During his absence he acquired a brother-in-law; the two quickly became inseparable companions. His oldest sister, Marguerite, had married Medard Chouart, a thirty-five-year old Three Rivers merchant. Chouart was prosperous enough to have acquired a tract of land on the edge of town. The parcel, stripped of its forest cover (probably for firewood), was a mass of brambles and berry bushes. Chouart, taking for his own the name of his estate, in the manner of a French aristocrat, styled himself Sieur des Groseilliers ("Lord of the Gooseberries"). It was a half-hearted jest that hardened into a title. Though he was substantially older than Radisson, the two became partners in exploration and enterprise. Radisson and Groseilliers—Caesars of the forest was the title Radisson gave them.

Groseilliers educated Radisson on the meaning of the Iroquois war. New France had suffered immense losses, in men and furs, ever since the Iroquois began attacking the Hurons of upper Canada in the 1640s. The passage to the rich fur lands of the upper Great Lakes, by way of the Ottawa River, Georgian Bay, and Lake Huron, had been virtually closed. Then in 1654 French Jesuits arranged a truce with the Iroquois and even won permission to establish a mission in their midst (probably at Onondaga, the central council fire of the Five Nations). Groseilliers promptly used the occasion to lead a party of traders into Lake Huron, exploring the lake as far south as the river (called de troit, or straits) leading into Lake Erie. He returned in 1656 with fifty canoes ("little gondolas of bark," the *Jesuit Relation* called them) loaded with Indians and beaver pelts. Commercially, New France was saved. The governor warned Groseilliers, however, that the fur trade was an official monopoly. Such opportunistic enterprise was not to be tolerated; he had to obtain permission for any future journey to the West and be prepared to split his proceeds with the governor and company of New France.

Radisson did not accompany Groseilliers on this initial foray into the West, probably because he was not yet back from Europe. But the following year, 1657, he accompanied a group sent to reinforce the Jesuit mission in the region later known as the Finger Lakes. One of the few survivors of Iroquois captivity, he was no doubt a valued guide and interpreter. While there he encountered his Indian "father" and "mother," a forgiving couple who "made much" of him. The Iroquois generally, however, were an unreliable lot, and before long the Jesuits received word that they were to be massacred. They escaped by staging a huge banquet, with singing and dancing for entertainment, and when the Indians, stuffed and exhausted, fell asleep, the missionaries fled for Canada. One of the Jesuits who recounted the incident gave credit for the scheme to "a young Frenchman who had been adopted by . . . the Iroquois."

Voyage to the Lake Superior Country

Radisson returned to find his brother-in-law eager for another western trip. What was the governor's warning to him? There was adventure, glory, and profit beyond the horizon. Old country monopolies stood no chance against New World enterprise. Groseilliers did, however, take the precaution of informing the governor of his plans. The mistrustful governor insisted on sending a servant with them. The Jesuits then learned of the scheme and wanted to send a representative or two. Groseilliers rejected all such keepers. He bluntly told the governor that he and Radisson knew what they were doing; it was a simple matter of "discoverers before governors." Radisson and he slipped out of Three Rivers by night, taking advantage of the fact that Groseilliers was captain of the city guard. When a sentry challenged them as they glided by the fort, Groseilliers answered with name and rank. The sentry replied, "God give you a good voyage." It was August, 1659.

The worst of the journey was the beginning. First there was the Long Sault, or lengthy rapids of the Ottawa River. Then a succession of lesser rapids and a falls near the present city of Ottawa. Whether pushing a canoe through frothing waters or carrying it around, it was hard work, though for a youth of twenty or so it must have been nothing short of high adventure. From the headwaters of the river, there was a short but difficult portage to Lake Nipissing. Then all was water and all downhill: French River, Georgian Bay, and Lake Huron. They were out of food by then, and the mixture of spruce forest and sphagnum bog through which they had passed yielded little game. But the straits leading to Lake Superior (Sault Ste. Marie) were teeming with whitefish, and the shoreline was alive with bear, beaver, and deer. They "showed themselves often," remarked Radisson, "but to their cost."

Indians accompanied them throughout. At the mouth of the Ottawa River they encountered, apparently by design, a party of Hurons returning home after selling their furs in Montreal. At Georgian Bay this bunch put them in the hands of the Cree, lords of the spruce-filled wasteland between the Great Lakes and Hudson Bay. The Cree, in turn, introduced them to the Menominees and Ojibwa (Chippewa) who inhabited the south

French Canada, ca. 1700

shore of Lake Superior. Radisson's own familiarity with Indian customs and facility with languages must have smoothed these transferrals.

Awesome Lake Superior presented new difficulties. Storms, or perhaps a persistent north wind, forced the voyagers to seek refuge on the shore for days at a time. But gradually they made their way along the south shore. Radisson recorded the principal landmarks in his journal—Keweenaw Point, where the Indians showed them great nodules of copper lying scattered on the ground, the Ontonogan River with its sloughs of wild rice, and finally Chequamegon Bay. The Indians left the two Frenchmen at the end of the bay and went overland to their village to seek help in carrying their baggage. Radisson and Groseilliers prudently built a small fort for themselves and ringed it with snares to warn of intruders. Then they went hunting to prepare a feast for their companions. Local residents turned up at the fort periodically out of curiosity, but none of them presented a threat. "We were Caesars," Radisson wrote, "being nobody to contradict us."

After a fortnight the Ojibwas reappeared with reinforcements, most of them apparently women. The Frenchmen had cached half their trading goods for future use; the women hoisted the remainder on their backs for the overland trek to the village. Radisson reimbursed their labor with a handful of trinkets, carefully keeping the amount low in order to avoid inflation. They reached the village after a march of four days through the woods. It was a beautiful country, Radisson observed, "with very few mountains [and] the woods clear." The lack of underbrush was probably due to Indian burnings as part of the hunt.

The location of the village where Radisson and Groseilliers spent the winter of 1659–1660 has been the subject of much conjecture. The usual guess is Lake Court Oreilles, where archaeologists have found remnants of a substantial Indian community. A better guess might be Lake Namekagon (or perhaps nearby Lake Owen where there are extensive Indian mounds). Had they gone as far as Court Oreilles, the latter part of the journey would almost certainly have been by canoe down the Namekagon River.

In any event, the Frenchmen were welcomed into the tribe and adopted by Indian families. During the winter the village split up to make hunting easier. Even so, there was much hunger. Even with snowshoes ("racketts" Radisson called them) the Indians could not catch up with the deer, and other game was in hibernation. They were starving by the time an early spring ice storm put a crust on the snow that gave the Indians footing and hampered the deer.

News of the white men meantime had spread across the northwest, and in spring the Sioux, neighbors of the Ojibwa to the west, sent a delegation to the village (Radisson calls them "Nation of the beefe," evidently because they lived on buffalo). After days of feasting and trading trinkets for beaver skins, Radisson and Groseilliers agreed to visit the Sioux country. The trip took seven days, after which they reached a colossal settlement of (so the Sioux claimed) 7000 people. Radisson noted the absence of trees; hence the village was evidently in the plains. The Indians lived in "cabins covered with skins" (teepees) and used grass for their cooking fires. Radisson does not say how they reached the Sioux homeland, but to get from the Lake Superior country to the western plains in seven days they must have gone by water—that is, down the Namekagon, St. Croix, and Mississippi rivers, then westward up the Minnesota River. The Sioux, who moved into the northern forests to hunt beaver during the winter, gave their guests 300 packs of beaver pelts, but the Frenchmen were able to carry only a few of them back. The journey back to Chequamegon Bay took twelve days—Radisson called them "easy journeys," again an apparent reference to an all-water route. Back on Lake Superior, they were delighted to find their cache of trading goods in good shape.

While with the Sioux, Radisson and Groseilliers promised to serve as intermediaries in ending a war between the Sioux and their traditional enemies, the Cree. A visit to the Cree involved a hazardous paddle across the western end of Lake Superior amid spring ice floes, but the Cree gave them a hearty welcome. Apparently they succeeded in their diplomatic mission (Radisson rarely records a failure at anything), and in addition swapped their remaining tools and trinkets for several boatloads of beaver pelts.

Radisson, who habitually extracted from the Indians all the geographical information they had, learned from the Cree of a great waterway to the north (the Albany River?) leading to an inland sea, which Radisson correctly surmised must be Hudson Bay. He instantly recognized the significance of this intelligence, for it promised a back door to the beaver country. A downriver trip to Hudson Bay would be easier and shorter than hauling furs all the way to Montreal, and it avoided the Iroquois menace. The vision of a northwest passage to Hudson Bay would dominate the rest of Radisson's life. So taken with it was he at this point that he included in his account of this western journey a trip from the Cree country to Hudson Bay. Since he arrived in Montreal toward the end of that same summer (1660), he clearly did not have time for such a trip. Why he would include a false account in a journal that is otherwise descriptively accurate will become clear in the course of our story.

The journey home that summer was uneventful until toward the end. Sweeping down the Ottawa River in August they came upon the grisly sight of dead Frenchmen tied to posts along the river bank. It was the remains of the Dollard Massacre, one of the famous incidents of Canadian history. In May, 1660, sixteen men led by Adam Dollard staved off an Iroquois attack and probably saved Montreal from destruction. Since the Iroquois went home after the battle, the Dollard party may also have saved the lives of Radisson and Groseilliers. On August 20 the voyageurs paddled into Montreal with their Indian companions. The market value of their furs came to a magnificent 140,000 livres (a livre was roughly equivalent to a Spanish dollar).

Men Without a Country

New France in 1660 was on the verge of collapse. The Iroquois attacks had destroyed the fur trade and so demoralized the colony's merchants that they threatened to return home. The arrival of Radisson and Groseillier with 60 boatloads of furs and friendly Indians restored the trade and revived spirits. Unhappily, the governor, far from welcoming them as heroes, clapped them in jail, ostensibly for having departed without his permission. He also claimed a good portion of the furs for the Company of New France. Groseilliers was too important a citizen to be kept in jail, and before long the two adventurers were on their way to France to seek justice from the king. They got only empty promises.

On their return from France they tried to organize a Canadian expedition to Hudson Bay, but petty politics again frustrated their design. The opposition this time came from the Jesuits, who were hoping to secure a portion of the fur trade for themselves. In 1661 the Jesuits attempted to reach Hudson Bay by way of the Saguenay River. The effort failed and drained the colony's meager resources. Neither governor nor merchants were in the mood to finance a further venture. Radisson and Groseilliers were once again left dangling.

The year 1662 found the intrepid pair in New England, a place where neither government nor church was likely to interfere with their dreams of empire. Boston merchants listened enthusiastically to their tales of beaver-rich lakes and rivers in the far west and provided them with a vessel to explore Hudson Bay from the Atlantic Ocean route. They penetrated no farther than Hudson's Straits, for the ship's captain, accustomed only to the West Indies trade, panicked at the sight of icebergs and insisted upon turning back.

The brothers-in-law remained in Boston for three years, and then in 1665 sailed for England to plead their case before another royal authority. Radisson, more often given to understatement than to exaggeration, said of the voyage simply that it was "a very bad time for the Plague and the wars." Indeed it was. England and the Netherlands had gone to war the previous year. A Dutch vessel captured their ship and took it to Spain to sell it. The brothers had to make their way to England from there and landed in the midst of an epidemic of bubonic plague. Nearly everyone had fled from London except Samuel Pepys, waspish neighbor of the Penn family and an indefatigable diarist. Pepys somehow met and befriended the two Frenchmen. He may even have induced Radisson to set down his adventures in writing. At any rate, Radisson began his memoirs while in London, and it was Pepys who preserved them for posterity. (Posterity unfortunately took its responsibilities more lightly; Radisson's memoirs remained buried in English family libraries for almost two centuries.)

Radisson and Groseilliers took their story of the northwest passage to the Privy Council, the body that was in charge of imperial affairs, and that group presented them to King Charles II. The king, intrigued, arranged for a vessel to take them to Hudson Bay, where they were to set up a fur outpost. The furs were to be marketed in England through a consortium of courtiers and politicos, among them James, Duke of York, and Prince Rupert, a cousin to the king. However, Dutch naval activity in the channel prevented them from sailing until the war ended.

While they waited Radisson spent his time writing a description of a trip he claimed to have made from Lake Superior to Hudson Bay back in the year 1660. So vague is the route he describes and so fuzzy the landmarks that he obviously manufactured the whole thing, probably from Indian accounts. Radisson evidently made up the story to keep alive the interest (and hence keep open the purses) of the courtiers who were financing him. Groseilliers (whom the English called Mr. Gooseberry) occupied himself with secret negotiations with various French spies. The French court, having belatedly recognized the strategic value of the two expatriates, was trying to woo them back into its service. But nothing, for the moment, came of the effort.

In 1668, with the Dutch war ended, the adventurers set out at last for Hudson Bay. Bad luck continued to plague Radisson, whose vessel ran into a severe storm off the coast of Iceland and had to turn back. Groseilliers, however, reached the bay and sailed along its shores to its southernmost tip, which he named James Bay. There at the mouth of a river, which he named Rupert, he built a fort and commenced trade with the Indians. Groseilliers and his men remained on the Rupert River through the winter, living comfortably on venison, rabbit, grouse, and salmon, and in spring they returned to London with a handsome cargo valued at £19,000. It convinced the English that there was profit to be made at the back door of New France.

In May, 1670, King Charles signed a charter for the Hudson's Bay Company, an institution that was to play a commanding role in the history of the Canadian West. Prominent among the eighteen charter members were the financiers backing Radisson and Groseilliers, but the two Frenchmen themselves were not included. Possibly they were regarded as mere employees of the company, a position that scarcely accorded with their importance in the operation. It was the first in a series of unkind cuts that eventually drove them back into the arms of France. The company's choice of governor for the new colony affords us a clue as to its general estimate of the men it sent to the frozen north. Charles Bayly was a Quaker who had been imprisoned in the Tower of London for writing inflammatory religious and political tracts. He was released on condition that he proceed to Hudson Bay and reside there as governor.

On May 31, the governor, the two Frenchmen, and assorted adventurers sailed for the bay in two royal frigates, the conveyances themselves an indication of the king's growing interest in empire. In the bay Groseilliers' ship headed for the fort on the Rupert River, while Radisson's struck westerly across the bay to the mouth of the Nelson River. He must have learned of this great waterway, which flows out of Lake Winnipeg, from the Sioux ten years before. The Sioux would have had easy access to it by way of the Red River and Lake Winnipeg. In any case, it was the passage to the fur country of which he had dreamed so long. Unfortunately, it was another twenty years before the Hudson's Bay Company realized that he was right.

There were signs of Indian habitation at the mouth of the Nelson River, but no Indians. So when it turned cold in early autumn, Radisson's group joined forces with Groseilliers' at the Rupert River. They got through the winter in fair shape, though several men died of scurvy (a vitamin deficiency disease caused by a lack of fresh fruit and vegetables). Groseilliers' trading policy of maintaining a firm and well-advertised price for beaver pelts (a half pound of beads for one skin, twenty skins for a gun) had kept the Indians happy and industrious. In spring the party returned to England with its usual rich cargo. Governor Bayly, taking seriously his bargain with the company, wanted to remain on the bay, but no one would stay with him.

The brothers-in-law remained in England for the next year, giving advice to the company on the trading goods to be shipped to the Canadian north. The company's records are dotted with notations of small sums doled out to the Frenchmen for their services. Before long the combination of aristocratic snobbery and middle-class penny-pinching began to irritate Radisson. The niggardly conservatism of the English seemed no better than the poorly informed indifference of his native France.

By 1675 French authorities in both Paris and Montreal had come to realize the importance of Radisson's and Groseilliers' discoveries. By then the Jesuits had succeeded in blazing a portage from the Saguenay River to the Rupert, and other coureurs de bois were utilizing the Lake

Winnipeg-Nelson River route. In Paris, Jean Baptiste Colbert, finance minister to King Louis XIV, undertook to breathe some life into France's flagging empire. A new and more energetic governor, Count Frontenac, had been sent to Canada (he, in turn, was responsible for the expeditions of Marquette and Joliet and La Salle down the Mississippi River) and secret negotiations were opened with Radisson and Groseilliers. In the spring of 1676 the pair slipped quietly across the English Channel for a meeting with Colbert. The French minister offered them triple the fee the English had been paying them, and the pair accepted. They were doomed to more disappointment.

A Pawn in the Game of Empire

The mid-1670s, Radisson and Groseilliers soon discovered, were not a choice moment for shifting sides. Early in the decade England's Charles II and France's Louis XIV had made a secret bargain that brought a temporary truce in the two countries' ancient rivalry. Louis provided Charles with a private subsidy that enabled him to govern without parliament, and Charles, in turn, declared war on their mutual rival, the Dutch. In Canada French authorities were reluctant to undertake any projects that might antagonize the English—as Radisson's scheme for seizing the Hudson Bay forts was certain to do. Frontenac, moreover, distrusted the turncoats, and worried that they had been sent over to sidetrack his plans to explore the Mississippi. Colbert, in fact, had sent the pair to Canada with no instructions whatsoever. Discouraged by their reception, Groseilliers returned to his long-suffering wife and his gooseberry patch, which must by now have become grown over with forest. Radisson joined an expedition to the West Indies, only to suffer shipwreck and the loss of all his belongings.

Shortly before he slipped out of England, Radisson, who seems to have been as cavalier in his attitude toward women as his brother-in-law, became married. His wife, whose first name he never recorded, was the daughter of an officer of the Hudson's Bay Company, Sir John Kirke. A loyal Englishman and a Protestant, Kirke refused to let his daughter accompany Radisson to Paris. Thus, upon his return from Canada, Radisson began making secret trips to England to see his wife. Before long the trips involved less romance than espionage.

By the end of the 1670s the French were beginning to realize that they were getting the worst of their cosy relationship with Charles II. The truce enabled the English to strengthen their hold on Hudson Bay. The expansion of their contacts with Indians eventually placed them in a position to siphon off the whole western fur trade. When Radisson returned in 1681 from one of his London visits with the news that the Hudson's Bay Company was planning a permanent settlement at the Nelson River, Colbert decided to act. Thus, in early 1682 Radisson found himself on his eleventh voyage across the Atlantic and his fourth visit to Hudson Bay.

Radisson paused in Canada long enough to clear his plans with Governor Frontenac and to pick up Groseilliers with a second ship. Arriving in Hudson Bay in August, 1682, the party steered straight for the western shore and the Nelson River. Two rivers enter the bay at the point—the Nelson River, which flows north from Lake Winnipeg, and, just across a sandy spit from the Nelson, the Hayes River, which arises to the east of Lake Winnipeg. The French party set up shop on the Hayes, and while Groseilliers superintended the construction of a fort, Radisson went inland looking for Indians.

In mid-September a cannon shot from across the sand spit told the Frenchmen they had company. Radisson went to investigate and found a settlement of New Englanders on the Nelson River. The Yankees had apparently arrived about the same time as the French (because the timing involved the right of prior claim to the river, the exact moment was the subject of bitter dispute between England and France for years thereafter). The New Englanders were interlopers, trading with the Indians on their own in violation of the Hudson's Bay Company's monopoly.

The New England captain was no match for Radisson, whose wits had been honed by years of wilderness survival. Radisson persuaded the young man that his own force was much superior (though they were in fact about equal) and grandly informed the captain that he was trespassing on French territory. He generously offered to let the New Englanders continue to trade under his protection, however, and the captain readily agreed.

A few days later another vessel steered into the Hayes River, a warship more formidable than anything possessed by either Radisson or the New Englanders. This, it turned out, was the official Hudson's Bay Company party sent to establish a permanent colony on the river. Radisson realized that if the English discovered his ships they would blow them right out of the water. To gain time, he lit a smudge fire, the traditional Indian trading signal. When a party came ashore, he pretended at first to be an Indian, then addressed the group in English, and finally told them they were intruding on French soil. While the English sorted all this out, nature intervened. An early winter storm swept newly formed ice from the bay into the estuary, and the English warship was sunk. The captain and fourteen of the crew were drowned.

That went far to even up the numbers. Radisson's only problem thereafter was to keep the English and the New Englanders from joining forces against him. This he did by simply not telling them about each other. With winter approaching he invited the New Englanders into his fort and locked the gates. So cordial was the French reception that the New Englanders were there a month before they realized they were prisoners. Radisson then burned their ship. The English meanwhile struggled through the winter in crude huts, and in spring, when they were too weak to resist, Radisson made them prisoners as well. He then loaded all the survivors on the two ships that he and Groseilliers had brought into the bay, together with the furs collected by the New Englanders, and sailed off in triumph. Jean Baptiste Chouart, Groseilliers' son, was left in charge of the fort on the Hayes River.

Radisson arrived in Quebec to find Canada under a new governor general, a cautious man inclined to obey the standing orders not to offend the English. He promptly seized Radisson's cargo of furs, fined him for starting a fight, and sent the New Englanders home. Once more Radisson and Groseilliers found themselves traipsing across the Atlantic in search of justice.

It eluded them as usual. Colbert was dead, and Louis XIV was preoccupied with preparations for a campaign into the Rhineland that would soon plunge Europe into another war. The imperial thrust had been sidetracked by an effort to set up a colony at the mouth of the Mississippi River, which had been claimed for France by La Salle in 1682. At this point Groseilliers disappears from the historical record. He may have simply given up and returned to his home at Three Rivers. He was, after all, sixty-five years old in 1684.

Allegiance at Last

As Radisson sat despondently in Paris in the spring of 1684, he was approached anew by agents of the English Hudson's Bay Company. His latest escapade had demonstrated for all that only he could master the northern outlet to the fur trade. Others might be sent to build forts and open trade, but with Radisson working for the French there was no assurance that they would last long. At the very least he had to be neutralized. For Radisson another turn of coat also had attractions. There was a fortune in furs at the Hayes River being stockpiled by his nephew, Jean Baptiste

Chouart. His past dealings with French authorities left no assurance that he would ever get them to market. Just that spring, moreover, Louis XIV decreed that a fourth of all furs collected in Canada had to be given to the governor and company of New France. His prospects were much better collaborating with the English.

The Hudson's Bay Company, having profited by its past errors, was inclined to be generous. It offered Radisson a salary of £50 a year and £200 worth of company stock; in return he was to capture and hold the settlement on Hudson Bay now going by the name of Port Nelson. There is no indication that Radisson informed the company that the fort there was commanded by his own nephew. Nor is there any mention in the agreement of the furs; Radisson apparently intended to market these on his own. He could claim them, after all, as spoils of war.

Having made its decision and having found its agent, the company was in a hurry. Radisson was allowed only a few days in London before he was sent off again to Hudson Bay, this time as commander of a fleet of three small warships. Young Chouart, true to his lineage, had gotten along splendidly with the Indians during Radisson's absence; he and his seven men had purchased and stockpiled 20,000 pelts. Although Chouart was expecting momentary relief from Quebec, Radisson managed to persuade him and his men to desert to the English cause. The group then hastily loaded the furs aboard ship and sailed for England. They passed the French relief vessels without seeing them in the straits leading to the bay. Radisson was back in London by October, 1684.

For once, he was treated as a hero. James, Duke of York, governor of the Hudson's Bay Company, made himself Radisson's patron, and the favor of course became trebly important when James became king in early 1685. The elevation to the throne forced James to resign as governor of the company, but he saw to it that his replacement, John Churchill, soon to become Duke of Marlborough, guarded Radisson's interests. There was a limit, however, to English gratitude and to the effect of royal patronage. The Hudson's Bay Company regarded the 20,000 furs as its own; neither Radisson nor Jean Baptiste Chouart ever received compensation for them.

Later that year, 1685, the company appointed Radisson superintendent of its Port Nelson facility. It would seem that the honor was due not so much to his royal patron as to the insistence of young Chouart and his fellow Frenchmen, who were expected to supply the outpost with men. It was tacit recognition by the company of the French facility for dealing with the Indians.

Radisson undertook his final voyage to Hudson Bay that summer. He remained at his barren but strategically vital outpost for two winters. In 1686 the French marched overland by the Saguenay route and captured the English forts on James Bay. An obvious retaliation for Radisson's seizures of the previous two years, it meant that full-scale war had come to the Canadian frontier, though it would be another three years before war was officially declared and longer still before England's American colonies became involved. Radisson's post was safe, for the French in 1686 lacked the ships to cross the bay. He returned home early in the following year, and he was thus spared the humiliation of surrendering to the sizable French fleet that captured the remaining British outposts in 1687. Commanding the fleet was Pierre Le Moyne d'Iberville, one of the several sons of Charles Le Moyne, old friend and business partner of Groseilliers. When the war ended a decade later the French held on to the Hudson Bay outposts.

Had Radisson the opportunist chosen at last the wrong side? For the moment it seemed so. The loss of its fur outposts left the Hudson's Bay Company in dire financial straits. It ceased paying dividends on its stock during the 1690s, and in some years was unable even to pay Radisson's meager salary. At one point he had to sue in court to obtain his pay.

He settled in London upon his final return from Canada and married a third time—each of his shifts in allegiance was attended by a marriage, though he never tells us what happened to the first two wives. By his second wife, Margaret, he had four children, perhaps more, and by his third wife, Elizabeth, he had three daughters. His final years could not have been very happy ones. For a man accustomed to the smell of spruce, the sight of wild rice bobbing on a misty lake, and the soft, rhythmic dip and splash of canoe paddles, adjustment to life in harsh, smoky London must have been difficult. And there were the constant financial problems.

England's fortunes improved, even if Radisson's did not. A new war broke out in 1702, as England and her continental allies tried to prevent Louis XIV from placing his grandson on the throne of Spain (a move that placed both France and Spain in the hands of the Bourbon family). Although called the War of the Spanish Succession, a better name might have been Marlborough's war, for John Churchill, Duke of Marlborough, friend of Radisson and William Penn, was the dominant figure. At Blenheim in southern Germany in 1704 he administered the first military defeat the French had suffered in Europe in half a century. In succeeding years he pushed the French out of the heavily fortified cities of the low countries (present-day Belgium). He was on the high road to Paris when Louis sued for peace.

At the peace table England demanded and received a vast extension of New World empire. France delivered up Newfoundland, Nova Scotia, and the land bordering Hudson Bay. Nova Scotia had been captured by an army of New Englanders in 1710, but Hudson Bay was won by Marlborough on the battlefields of Europe. At the end of the war England's possessions virtually encircled New France, and England's ultimate conquest of Canada seemed only a matter of time.

England's recovery of the Hudson Bay forts also revived the fortunes of the Bay Company. Port Nelson became a major fur entrepot; using Radisson's passage to Lake Winnipeg, trappers and traders fanned into the fabled hinterland of beaver-rich lakes and streams extending to the edge of the western prairies. Radisson unfortunately did not live to see his vision come true. He died in 1710 before the war ended.

SUGGESTIONS FOR FURTHER READING

Grace Lee Nute, *Caesars of the Wilderness* (1943, reprinted 1978), is a joint biography of Radisson and Groseilliers. In making sense of Radisson's mysterious journals, Nute performed a classic piece of scholarly detective work. The journals themselves, discovered in an English library 150 years after Radisson's death, were published by Gideon D. Scull, ed., *Voyages of Pierre Esprit Radisson* (1853, reprinted 1943). Thomas B. Costain, *The White and the Gold: The French Regime in Canada* (1954), is especially recommended for those who would explore further this oft-neglected part of American history. Despite its title, the focus of the work is the seventeenth century.

7

The Brothers Le Moyne:
Maccabees of New France

Sometime during the summer of 1682 an important though informal meeting took place in Montreal, the Canadian fur trading capital located at the point where the Ottawa River flows into the St. Lawrence. In the center of the group were Radisson and Groseilliers, newly arrived from France with orders to capture the English outposts on Hudson Bay. With them was Louis Joliet, professional soldier who in company with Father Marquette had discovered the Mississippi River a decade before. A late-comer to the group was another soldier, Sieur de la Salle, who had pen-etrated to the mouth of the Mississippi just the previous April. There too were several Montreal fur merchants, seated perhaps on the edge of the circle, in deference to the soldiers and pathmarkers. The most promi-nent of these was Charles Le Moyne, a man whose exploits as trader and Indian fighter were legendary. His services had earned royal rec-ognition and a landed estate that he called Longueuil. Now approaching his sixtieth year of age, Le Moyne was still respected for his knowledge of the frontier.

The meeting agreed to finance Radisson's expedition to Hudson Bay that summer, the voyage that resulted in French seizure of the posts on the Nelson and Hayes rivers. The group also agreed to seek a charter from the king as *La Compagnie du Nord*, the Company of the North. So organized, they felt they could contest the English Hudson's Bay Com-pany for control of the western fur trade. King Louis dallied until 1685 before granting the charter, and in the meantime Radisson switched back to the English service. But the company pressed on and even won control of Hudson Bay for a time. Prime among its servants were the sons of Charles Le Moyne, whose fierce loyalty to the cause of New France stands in sharp contrast to the opportunism of Pierre Radisson.

Charles Le Moyne was the son of an innkeeper of Dieppe, a seaport on the Norman coast of France. He had come to Canada at the age of seventeen and settled in Montreal in 1646, just four years after the village was founded. He earned his reputation as an Indian fighter in the Iroquois wars, which began in the very year he landed. He quickly mastered the Indian languages, including that of the Iroquois, and employed his skill in both war and commerce. Within a decade he was one of the wealthiest merchants in the city. In 1654 he married Catherine Thierry, who had come to Canada in company with her uncle, Antoine Primot, another fast-rising trader. Two years later was born the first of fourteen children, two of whom died in infancy—ten sons and two daughters survived.

The innkeeper's son did what he could do to attach gentility to his family fortune. He developed the custom of giving his sons informal titles, taken from localities in his native Normandy. Charles, the eldest, was given the title of the family estate, Longueuil (named Baron Longueuil by the king after his father's death, Charles ultimately fulfilled the dream of gentility). Being the eldest, Charles took over both the family estate and the fur business, which he managed with skill and profit. His brothers all became soldiers, a role not unusual for younger sons in those days. But what soldiers they! Jacques de Saint-Helene, born in 1659, masterminded the expeditions that devastated the New York-New England frontier at the outset of the French and Indian wars. Pierre d'Iberville, born in 1661, was perhaps the greatest soldier Canada ever produced. Equally at home on land and sea, Iberville never lost a battle on either element, and he battled the English from the foggy shores of Hudson Bay to the sunny strands of the West Indies. Sharing Iberville's adventures and seconding his commands were his younger brothers, Paul de Maricourt (1663), Joseph de Serigny (1668), Louis de Chateauguay (1676), and Jean-Baptiste de Bienville (1680). Bienville is justly famed in his own right as founder of New Orleans and father of Louisiana. No family in all history can equal the record of the Le Moynes, except perhaps the Biblical Maccabees, who led the Jews in revolt against the Roman Empire.

Undeclared War in Hudson Bay

When he granted a charter to the Company of the North in 1685, King Louis XIV conferred on it the shores of Hudson Bay in the vicinity of the Nelson River, gateway to the western fur trade. It was one of those grand and useless gestures to which French kings were so often given. The Nelson River was actually in the hands of the Hudson's Bay Company, and Louis had no intention of supplying the Company of the North with soldiers to conquer it. For all of that, Louis might as well have granted the rest of Hudson Bay, including James Bay, to the company, for that too was in the hands of the English.

Although Louis was technically at peace with the English in 1685, his grant was an implied permit for the company to do something on its own. The company was happy to try, since the deflection of furs to the north and away from the Great Lakes routes threatened ruin to Montreal. In the early weeks of 1686 the company organized an expedition in Montreal. Pierre de Troyes was given command; among his lieutenants were three young Le Moynes, Jacques de Saint-Helene, Pierre d'Iberville, and Paul de Maricourt.

The tiny army, told to find an overland route to James Bay so as to take the English forts there by surprise, got under way in mid-March, 1686. The snow was still deep on the ground, so deep that they could not make the usual portage at the Long Sault rapids of the Ottawa River. Instead they had to wade their canoes up through the icy falls. They followed the familiar trade route to the upper Great Lakes blazed by Radisson and Groseilliers a quarter century before. At the Mattawa River, a tributary of the Ottawa, the party turned northward toward Lake Abitibi. It was early June before they struggled across the divide and camped on the lake, whose waters flowed northward to the bay.

Fort Hayes, situated on James Bay, a few miles below the confluence of the Abitibi and Moose rivers, was completely unprepared. Not even a sentinel was posted when the French appeared before its gates at dawn on June 19. Iberville and Sainte-Helene, sent to make a diversionary attack from the rear while Troyes battered down the main gate, simply climbed the palisade and dropped into the enclosure. They opened the gates for their comrades and then rushed the log redoubt where the English defenders, now fully awake, lay waiting. A spirited exchange of fire ensued until Iberville, pistol in one hand and knife in the other, threw himself against the door and broke it open. Sainte-Helene and the others followed, and the English gave up. There were only fifteen left to take prisoner.

The English at Fort Hayes put up a surprisingly stiff fight considering they were only civilian employees of the Hudson's Bay Company. Although an empire was at stake, the English were no more prepared than the French to send professional soldiers into the far north. The other English outposts on James Bay—Fort Charles at the Rupert River and Fort Albany at the Albany River—were just as weak. Caught unprepared by the fast-moving French, they surrendered without even a struggle. At Fort Charles was an added bonus, a warship belonging to the Hudson's Bay Company. Iberville slipped aboard this vessel under cover of night, stamped on the deck to awaken the crew, and captured them as they came sleepily running up from below.

At Fort Albany another vessel was discovered, though this one was too leaky to be of much value to the French. They accordingly loaded their prisoners on it and sent them off to Port Nelson. Troyes then returned to Montreal, carrying 50,000 captured pelts, more than enough to reimburse the Company of the North for its expenses. The Le Moyne brothers, with 40 men at their command, were left to stand vigil over James Bay through the winter. Iberville and Sainte-Helene went back to Montreal the following year, leaving Paul de Maricourt in charge of the bay.

Trouble greeted Iberville on his return to Montreal. Shortly after he had left on the expedition, one Mlle. de Belestre, aged nineteen, appeared in court to accuse Iberville of having seduced her and of being the father of her expected child. She apparently did not demand marriage and even informed the bailiff that she would not take care of the child when it arrived. But, quite understandably, she wanted Iberville to pay medical and other expenses. Iberville, who did not deny the charge, replied with the common, if utterly irrelevant, defense that the young woman was of poor repute in the community. Before anything further happened, however, the governor intervened by sending Iberville on a mission to France to report on the situation at Hudson Bay. Whether the governor acted out of duty or solicitude for a Le Moyne is not entirely clear.

Iberville received a warm welcome in Paris. The victories on Hudson Bay had rekindled the king's interest in the empire. The English had protested the seizures but were clearly in no mood for war; indeed, James II had troubles enough at home. Thus Louis was amenable to further adventures in the bay. The Company of the North had asked for one of the king's own ships to pick up the furs that were being collected on James Bay. This was granted, and Iberville was given command of the *Soleil d'Afrique* along with a commission in the French navy. At age 27 he had his first independent command.

When he arrived back in Quebec in June, 1688, the governor named him commander-in-chief of all the French posts on Hudson Bay and ordered him to proceed immediately to his station. The paternity suit was still pending, but the governor's order took precedence. Iberville sailed, and in his absence the court ordered him to provide for the child. It seems likely that he did, since there is no further record of the matter.

Iberville reached the mouth of the Abitibi River without mishap, took on the furs his brother had collected in the past year, and started for home. Just as he cleared the river, however, he encountered two English vessels, fur carriers belonging to the Hudson's Bay Company. Since these were no match for a French man o' war, the English offered a deal— they would all trade with the Indians without fighting each other. Iberville negotiated with them for a time, but then, his suspicions aroused by an Irish desertcr (who may have had an axe of his own to grind), Iberville attacked and captured the English ships. With his expanded fleet he sailed off to the Moose River, where he found another English ship and captured it. Then, leaving his warship at the disposal of his brothers (Sainte-Helene had come overland with reinforcements for the forts), Iberville sailed the largest of the English ships back to Quebec. The Hudson's Bay Company estimated its losses in ships and furs at £15,000. So pleased was the governor of Canada that he asked the king to give Iberville a regular commission as a lieutenant in the French navy. King Louis, who never seems to have denied Iberville anything, agreed. It was an unprecedented honor for a Canadian.

The Conquest of Hudson Bay

Shortly after Iberville's return to Quebec, war between England and France was officially declared. It resulted not from the New World conflict, but from the dynastic quarrels of Europe. To resist French aggression, Austria, the Netherlands, and various German principalities formed an alliance called the League of Augsburg. Architect of the alliance was William of Orange, Stadtholder of Holland, son-in-law of James II, and a lifelong foe of Louis XIV. In hopes of bringing England into the alliance, William in 1688 accepted the offer of the English crown, an offer tendered by a group of politicians and churchmen disenchanted with James II. After becoming king, William signed England into the League of Augsburg and declared war on France in June, 1689. The war greatly simplified matters for Iberville and the Company of the North. They could now plan openly the total conquest of Hudson Bay.

That scheme had to wait, however, for the governor had other ideas. To forestall an English attack on Canada, Frontenac organized raids against the New York-New England frontier. One division, commanded by Sainte-Helene, was to proceed by way of Lake Champlain to Fort Orange (Albany). A second army was to march eastward into Massachusetts.

Sainte-Helene's force left Montreal in the wintry darkness of February, 1690. The choice of season, of course, was to make the surprise complete. Armies did not campaign in the winter in that period of history because there was no forage for horses, and they needed horses for their enormous trains of baggage and artillery. Sainte-Helene's woodsmen carried their belongings on their backs and marched on snowshoes. The route, by way of the Richelieu River and Lake Champlain, would become a standard invasion path in the wars of the next century, climaxing with Burgoyne's march during the American Revolution. Iberville accompanied his brother, apparently without formal command.

It required six days of trudging through the snow to reach Lake Champlain, and several days more to traverse the length of that long icy finger nestled between the Adirondacks and the Green Mountains. When the army reached the Hudson River, Sainte-Helene announced a change in plans. Instead of well-fortified Orange, they would descend instead on the smaller village of Schenectady below the mouth of the Mohawk River. Sainte-Helene's Indian allies, who had little stomach for fortified palisades and to whom one dead white was as good (or bad) as another, apparently dictated the change.

The French detachment appeared on the edge of the sleeping community at midnight on February 19. In the middle of town was a fort, but no one was on guard. At a signal the French burst into the fort and slaughtered the garrison. The Indians then ravaged the town, killing everyone in sight. Whether Sainte-Helene lost control of his allies or approved their deeds is not clear. Perhaps he considered it just retribution for the savage attacks of the Iroquois, armed and abetted by the English, on Canada. The war party then headed for home, taking along some fifty horses to carry their plunder. Most of the horses were eaten along the way.

On his return from Schenectady, Iberville set sail for Hudson Bay. The Company of the North was determined to eliminate the remaining English posts at the mouths of the Nelson and Hayes rivers, and Governor Frontenac concurred. Iberville was given two ships, one of which he placed under the command of his brother Maricourt. When he dropped anchor in the Hayes River (apparently a better anchorage than the nearby Nelson River, even though the latter was the more important waterway because of its link with Lake Winnipeg), Iberville encountered three ships of the Hudson's Bay Company, all larger than his own. He beat a hasty retreat, aided by some rocky shoals that grounded one of the English vessels. Rather than call the expedition a failure, he descended on an undefended English outpost, a sort of fur depot for the Indian trade, and seized its stock of peltry. This booty he sent back to Quebec with Maricourt, while he himself wintered in the bay. Iberville spent the winter in profitable exchange, and returned to Quebec in October, 1691, with a beaver cargo worth 80,000 livres. He was rapidly becoming one of the wealthiest men in Canada. As so often, empire-building and fortune-hunting went hand in hand.

In Iberville's absence Quebec had been attacked by an army of New Englanders commanded by Sir William Phips, governor of Massachusetts. The attack failed, but Sainte-Helene was mortally wounded in the fighting. Second oldest of the Le Moyne brothers, he was the first to die in battle. Iberville sat through his brother's final hours, and then set sail for France. Realizing that the Company of the North lacked the resources to battle both English and their American colonists, he hoped to interest the king in his plans for conquering Hudson Bay.

The French Court, to whom Iberville was already something of a hero (and, because of his colonial birth, perhaps something of an oddity) greeted him warmly. He was promoted to captain in the navy and given command of an entire squadron, headed by a thirty-eight gun frigate. Unfortunately, with a misdirection of energies so characteristic of bureaucracies, the ministry ordered Iberville to convoy merchant vessels across the Atlantic before proceeding to Hudson Bay. The merchant vessels were so slow that it was autumn before Iberville reached the St. Lawrence, much too late in the season to attempt a journey into Hudson Bay. He was back in Paris the following year (1693) and again received a small squadron. These vessels proved utterly unseaworthy; Iberville barely coaxed them as far as the St. Lawrence, with no chance of proceeding on to the bay. The deterioration of the French navy, which would ultimately cost France her North American empire, was already being felt. In the meantime, while Iberville sailed futilely back and forth across the Atlantic, the English recaptured the forts on James Bay. The French never got them back.

By 1694 both the Company of the North in Canada and the ministry in Paris were becoming leery of Iberville's plans for the conquest of the frozen north. Vast sums had been appropriated for his expeditions with no tangible result. In Quebec, Governor Frontenac was openly critical of Iberville for not having pushed on to Hudson Bay, leaky ships or no. Thus, in the spring of 1694 Iberville, in order to secure a new expedition, had to agree to finance it himself. The king loaned him a pair of warships, but Iberville had to provide food and pay wages for the crews out of his own pocket. He could reimburse himself out of any furs taken, but the forts he captured were to be turned over to the Company of the North. The arrangement, a curious blend of profit and patriotism, was reminiscent of Queen Elizabeth's secret contracts with her "sea dogs," Hawkins and Drake. And like those early nemeses of the Spanish Main, only the gossamer thread of royal sanction saved Iberville from being labeled a pirate.

As usual, he took along a brother to command the second ship, this time twenty-six-year-old Joseph de Serigny. Iberville's wife also accompanied him as far as the St. Lawrence settlements. They had been married in Quebec the previous year, and he had taken her to France for a honeymoon. She gave birth to a son on this homeward voyage, but for the next few years Iberville was too busy to pay much attention to either of them.

In Quebec, Iberville recruited a small army of 110 Canadian woodsmen, together with half a dozen Indians. None of them came cheaply—pay advances and food supplies cost Iberville 110,000 livres before he even started. Another brother joined him, nineteen-year-old Louis de Chateauguay, and a cousin, Jean-Baptiste Le Moyne de Martigny.

They sailed for Hudson Bay on August 10, 1694, and anchored at the mouth of the Nelson River on September 24. His target was a newly constructed fort on the Hayes River just across the narrow spit that separated the two waterways (the English seem to have temporarily abandoned the post at the Nelson River). The English quickly spotted his ships, depriving Iberville of surprise, and he was forced to lay siege to the log palisade. In an early stage of the operation, young Chateauguay ventured too close to the English works and a musket shot killed him.

It took Iberville several days to land the ships' cannon and set them up for a bombardment. When all were at last in position on October 13, he demanded the fort's surrender. The English asked only to be given a peaceful night's sleep; Iberville acceded, and the fort surrendered the next day. Iberville spent the winter at the post, gathering a haul of 45,000 pounds of beaver from the Indians. He lingered there through the following summer as well, waiting for the annual convoy of English fur ships, which he fully expected to capture. The English failed to appear, however, and in September he sailed for France, leaving Martigny and another officer in joint command of Port Nelson. The furs, which he sold in Paris, paid only half the expenses he had incurred, but Iberville expected to recover the rest of the money from future trade. To help him out, the king gave him a three year monopoly on Hudson Bay.

On Land and Sea: Newfoundland to James Bay

Iberville returned to Paris to find the royal court bursting with bigger plans than ever. The successful defense of Quebec, together with Iberville's victorious foray into Hudson Bay, inspired Louis' ministers to undertake a major offensive. Iberville, who was to command the expedition, was to attack first Fort William Henry at the mouth of the Pemaquid River in New England (Maine). This new, stoutly built edifice dominated the Bay of Fundy and thus gave the English influence among the Indians of Acadia (modern New Brunswick and Nova Scotia). Thus it both protected New England and promoted English interests in the maritime provinces. Iberville was then to proceed to Newfoundland, where English and French settlements lived side by side in uneasy truce, and secure that island for King Louis. Then, with what strength remained, Iberville was to push on to Hudson Bay and capture the remaining English forts there. To carry out this mission Iberville was given three warships; any troops he needed he was to recruit in Quebec.

The French government's faith in Iberville, it must be said, was unbounded. Iberville himself might well be pardoned had he pointed out the difficulties involved in such a multiple venture, but that was not in his character. Instead he joyfully accepted the assignment, asking only that his brother, sixteen-year-old Jean-Baptiste de Bienville, be allowed to accompany him as personal aide. It took him two years, instead of the anticipated one, but he very nearly succeeded in carrying through the threepoint parlay.

The taxpayers of Massachusetts had poured £20,000 (not all of them willingly) into the construction of Fort William Henry, and it stood boldly on the boundary between English and French claims in the Bay of Fundy. It was built of stone, its walls six feet thick and more than twenty feet high. Iberville anchored at the mouth of the Pemaquid River in mid-August, 1696, and scouted the situation. He found that by placing his vessels in certain positions the walls of the fort actually protected him. So thick were the walls that they limited the movement, and hence the lateral range, of the fort's cannon. Iberville placed his ships in a spot where only one of the New Englanders' cannon could reach him and began a bombardment, lobbing cannon shot over the walls with considerable effect. Having thoroughly demoralized the defenders, he sent in a demand for surrender, threatening that if he had to mount an assault it would be led by savages, who would show no mercy. The fort surrendered.

Iberville shipped the garrison of Massachusetts militia off to Boston (where the commander was promptly jailed for surrendering too easily) and then destroyed the fort. Its artillery was added to his own armament, and its muskets he gave to the Indians. The Indians, whose own confidence in Iberville matched that of Paris, offered to attack Boston if he would lead them. Iberville demurred, since that was not part of his instructions, and sailed off for Newfoundland.

Newfoundland, which contained neither mineral wealth nor substantial amounts of beaver, had been largely overlooked by imperial expansionists. A handful of fishing villages dotted its Atlantic shoreline, most of them on the Avalon Peninsula, which is connected to the mainland by a narrow isthmus. The English settlements, totaling about 2000 people, were on the eastern side of the peninsula. Their capital was St. John's, North America's easternmost port. The French claimed the island by right of discovery, but their own settlement was a run-down fishing community at Placentia on the western side of the peninsula. French officials, however, regarded it of considerable importance as a place of refuge for ships entering the Gulf of St. Lawrence. By capturing the neighboring English villages they would not only protect their own, they would add to the convenience of their shipping.

Iberville dropped anchor in Placentia harbor on September 12, 1696, having occupied less than a month in his assault on New England and well within his timetable of conquest. At Placentia, however, things began to go wrong. The French governor was absent—attacking the English villages on his own initiative, as it turned out—and when he returned emptyhanded he was in no mood to cooperate in a new venture. Paul de Maricourt, who had been sent to Quebec for reinforcements, had run into difficulties there. Governor Frontenac was likewise on an expedition, and Maricourt had to wait until he returned. Iberville sat restlessly in Placentia for weeks, occupying himself by exploring the neighborhood and absorbing information. At last the reinforcements arrived, a mere eighty men, but a specially selected lot.

Iberville persuaded the Placentia governor to add a few more, and on the first day of November he set off with 120 men. Bienville, the only brother along on this venture, still functioned as aide. They crossed the heart of the peninsula, an area largely unexplored by Newfoundlanders, who were glued to the sea, and descended on the English settlements from the rear. Iberville gobbled them one by one; the only resistance he met was in St. John's. The citizens of that town put up a spirited defense from their small fort until Iberville had his Indians cut the scalp off one of his prisoners and then sent the pain-crazed man into the fort as an example of what further resistance would bring. It was a deed matched in ferocity only by Sainte-Helene at Schenectady.

After the surrender, Iberville sent the residents to England on a ship that happened to be lying in the harbor, and then burned the town. On Christmas Eve he resumed his march with the intent of destroying every English settlement on the coast. The shock that one feels for Iberville's brutality yields almost immediately to admiration for his ability to conduct a winter campaign in a pathless wilderness. His men had snowshoes, which they fashioned for themselves, but still they fell into drifts so deep that some were buried alive. Every river was a treacherous impediment, for the thickness of the ice varied with the speed of the unseen current below. Yet he captured every village but one, that one on an island that he could not reach. He returned to Placentia with 700 prisoners and some booty, most of it salted fish.

Devastating though it was, Iberville's swath of destruction accomplished little. The outraged English simply sent over a naval squadron that reestablished their claim. By the time it arrived, Iberville was in Hudson Bay. The detached observer might well wonder if he—and France— had attempted too much. Iberville himself must have had a doubt or two when he learned from his brother Serigny that the British had recaptured Port Nelson the previous summer (while Iberville was at Pemaquid). That unraveled all the French achievements (beginning with Radisson and Sainte-Helene) of the past ten years.

Shocked by the loss, the French king moved to reinforce Iberville for his Hudson Bay enterprise, the third leg of the king's grand design. An additional squadron of five ships was assembled at La Rochelle that winter, together with a ten-month stock of provisions. Serigny was placed in command and told to deliver the vessels to his brother at Newfoundland. It was a stormy crossing; the ships were battered and the crews racked with scurvy when Serigny put into Placentia harbor in May, 1697. Forced to make repairs, Iberville's departure for the bay was delayed until July.

He could not have left much earlier in any case, for the bay was covered with ice until mid-summer. As it was, his squadron encountered a morass of floating ice in the straits leading to the bay. The huge floes crushed one ship altogether and imprisoned the others for three weeks. At last Iberville's flagship, the *Pelican*, freed itself and started off for Port Nelson, leaving the others to come when they could.

Iberville anchored in the mouth of the Hayes River on September 4 and sent out a party to round up Indians for information on the English defenses. At that juncture he spotted three sails on the horizon. Ever alert, he sailed out to meet them and discovered that they were English— the Hudson's Bay Company's annual fleet. But, because of the war, they were better armed than the company's usual fur carriers. The squadron included the *Hampshire* (56 guns), the *Dering* (36 guns), and the *Hudson's Bay* (32 guns). Iberville's *Pelican* had but 44 guns; in addition he had put ashore a fourth of his crew to look for Indians. Yet he felt he had to fight. If the English ships made it into the river and reinforced the fort, Iberville's entire squadron would be unable to dislodge them. The ownership of Hudson Bay had to be decided now.

As the English ships advanced in battle formation, Iberville boldly steered for the largest, the *Hampshire*. Thinking he was about to be boarded, the Englishman backed off out of range. Iberville then wheeled toward the smaller vessels, pouring a murderous broadside into each as he passed. The *Hampshire* then joined the fray, and for three hours the four ships hammered away at one another. On one passage the English commander, seeing the *Pelican's* broken masts and shattered rigging, called on Iberville to surrender. When Iberville refused, the Englishman took out a bottle of wine and drank a toast to his foe and invited him to dinner when it was over. Iberville replied with a similar toast and invitation. (Where all the wine came from in the midst of battle remains one of the minor mysteries of the affair.)

Pleasantries completed, the English commander decided to board the *Pelican* in order to force things to a conclusion with infantry combat. Iberville, whose crew was badly outnumbered, could not afford to let him, but his ship was too damaged to get away. The Englishman bore in and fired a round of grape, small shot designed to kill men rather than damage the ship. Iberville replied with the heaviest shot he had, a broadside aimed right at the waterline. At that range it was devastating. The *Hampshire* filled with water and sank on the spot, carrying her gentlemanly captain with her. Iberville then turned on the *Hudson's Bay*, as this was the vessel nearest the river. Its captain promptly struck his colors. The other English ship fled. Iberville started in pursuit but gave up; his vessel was too badly damaged. Together with his prize, he anchored again in the Nelson River to await the arrival of Serigny and the rest of the squadron. The battle, given the odds, is the most remarkable victory in French naval history— the most remarkable perhaps in the history of any nation.

That night a northeasterly gale blew up, accompanied by driving snow. The two damaged ships bobbed helplessly in the mouth of the river, pushed gradually by the wind toward the muddy shore. Iberville, with only one undamaged lifeboat, ferried his crew with repeated trips to shallow water where they could wade ashore. It was a trip of several miles because of the huge tides in those northerly latitudes, and eighteen sailors died of exposure. The next day they crossed the peninsula toward the fort and saw, lying placidly at anchor, the rest of the French squadron. Possessed once again of ships, Iberville prepared to attack.

The English commander at Port Nelson, the same man who had surrendered so meekly to Iberville three years before, was determined to fight this time. Iberville took the heavier cannon from his ships, lined them up around the fort, and began a bombardment. After a few hours of this he demanded surrender. The English commander, hoping to get better terms by an early capitulation, asked if he would be permitted to keep his furs. Iberville, who had expenses of his own and never operated at a loss, refused. The bombardment resumed, and the fort surrendered the next day.

Iberville then had to make some fast decisions, for winter was once again at hand. Ice was already forming in the bay. Ice floes, storms, and battle had reduced him to two seaworthy ships—not enough for an assault on the English outposts on James Bay. Nor had he enough supplies to spend the winter with his entire force. So he set out for home, leaving his cousin Le Moyne de Martigny, in command of Fort Bourbon, the new name for Port Nelson.

Iberville never returned to the Great Bay of the North. The Treaty of Ryswick, which ended the war that same year, 1697, acknowledged the military stalemate. The French were left in control of the vital Nelson River gateway, while the English remained at James Bay. Both sides seemed to recognize the futility of capture and recapture of wilderness outposts. When the English finally won title to Hudson Bay, they did it by defeating France on the continent of Europe.

Iberville too realized that there was nothing further to accomplish in the frozen north. As the century came to a close, he embarked on a new career—an effort to establish a colony at the other end of the French empire, Louisiana.

Iberville in Louisiana

Robert Cavelier, Sieur de la Salle, dreamed of a French colony at the mouth of the Mississippi River. With a rich continent to tap and direct access to Europe by way of the Gulf of Mexico, such a settlement was certain to become one of the great entrepots of the world. In 1684, two years after his initial journey down the Mississippi, La Salle set out for the Gulf of Mexico with a group of colonizers. Weak on navigation since he was not a sailor, he missed the entrance to the river and landed on the coast of Texas. (The mouth of the river was obscured by wooded debris built up over the centuries.) He settled on Matagorda Bay (the mouth of the Colorado River), which he supposed was a western branch of the Mississippi delta. His ships were wrecked and his men fell prey to Indians. After two years La Salle started overland to seek help from the French outposts in the Illinois country. His men mutinied along the way and killed him.

The dream of a French settlement in Louisiana remained very much alive, however, though further efforts were delayed by the War of the League of Augsburg. When peace returned, the Comte de Pontchartrain, head of the Ministry of Marine, together with his son and assistant, Count Maurepas, revived the idea. Together they secured the eager assent of the king. The potential opposition of Spain, which claimed all the territories bordering the Gulf of Mexico, was the one remaining obstacle. That was seemingly removed by the death of Spain's King Charles II, with neither children nor brothers to succeed him. Charles willed his throne to the grandson of Louis XIV, who had, through a devious chain of marriages, some claim to it by birth. Louis' attempt to enforce the claims of his grandson would eventually provoke another European war (1702), but in the interim the family tie left France with a free rein in the Gulf of Mexico.

The question of who should command the expedition was easily resolved. La Salle had foundered on a navigational error; a sailor might have better luck in finding the elusive mouth of the Mississippi. Maurepas approached Iberville, newly returned from Hudson Bay with battered ships and scurvied crew. Iberville was willing, even eager. The colonization of Louisiana would deter English expansionism into the southwest and improve the French position in North America. Iberville knew that the Peace of Ryswick was but a lull in the struggle for the control of North America. Louisiana offered a fertile theater of operations when war broke out anew.

The plan called for Iberville to stop over on the island of Santo Domingo, the western half of which was a French colony (Haiti). There Iberville would pick up some small rowboats (pirogues) to explore the Mississippi and to recruit additional men. Iberville was even willing to hire buccaneers (so nicknamed because of the practice among West Indies pirates of taking the dried meat of wild pig, "boucan," to live on at sea), provided they were "gentle, peaceful, and obedient." The qualification sounds naive until one remembers that the line between piracy and privateering (of the sort that Iberville carried on) was a very tenuous one. In stopping at Santo Domingo, Iberville may also have hoped to soothe the feelings of the French governor there, who had already voiced objections to a colony on the Mississippi. The governor considered the site uninhabitable, and he did not wish to antagonize his Spanish neighbors, who had already announced the intention of establishing a colony at Pensacola. In deference to the governor's wishes, Count Maurepas instructed Iberville only to explore the river and chase out any Anglo-Americans he might find (South Carolina fur traders were rumored to be active in the area).

Iberville set sail from France in October, 1698. Accompanying him were Joseph de Serigny, Jean-Baptiste de Bienville, Gabriel d'Assigny, and Antoine de Chateauguay. The last of these, being the youngest and last of the brothers Le Moyne, was only fifteen years old. Four had been killed in battle; the remaining two, Charles de Longueuil and Paul de Maricourt, remained in Canada. Of those who followed Iberville to Louisiana, Serigny, the oldest and closest to Iberville after the death of Sainte-Helene, remained a naval officer until, near the end of his life, he was appointed governor of the port of Rochefort, France. Chateauguay, the second of that name, ultimately became a highly successful colonial official, serving as lieutenant of Martinique for a time and then governor of French Guiana. Of Jean-Baptiste de Bienville, founder of New Orleans and nearly lifelong governor of Louisiana, we shall have more anon.

Iberville picked up his pirogues in Santo Domingo and about a dozen buccaneers, none of whom, interestingly, knew where the Mississippi was, and sailed again on the last day of December. Toward the end of January, 1699, he dropped anchor at Pensacola, doubtless to reassure the Spanish as to the French presence in that area. The Spanish, who were still in the process of constructing a fort, were communicative, if not exactly hospitable, but they knew little about English activities in the area and even less concerning the whereabouts of the Mississippi.

Steering west from Pensacola, Iberville made his way carefully, for the waters were shallow, uncharted and full of mysterious islands. He explored Mobile Bay far enough to satisfy himself that it was not the Mississippi, and then groped his way west to modern Biloxi. There, inside the low, sandy islands that separate Mississippi Sound from the Gulf, he anchored his fleet, and took to his pirogues for further exploration. On his first excursion ashore Iberville encountered a hunting party of Indians. They seemed sociable enough, rubbing their hands on their heads and bellies and then on those of their guests in an obviously friendly sign of salutation. Iberville replied with the same greeting, and then enticed a few of the braves on board his ship, where he gave them presents. Good Indian relations were important if he wished to colonize; besides, they might be able to show him the Mississippi.

The Indians went off to hunt food for a feast, but they were gone so long Iberville resumed his search without them. A late February cold front swept along the coast, and Iberville's tiny craft was buffeted by a chill north wind as he poked along the crooked lowland of alternate mangrove and sand spit. On March 2 he spotted something different, a rocky palisade so it seemed, and he steered for it. It turned out to be masses of driftwood, greyed by weather, and deposited there by some primeval torrent. Slipping past the driftwood through a narrow channel, he entered the quiet waters of a slow-moving river, its waters a sickly white in contrast to the brilliant azure of the Gulf. In appearance, it seemed to match La Salle's description of the mouth of the Mississippi, but then river deltas looked much alike. Iberville had to be sure.

Iberville had with him about twenty men, half Canadians and half buccaneers, his brother Bienville, and about three weeks' worth of provisions. Rowing slowly against the current, they moved up river, past one fork, then another (Iberville had entered the North Pass of the many-fingered Mississippi delta). Some sixty miles or so above the curls where the city of New Orleans now stands they came upon the village of the Bayogoulas. This was the tribe whose hunting party Iberville had befriended on the Gulf. They welcomed him with the customary stomach caress and prepared a feast of palm root, beans, and corn, fried in bear grease. It was not Parisian cuisine, but the French, running low on provisions, dined hungrily.

The friendly Bayogoulas offered guides and an introduction to their neighbors to the north, the Houmas. The boundary line between the two tribes was marked by a red-stained pole along the river bank, adorned with fish and animal heads. The French translated the Indian name for the marker as Baton Rouge, and the place-name has stuck.

The Houma village rested on a fork where a major tributary (the Red River) joined the Mississippi from the west. Even to this point in his journey Iberville was not positive he had found the Mississippi. La Salle had said that the Mississippi forked into two main streams at a point about ninety miles from the Gulf. Iberville had seen no such fork and he worried. The Bayogoulas assured him there was none, but he thought they might be deceiving him, either from some deliberate purpose or from

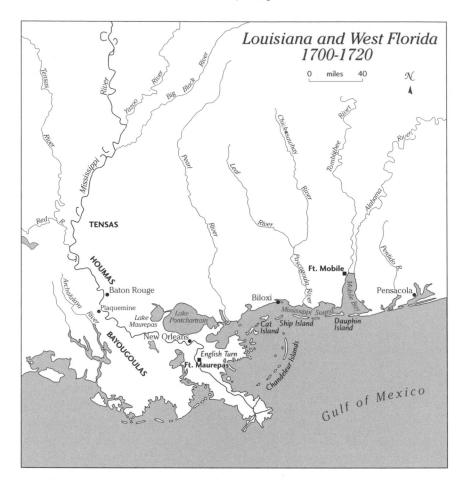

Louisiana and West Florida 1700-1720

0   miles   40

a misleading sense of etiquette. Only when the Houmas, questioned privately, told him the same thing, did Iberville at last conclude that he was on the right river. Satisfied of his discovery, and running short of both trading goods and time (if he was not back in ten weeks his ships were ordered to sail for France), Iberville on March 23 started back down stream, taking along a Bayogoulas warrior as guide.

Near the site which the French later named Plaquemine, the Indian pointed out a short-cut to the Gulf. Since the stream was too small for the pirogues, Iberville sent them on down the river with Bienville, and he set off in a canoe. The going was rough, fifty portages on the first day, and the Indian deserted him on the second. The stream fed ultimately into two brackish lakes, which Iberville named Maurepas and Pontchartrain, and from there through a pass into the sound where his ships lay. He arrived only two hours ahead of Bienville; the short-cut had saved mileage but not time.

It was time now to build a fort to establish the French presence in the area and then head home for supplies and reinforcements. The spot Iberville chose was right at the entrance to Biloxi Bay. It was easily defended, yet accessible from the Gulf, and thus could be easily supplied. Leaving Sauvole de la Villantray (one of Iberville's few associates who was not a Le Moyne) in command, with Bienville as his second, Iberville departed for France.

Six months later, January 8, 1700, he was back, in command now of a fine forty-six gun frigate, still smelling of oak sap and tar, fresh from the shipyards at Bayonne. With him was a somewhat smaller warship and two sailboats for exploring the Mississippi. With him, too, were 100 new colonists, many of them seasoned Canadians. The commitment in men and ships reflected the French court's growing enthusiasm for the Louisiana venture. The governor of Santo Domingo had been overruled; France would plant a permanent colony on the Gulf of Mexico. In deference to Spanish sensibilities, however, the King warned Iberville not to molest Pensacola, nor even to take possession of the site if he found it abandoned.

Not surprisingly, given able leadership, a mild climate, and friendly Indians, the settlement on Biloxi Bay had fared well in Iberville's absence. When the fort was finished, Sauvole had sent Bienville to explore Mobile Bay and the Gulf Coast. While investigating the Mississippi River delta, Bienville encountered an English ship, part of an English colonizing effort. Bienville managed to persuade the English captain that the French had title to the region, by right of discovery, and that they had settled it in overwhelming numbers. It was a bold front, but it worked. The English discreetly retired. Had they been more insistent, the history of Louisiana, indeed of all America, might have been quite different.

Happy with Sauvole's management of the fort and too restless to involve himself in the mundane details of colonization, Iberville mounted a new expedition into the interior. Besides further exploration, he planned to build a fort on the Mississippi in order to solidify the French claim to the river. The site chosen was on a high bank of the river, which the Indians claimed was never inundated even in high water, and about thirty miles south of the portage to Lake Pontchartrain (New Orleans).

While they were constructing the fort, birchbark canoes appeared in the river, an unfamiliar sight in those southern latitudes. It was a party of Canadian fur traders, led by Henri Tonty, lieutenant of La Salle's and now governor of the Illinois country. Tonty, an old acquaintance of Iberville's, had come south to cement relations among the French settlements. He brought some trading goods with him, no doubt to explore the possibilities of exchange in the vast river basin. The meeting of Tonty and Iberville represented in symbolic fashion the maturing of New France, soldier and fur trader exploiting a vast domain, from the Gulf of St. Lawrence to the Gulf of Mexico.

When Tonty departed for home, Iberville went north to the Red River for further exploration. He might have gone on to the Arkansas River—the only major tributary of the lower Mississippi that had so far escaped French examination—but he came down with a fever and had to return to Biloxi.

On May 28, 1700, Iberville weighed anchor once again, but this time he did not proceed directly to La Rochelle. He steered instead for the English colonies and put into New York with a request for food and water. The request was reasonable enough, but it was also pretext. The conquest of English North America was never far from Iberville's thoughts. New York, with its excellent harbor and French-speaking minority (Flemings and Walloons who had settled there when it was a Dutch colony), was an ideal target. The English granted Iberville's request for supplies with what grace they could muster, though they detailed a barge to keep watch on his activities. Iberville blandly proceeded to map the harbor, taking soundings from Sandy Hook to the tip of Manhattan. When the English barge became too nosy, he shifted his activities to the night. Then, brimming to the gunwales with victuals, water, and strategic data, he sailed for France, leaving the governor of New York penning frantic requests to London for aid in building fortifications.

Iberville came away from New York with more than military intelligence. He was impressed with the strength and security of the English colonies, a strength that came from the sheer weight of numbers. Independent farmers, as proficient with a gun as they were with axe or plow, were not as mobile as France's churchmen and fur traders, but the territory they did lay claim to was more firmly held. By contrast, there was a frailty to the French empire that troubled Iberville. He thus returned to France with a plan for strengthening the Louisiana colony, a plan that he presented to Maurepas, who, on the death of his father, had become Minister of Marine and Comte de Pontchartrain. Combining the English and French modes of settlement, Iberville wanted to send farmers to reinforce the colony on Mobile Bay, while tying the Indians to the

French cause by building forts at strategic points along the Mississippi. Envisioning himself as lord of this vast domain, Iberville also asked the grant of a tract of land in the vicinity of Mobile Bay, to be known as the county of Iberville.

Pontchartrain agreed to everything except the land grant (it may have reminded him too much of the feudal baronies that had troubled the French crown for centuries), and Iberville returned to Louisiana in January, 1702. Illness, however, prevented him from carrying out his grand scheme. He was laid up for weeks with the sort of fever (malaria, perhaps) that had struck him down the previous year. Bienville did what he could to salvage his brother's dream. He and the capable Henri Tonty visited the Choctaw and Chickasaw villages to the north of Mobile Bay, and returned with a band of chiefs who were prepared to sign a friendship agreement. Rising from his sickbed, Iberville staged a peace conference that cemented those two powerful Indian nations to the French interest, and then he returned to France. His plan for establishing forts at the mouths of the Ohio, Missouri, and Arkansas rivers would have to wait for a later day. Iberville planned to return to Louisiana the following year, but the European war intervened. There were other, more pressing, demands on French resources. Another Louisiana expedition was authorized for 1704, but Iberville took sick again and it sailed without him. In 1706 he received a new command, the largest squadron of his career. He sailed for the West Indies sugar isles, conquered and sacked the strongly fortified island of Nevis. On the way home he was stricken with yellow fever and died aboard his flagship, July 9, 1706. The Louisiana enterprise, meantime, had fallen to twenty-two-year-old Jean Baptiste Le Moyne, already familiar to us as Sieur de Bienville.

The Le Moynes and New France: The Ending

Bienville, who inherited command of the forts at Biloxi and Mobile after his brother's departure, faced a sea of troubles. The long anticipated fight over the Spanish Succession burst forth in 1702, and the conflict quickly spread to North America. Bienville expected a British squadron to appear in the Gulf at any time, and, though one never materialized, rumors kept his colony in constant tension. The Indians, too, caused him difficulty. Bienville kept his nearest neighbors, the Mobile and Alabama tribes, under control with a mixture of bribes and threats, but the more distant and ferocious Choctaws were beyond his reach. In violation of the agreement they had made with Iberville, the Choctaws attacked both the

French and their Chickasaw neighbors with indiscriminate zeal. Bienville accused South Carolina fur traders of inciting the Choctaws, but it is unlikely that the tribe required any outside inspiration. The foreign intrusion upon their lands itself was probably good enough for war.

As allies, the Spanish were no help. Bienville was too chivalrous to say so, but he would have been better off had they sided with the English. Their method of fighting a war was to shut themselves up in their forts and scream for help whenever a British warship or a band of Indians appeared in the vicinity. Every month or so a Spanish vessel came careening into Mobile Bay to ask for help, and Bienville had to thin his own defense in order to render aid to Pensacola or Appalachicola. He was convinced that without his help the Spanish would have been forced to abandon their holdings in western Florida.

Bienville, one suspects, contributed to his troubles. He had neither the courtly charm nor the inspiring charisma of his older brother. His age too was a handicap, for he was called upon to direct men older and more experienced than he. In 1706, Pontchartrain, responding to a series of complaints from Mobile, removed him from command. The Minister of Marine instructed Bienville, however, to remain in Mobile until his successor arrived. Because of the war, the new governor was unable to find a way across the Atlantic, and Bienville remained de facto governor for another six years.

In 1712 Antoine de la Mothe Cadillac appeared in Mobile Bay to take over the governorship. Bienville remained in the colony to tender advice, a service which Cadillac, a veteran of the Indian wars in the North and founder of Detroit, did not want. The Indian fighting subsided, but friction in the French settlements on the Gulf continued.

Cadillac was the choice, not of the king or Pontchartrain, but of the new proprietor of Louisiana, Antoine de Crozat, a merchant of Paris. Pressed hard by Marlborough on the battlefields of Europe, Louis XIV sought to ease his imperial burdens by transferring Louisiana to a profit-minded businessman. Crozat was to manage the colony for fifteen years; he lasted only five. In 1717 he returned his profitless enterprise back to the crown. His lieutenant, Cadillac, fared no better. Distressed with the slovenly appearance of his settlement and the seeming indolence of its citizenry, Cadillac sent a stream of petulant complaints back to Paris until Pontchartrain lost patience and dismissed him. Bienville once again found himself governor.

By the time Crozat returned Louisiana to the French crown, Louis XIV was dead; Hudson Bay, together with Newfoundland and Nova Scotia, had been lost to the English. Stung by these losses, the Duke of Orleans, regent for the infant Louis XV (a great-grandson since Louis XIV had outlived both his children and his grandchildren), planned to strengthen France's remaining possessions. Orleans' vision was strong enough; his wits were not. The regent fell under the influence of a Scots promoter named John Law, who convinced him that Louisiana could be developed and populated through private investment. The regent accordingly gave his blessing to the formation of a Company for Louisiana or the West, which raised capital for the enterprise by selling stock. To attract investors Law pictured the Mississippi Valley as an El Dorado, a cornucopia of furs and precious metals. Inspired by the duke himself, who managed to involve both the royal bank and the royal mint in the scheme, investors by the hundreds crawled over one another to share in the bonanza. Reorganized as the Company of the Indies, Law and his fellow promoters undertook to manage not only French finances but the French empire.

In 1718, Pontchartrain, still Minister of Marine, sent Bienville a flash warning to expect a horde of new settlers. The company was sending out shiploads of prospectors. Bienville was equal to the emergency. Displaying an administrative capacity typical of his family but hitherto untapped by his superiors, Bienville began organizing his colony for the onslaught. Since the forts at Mobile and Biloxi were already strained to capacity, a new site had to be found. Bienville remembered the spot pointed out to him by the Indians, where a short portage trail connected the Mississippi with Lake Pontchartrain. The river curled sharply at that point, carving a deep channel next to the river bank. Even deep-bottomed sailing vessels could tie up to the shore. A seaport there could become a depot for the entire Mississippi Valley. Bienville honored the regent by naming the site New Orleans.

Bienville was laying out the first rude buildings in his city in the summer of 1718 when the colonists began to arrive. The Louisiana company, with dazzling promises of free transportation as well as free food and lodging until the colonists reached their new homes, had no trouble attracting volunteers. Shipload after shipload steered into Mobile Bay—800 people arrived in the month of August alone, doubling the size of the colony in a matter of days. Bienville struggled to accommodate the immigrant horde. He filled every building in every town he had and even sent 200 up river to the Illinois country. But the immigrants themselves were of little help. Many were derelicts fresh from French prisons; others were mere adventurers who expected to reap a fortune but not earn it. In a plaintive report home Bienville asked the Company of the Indies to include in the next batch at least a few who knew how to build shelters for themselves.

The company ignored his pleas, and the French government complicated his life further by going to war with Spain. Joseph Le Moyne de Serigny arrived with the news in April, 1719. Bienville, though he had troubles enough, realized that this was his long-awaited opportunity to seize Pensacola, an opportunity too good to pass. Serigny, who had been sent to Louisiana to map the Mississippi delta, was happy to delay his own plans for the sake of military adventure. Chateauguay, who had been in the colony since its inception, also volunteered his services.

By mid-May Bienville had a small army ready; he commandeered three of the company's immigrant ships and sailed for Pensacola. At Isle Sainte Rosa, lookout post for Pensacola Bay, Bienville landed unobserved and silently overpowered the small garrison. Donning the Spaniards' uniforms, the French waited for a new guard detail to come out the following morning and seized it too. Then, garbed in Spanish uniforms, the French sailed the guardboat across the bay, entered the fort, surprised the sentinels, and captured the whole place. Bienville sent his captives off to Havana in two of his vessels, left a detachment in the fort with Chateauguay in command, and returned to Mobile.

The whole operation was one worthy of a Le Moyne, even an Iberville. So was the sequel. The governor of Cuba seized the French ships when they entered Havana, filled them with Spanish soldiers and sent them back to Pensacola. Chateauguay, badly outnumbered, was on the point of surrender, when Serigny, followed closely by Bienville, came to his rescue. After some inconclusive fighting, the Spanish sailed away. When the war ended young Louis XV married his cousin, the Infanta of Spain, and obligingly gave back the port of Pensacola. The war had been only a family quarrel, so far as the Bourbons were concerned. The Le Moynes would have to make the best of it.

In the meantime France was in the grip of a speculative mania known as the Mississippi Bubble. By 1720 the Company of the Indies was financing itself by issuing paper money, and it was not long before its obligations far exceeded the amount of gold available. The regent tried to shore up the company's paper by accepting it in payment of taxes, but the impact was only temporary. Since its credit depended on maintaining the "boom" psychology, the company kept up the stream of immigrants, scraping hospitals and asylums for "volunteers," even kidnapping people from city streets. Biloxi and Mobile had no room for them, so the company's ships dumped their wretched cargoes on islands in the Gulf. Bienville lacked the facilities to move them inland; they died by the hundreds.

Then the bubble burst; the company admitted its insolvency. With government approval it discharged its obligations at a fraction of what it owed. Thousands of investors were ruined; the company survived. John Law, the spellbinder, slipped quietly out of the country. Incredibly, the King and Orleans, as slow to learn as any Bourbon, let the company retain its concessions in Louisiana. The company promptly blamed its troubles on Bienville and recalled him to Paris. Chateauguay was left in charge of Louisiana until a new governor appeared; then he too was called home.

Bienville, who never married, spent the next few years in poverty and isolation, an inference we draw from the fact that there is no mention of him in any public record. He got his revenge in 1731, however, when the company, bankrupted by continual Indian wars, surrendered its charter and its colony to the king, and Louis XV restored Bienville to his post as governor.

Bienville ruled over Louisiana for the next decade. They were years of peace in Europe and America, an interlude in the century-long Anglo-French struggle for control of the continent. Bienville brought peace to his own frontier by arranging a truce with the powerful Choctaws. When the English founded the colony of Georgia in 1732 to give themselves better access to the southern fur trade, Bienville responded by sending his Indians to intercept their caravans. For the moment he held the English at bay. Gradually the immigrants were assimilated; many of them even found the riches that had beckoned them to John Law's New World Garden. The pine forest yielded to sugar plantations; New Orleans showed promise of becoming the great commercial entrepot that Bienville planned. When he departed at last in 1742, Bienville's Louisiana—for surely it was his—could be counted a success. He himself felt weariness, rather than elation, however, for he had grown old and tired.

Bienville spent his remaining years in Paris in quiet solitude. He emerged upon the stage of history only once more, in 1764, to protest the transfer of Louisiana to Spain. By the treaty of the previous year, which ended the Seven Years' War (French and Indian War to Americans), the French empire was dismembered, with the English taking everything east of the Mississippi River, including Canada; the land west of the Mississippi, together with New Orleans, went to Spain. Bienville was ignored; his petition never reached the eye of the king. His was a voice from another age. Louis XV, as debauched and ignorant a man as ever occupied a royal throne, had forgotten, if he ever knew, that the French crown had once commanded a Bienville and an Iberville, even a Sainte-Helene, a Maricourt, a Serigny, and a Chateauguay. New France died with the Le Moynes and the giants of their generation. The royal fool simply wrote *finis*.

SUGGESTIONS FOR FURTHER READING

Nellis M. Crouse, *Lemoyne d'Iberville: Soldier of New France* (1954), is a well-executed study of the most famous of the Le Moynes. Grace E. King, *Jean Baptiste Le Moyne, Sieur de Bienville (1892)* is dated but thorough. Joseph Lister Rutledge, *Century of Conflict, The Struggle between the French and British in Colonial America* (1956), covers the wars for empire, as does Howard Peckham, *The Colonial Wars, 1689–1762* (1964).

8

Edward Teach:
The Story of Blackbeard the Pirate

No one at the dawn of the eighteenth century made any effort to separate the spheres of business and government. National interest and private profit went hand in hand as the career of Le Moyne d'Iberville so well attests. Nor was there any nice distinction between trade and war. Wars, in fact, were commonly fought for the sole purpose of opening the paths of trade. In one form or another, war was supposed to make a profit. In pursuing their related interests, kings and merchants relied heavily upon one another. Kings rarely had enough money to maintain a standing navy; hence in time of war they commissioned private warships to prey on the enemy. Occasionally these "privateers" sailed in battle formation with the king's vessels; more often they went off on their own, scouring the seas for unarmed merchantmen unfortunate enough to be flying the wrong flag.

Henry VIII, the first English sovereign to build a seagoing fleet, began the practice of commissioning privateers. Elizabeth transformed it into an art. Her "sea dogs" broke the Spanish monopoly on the New World and laid the foundations for the English empire. In the succeeding century the quadrangular oceanic rivalry among England, France, Spain, and the Netherlands made privateering a standard feature of warfare. And before long the line between privateering and piracy became blurred, as greedy captains seized every weaker vessel they came across.

They can scarcely be blamed. Poor communications and bewildering *renversements des alliances* among the monarchs of Europe made privateering a chancy business. A captain who nabbed an enemy merchantman on the high seas might well discover that he had a friend and ally in tow by the time he reached port. In the course of the century the English fought the French once, the Spanish twice, and the Dutch three times. Under such conditions the privateer found it simpler and often safer to board any vessel he chanced upon, steal the cargo, enlist the crew (stranding on a deserted beach any who would not join him), and burn the evidence. By the end of the seventeenth century every ocean the world around was infested with privateer-pirates. Nourished

*Edward Teach (1680?–1718). A walking arsenal who inspired awe and fear—
that is the image Blackbeard cultivated, and it is certainly the impression con-
veyed by this sketch, which was drawn specifically for "A General History of the
Lives and Adventures of the Most Famous Highwaymen, Murderers. . ." (1736).
(Rare Book Division, The New York Public Library.)*

by the intermittent warfare that engaged Europe from 1689 to 1714, piracy entered its golden age.

The American colonies found the pirates a reliable source of exotic goods and hard cash. Like underdeveloped countries everywhere, they were chronically short of money. Such gold and silver as they were able to earn, principally by trading with the West Indies, trickled off to Britain to pay debts. Imperial authorities frowned on colonial paper money, though in time of war they sometimes found they had to permit a run of bills in order to secure the colonists' military cooperation. In any case, no one but colonists accepted colonial paper. Thus a pirate with a sea chest full of Spanish dollars (pieces of eight) was a welcome sight in American seaports; he was an important link in the international balance of payments.

Colonial governors had standing orders to prosecute pirates, but obedience to instructions depended on the individual and the circumstances. In wartime, when British attention was centered elsewhere, pirates freely roamed the streets of American cities, selling their loot and spending the proceeds in taverns and bawdyhouses. William Markham, Penn's lieutenant governor in the 1690s, was accused of harboring pirates in Philadelphia, though the accusation rested principally on the fact that he had allowed his daughter to marry one. Governor Benjamin Fletcher of New York became the target of a royal inquiry after he issued privateering commissions to a band of notorious pirates. Fletcher's lame excuse was that he was trying to "reclaim" them to an honest livelihood. Left unsaid was the fact that some of the most prominent merchants of New York, political allies of the governor, were retailing pirated goods.

Pirates were so prevalent on the American coast in the spring of 1700—a brief interval between King William's and Queen Anne's wars—that one imperial official described sailing conditions as a continual state of war. The West Indies were even more deeply infested, for the Spanish treasure ships, coming from Cartagena (Columbia) and Porto Bello (Panama) were an inviting target. The treasure ships sailed in convoy across the Gulf of Mexico to Havana and then through the Florida Straits into the North Atlantic. Pirates congregated at strategic intercept points—the Mosquito Coast of Honduras, the island of Jamaica, the Bahamas. Pirates, contrary to the popular impression, rarely buried their treasure. They spent their earnings, just as honest folk do. And the buccaneers of the West Indies, surrounded by hostile Spanish dominions, found the English colonies a good place for a holiday. A prize or two picked up en route simply added profit to pleasure.

Next to the West Indies, the largest concentration of pirates was on the island of Madagascar in the Indian Ocean. From Madagascar, or to be more precise, the tiny island of St. Mary's adjacent to it, pirates roamed the Indian Ocean, the Red Sea, and the Persian Gulf. The Red Sea, a trading artery that connected the Mediterranean world with the Orient, yielded fabulous plunder in silks, spices, and precious metals. American colonists trafficked with these pirates as well. Several New York merchants maintained brokers on St. Mary's, trading rum, firearms, and gunpowder for "Arab gold." In 1699 one such broker, after loading his ship with jewels, ivory, muslins, and gold, offered to transport the pirates themselves to New York for a fee of 100 pieces of eight. Twenty-nine of the brigands accepted the offer, with the understanding that each was allowed to take along a chestful of wares on his own for sale in New York. The total value of the cargo was close to £50,000, a major infusion of capital into New York City's economy.

Association with pirates was, not surprisingly, a mixed blessing. They were rowdy on shore and undiscriminating in their captures at sea. American shipowners fell prey to them as often as any other. The problem grew steadily worse after 1700 because much of the fighting in Queen Anne's War took place in the New World. Every contestant eagerly commissioned privateers, and pirates accepted commissions because such documents legitimized their activities. Some of the more enterprising privateers carried commissions from several countries and a trunkful of battle flags.

The Carolinas were particularly troubled by pirates. Rather new settlements, they were thinly populated, poorly governed, and distracted by Indian wars. Their coastline, a blend of sandy capes, shallow lagoons, and lush islands, provided ideal habitat for lawbreakers. The Carolinas tolerated the pirates for a time because they were a source of profit and, as privateers, they sailed under the cloak of patriotism. But when the war ended in 1714 and the brigands blandly continued their activities, Carolinians turned against them. No one contributed to this change of heart more than Edward Teach, the notorious Blackbeard. His life spanned the golden age of piracy, just as his death helped mark its end.

The Brethren of the Coast

Edward Teach (or Thatch, as it was sometimes spelled), was an Englishman, born in the west country seaport of Bristol some time around the year 1680. But his story begins not in that place or time, but on the small, barren West Indian isle of Tortuga some decades earlier in the seventeenth century. Tortuga had one advantage—its location. It lay near the coast of Hispaniola (later French Haiti) at the northern end of the Windward Passage between Cuba and Hispaniola. The passage was one of the two principal entry points from the North Atlantic to the Caribbean (the other being the Leeward [Mona] Passage between Hispaniola and Puerto Rico), the gateway to the Spanish Main.

French Huguenots were the first Europeans to settle Tortuga, about the middle of the sixteenth century. They created a loosely structured, brotherly community that attracted vagabonds and fugitives from all over the Indies. Brethren of the Coast they called themselves, and they made a modest living selling dried beef and pork to vessels starting the long haul across the Atlantic. The Indians had showed them how to dry meat on racks of green wood over an open fire pit called a boucan. (The strips of dried meat were also called "boucans.") Thus the Brethren won the nickname of boucaniers. When the cattle gave out on Tortuga, the Brethren built boats and sailed to Hispaniola, where cattle abounded. Their craft, designed and built by the Dutch among them, were swift, lean, and

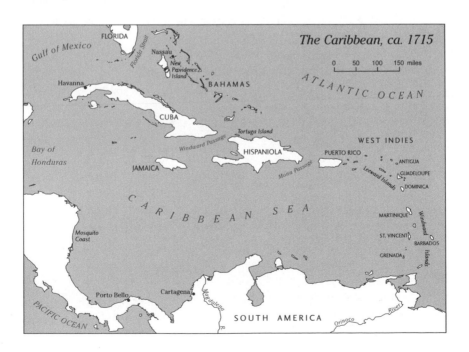

The Caribbean, ca. 1715

sloop-rigged. The Dutch called them *frei-botes*; hence their sailors were *freiboteros*. The English converted that to *freebooters*; like *buccaneers* it eventually became a synonym for pirates.

The altered meaning of words reflected changes in the island community. In the 1670s the Spanish seized Tortuga as part of a campaign to eliminate foreign influences from Hispaniola. Forced into exile, the Brethren turned outlaw, enlisted the aid of other outlaws, and recaptured the island. Tortuga thereafter was a pirate haven, and the fame of the Brethren spread across the Indies. Their recruits carried the title "buccaneer" to Madagascar and the Red Sea.

A lad reared in Bristol, such as Edward Teach, would have been irresistibly drawn to the sea, and to the West Indies. Second in size among English cities only to London itself, Bristol was the major center for American trade—and for privateering. In 1708 when the Crown, as an inducement to privateers, relinquished its traditional one-fifth share of privateering enterprises, a syndicate of Bristol merchants hastily organized a round-the-world expedition. Woodes Rogers, scion of an old Bristol seafaring family, was placed in command of the enterprise, which included two ships and more than 300 men. During the next three years Rogers plundered his way around the world, returning to Bristol in 1711 with a fabulous haul estimated at a quarter to a half million pounds in value.

Teach may have served on the Rogers expedition. His activities in connection with Rogers in later years indicate that the two were old acquaintances. It is more likely, however, that Teach was in the West Indies by this time. Captain Charles Johnson, who wrote, perhaps from first-hand knowledge, A *General History of the Robberies and Murders of the Most Notorious Pirates* in 1724, states that Teach sailed on privateers out of Jamaica during Queen Anne's War, and that he "often distinguished himself for his uncommon boldness and personal courage." The Brethren of Jamaica provided Teach his apprenticeship in the art of plunder.

When the war ended, Teach, along with other privateers, turned pirate. Since Jamaica frowned on such activity, the Brethren were forced to change bases. New Providence Island in the Bahamas suited them fine. It lay athwart the Florida Straits, the principal highway for Spanish treasure ships. During the war New Providence and its village of Nassau had been sacked twice by the French and Spanish; it had neither organized community nor law enforcement. The pirates set up a shantytown of tents and palm-leaf shelters; traders, barkeepers, and prostitutes moved in behind them.

At New Providence, late in the year 1716, Teach joined the crew of

Captain Benjamin Hornigold, who was the most widely respected and feared of all the Brethren of the Coast. Teach's courage and ferocity in battle early attracted Hornigold's attention, and before the year was out Teach found himself in command of a sloop of his own, armed with six cannons and a complement of seventy men. During the spring and summer of 1717, Hornigold and Teach sailed northward along the American coast, plundering, but rarely destroying, coastal schooners carrying flour, wine, and fish from colony to colony. In September they were spotted on the Eastern Shore of Virginia, with their vessels drawn up on the beach and tilted (a process known as "careening") so their barnacles could be scraped off. A month later Teach was in Delaware Bay seizing ships headed for Philadelphia.

In the autumn the partners in piracy returned to the West Indies. Off the island of St. Vincent they came upon a large French merchantman, of a size that neither could have captured single-handedly. Like wolves, they closed in from the Frenchman's rear quarters, then let fly simultaneous broadsides that killed or maimed half the French crew. The prize was the richest of Teach's career—gold dust, silver plate, coins, jewels, and cloth enough to make each pirate wealthy for life. Hornigold seized the opportunity and retired from his risky occupation, purchasing a sugar plantation on New Providence. When, a few months later, Woodes Rogers arrived in the Bahamas with a governor's commission and a pardon for all pirates willing to surrender, Hornigold took advantage of the offer.

Teach was still too young and restless for such a life. Instead he looked over the French merchantman for its potential as a warship. Deciding that she might do—he sacrificed some speed compared to his previous vessel but gained immensely in armament and size of crew—he asked Hornigold for permission to make her his own. Hornigold agreed, they shook hands, and Teach sailed off in search of new criminal adventure. The two never saw each other again. In later years Hornigold "boasted as his chief distinction that he had been the one to discover and train the great Blackbeard."

The Making of Blackbeard

With the sardonic humor characteristic of the hyperconfident outlaw, Teach named his new vessel the *Queen Anne's Revenge*. He made her into a floating fortress, bristling with 40 cannon and a crew of 300. He was soon given an opportunity to test his crew (many of them French recruits) and establish a reputation of his own. Cruising in the vicinity of St. Vincent, in straits frequented by British ships passing between Barbados and Jamaica, he came upon a huge and well-armed merchantman. After a lengthy engagement the British vessel struck her colors. Teach transferred the cargo to his own ship, put the crew ashore on St. Vincent, and burned his prize.

Angered at Teach's effrontery when pirates everywhere in the British islands were accepting the royal offer of pardon, the governor of Barbados sent a thirty-gun warship in search of him. The man o' war found Teach still lurking among the Windward Isles and closed in for the kill. To the British commander's surprise, Teach prepared to do battle. Pirates usually ran from situations where defeat was likely and even victory carried no reward. Perhaps Teach lacked the speed to escape; more likely he was simply hungry for a good fight. The two vessels engaged in a running battle for several hours, until the pirates' superior armament began to show. Badly damaged, the British ship broke off the fight and hobbled back to Barbados. With it went a measure of respect, bordering on fear, for the pirate Blackbeard.

When Teach began to grow his famous beard is not really clear, but it must have been about this time. It was an awesome set of whiskers. Jet black and several inches long at the chin, it stretched high up his cheekbones to his wild and fiery eyes. Parts of the beard were twisted into pigtails held in place by ribbons. Lighted matches (made of hemp cord dipped in saltpeter and limewater) dangled from under his hat, exaggerating the fire in his eyes and giving his features a ghastly glow. Across his chest was a bandolier containing half a dozen loaded pistols, while at his waist was a long, curved cutlass. The overall effect must have been one of a walking arsenal; an awesome blend of human cunning and animal ferocity coexisting in uneasy equilibrium.

Teach himself tried to convey the impression among his men that he was akin to the Devil. To prove it—and not much proof was required among that simple, superstitious folk—he challenged them to help create a hell on earth. When several of the more venturesome ones agreed, Blackbeard led them down into the hold of the ship, closed the hatches and set fire to several pots of brimstone. The crewmen were soon screeching for air, while Blackbeard sat there calmly inhaling the sulfurous smoke, perhaps shaking his head once in a while to make his matches dance. Then, having dispelled all doubts about his nefarious relationships, he set them free. The story, of course, grew better in the telling as it spread from cookfire to bawdyhouse across the Indies.

There was solid sense beneath all this flummery. It was, after all, a form of psychological warfare. Terrorized by the mere mention of Blackbeard's name, his victims were defeated before they even began to fight. More than one prize surrendered without any fight at all, in the hope that by submitting to his mercy they might appeal to whatever tiny shred of humanity there was in him. And Blackbeard usually responded to such humility. After considerable bluster, and occasionally a random execution for the sake of show, he usually landed his captives unharmed on some isolated beach. Sometimes he even let a merchant vessel continue on its journey after he had stripped it of everything of value.

The image-making also helped Blackbeard resolve the chronic problem of leadership. Lacking the legitimacy that cloaked the authority of the ordinary ship captain, a pirate captain was no more than a *primus inter pares*, a first among equals in a jungle without honor. He owed his position, even his very life, to success in the chase. If prizes eluded him, he had only his own strength, wits, and brutality. A reputation for ferociousness bordering on the supernatural, such as Blackbeard had, was a precious dab of life insurance.

Even so, he had troubles enough. A log kept in the last months of his life reveals the unease that pervaded a pirate ship. "Such a day," he wrote without giving the date, "rum all out—our company somewhat sober—a damned confusion among us! Rogues a plotting—great talk of separation—so I looked sharp for a prize—such a day, took one, with a great deal of liquor on board, so kept the company hot, damned hot, then all things well again."

The Siege of Charleston

While prowling the Bay of Honduras in the spring of 1718, Blackbeard came upon a sloop of ten guns flying the black flag of a pirate. The captain of the tiny vessel boldly heeled his craft alongside the *Queen Anne's Revenge* and inquired through his speaking trumpet whom he had the honor of addressing. Blackbeard, amused at such effrontery, bellowed, "A Brother of the Coast!" and invited the stranger aboard. There was no need to provide his own name; his face did that.

The stranger turned out to be Major Stede Bonnet, a planter of Barbados, who had been driven to piracy by boredom. Fast friends midway through the first bottle of rum, Bonnet and Teach decided to cruise together as partners. Within a few days, however, it became apparent that Bonnet knew nothing of sailing or navigation. Indeed, whatever he knew of piracy itself probably came from reading books (he is, at any rate, the only pirate of record who made one of his captives walk the plank). Observing this flaw in his partner, Teach simply removed him from command and placed one of his own men in charge of the companion vessel. Bonnet was made second in command of the *Queen Anne's Revenge*. It is a measure of Teach's leadership ability that this *coup* was accomplished without serious opposition from either Bonnet or his men.

A few days later, off the Mosquito Coast of Honduras, the allies persuaded a merchantman from Jamaica to join them. To ensure loyalty within his enlarged command, Blackbeard put half the Jamaican crew aboard his own ship and put some of his own men on the newcomer. The advantage of large-scale operations was almost immediately evident. Sailing into the Bay of Honduras, the pirate fleet encountered a large merchantman from Boston and four small sloops from Jamaica. A single cannon shot from the *Queen Anne's Revenge* was sufficient to send the crews of all five vessels rowing to shore. Blackbeard removed the cargo and then burned the large ship because the town of Boston had recently hanged a Brethren of the Coast. The sloops were let go, except for one which was burned because the owner protested the loss of his goods.

The pirate fleet stopped in Havana, Cuba, to sell their loot and then headed for the American coast for a summer cruise. Near the end of May, 1718, they appeared outside the harbor entrance of Charleston, South Carolina. With stunning audacity Blackbeard proceeded to blockade the busiest port in the southern colonies. He seized and stripped eight or nine vessels before Charleston authorities, their suspicions aroused by the sudden decline in imports, discovered him. With each vessel that he captured, Blackbeard carefully interrogated the passengers and crew, seeking information about the defenses of Charleston and the number of ships in its harbor. Such was the terror he inspired that his captives readily spewed forth everything they knew. There were eight ships in the harbor, he learned, of armament too weak to present a threat to him. At the same time, the harbor defenses were such that it would have been dangerous for him to enter.

It was time to move on; a bit of luck afforded him a parting shot. Among his prisoners was Samuel Wragg, wealthy planter and member of the governor's council. A valuable hostage indeed! Teach summoned a general council of his crews. It was decided to demand of Charleston a chest of drugs in return for Mr. Wragg. It might seem a quixotic request—unless there was some peculiar ailment running through the pirate fleet. Had they picked up a venereal disease during the Havana stop-over? Blackbeard was a notorious lecher. Was the captain himself infected?

There ensued a low-comedy melodrama of the sort relished by eighteenth century literati. Blackbeard sent one of his captives into town garbed, for credibility, in Blackbeard's own scarlet cloak. Two pirates accompanied him and the trio was given two days to accomplish its mission. If harm came to the pirates or if the timetable was missed, Blackbeard vowed to cross the bar, burn every ship in the harbor, and "beat the town about their ears." The envoy missed the deadline because their small boat capsized in a squall as it entered the harbor, and they had to swim to shore. Then, after collecting the drugs from the willing (and no doubt much relieved) Charlestonians, the trio became separated. The two pirates had been sidetracked, and were busy touring every tavern in town. After retrieving his comrades, the envoy returned to the pirate fleet just as Blackbeard was entering the harbor with plans to bombard the city. Tension eased. Blackbeard released his captured vessels and prisoners and sailed away. Humiliated Charleston plotted revenge.

A Home in the Carolinas

King Charles II, with the inconsiderate audacity common among kings and empirebuilders, granted the Carolinas (named after himself) to a consortium of royal favorites. The English king had nothing more than a technical claim to the landscape. Indians were the resident owners, the French were the first European settlers, and pirates were the most common visitors. The Atlantic coast from Florida north to Chesapeake Bay was a near-ideal environment for piracy. It was a maze of sandy capes, tide-washed sea islands, and shallow sounds. A pirate familiar with the landscape could slip through a hidden channel into waters where no man o' war dared venture. There he could careen his ship and rest his men, while gorging on oysters, soft-shelled crabs, and wild fowl.

The first English settlers, most of whom came from the West Indies, were accustomed to pirates and happy to trade with them. They had little choice, for the lords proprietors, being interested only in their own profit, provided the settlements with no funds for defense. The settlers, in fact, had bigger problems than pirates. The Spanish, who considered this area to be part of Florida, were a constant menace, and the Indians naturally resented the intrusion upon their lands. There was chronic Indian warfare after 1700. Indeed, the South Carolinians had just ended a long, exhausting struggle with the Yamassee when Blackbeard appeared off Charleston harbor.

After his Charleston caper Blackbeard began to think of retirement. His was a dangerous occupation, and he was no fool. Every day the odds of death or capture grew shorter. In Charleston, moreover, he had picked up some news that changed the nature of the game. King George I in 1717 had issued a proclamation offering to pardon all pirates who surrendered promptly. To encourage surrender he sent a squadron under Woodes Rogers to clear pirates out of the West Indies. The golden age of piracy was coming to an end; Blackbeard may have felt it too.

First he had to secure his financial future, and he did it in characteristic fashion—by robbing others. His four-ship fleet contained a fortune in plunder, but if it were fairly divided there was not much for each man, at least not enough to satisfy Blackbeard. So, in June, 1718, on pretense that the fleet needed careening, he sailed into Topsail Inlet, just north of Cape Fear, and deliberately ran the *Queen Anne's Revenge* aground. His second in command, Israel Hands, who had been brought into the scheme, likewise grounded his vessel. That left intact Major Stede Bonnet's vessel, the *Revenge*, and a small sloop. The sloop had been used primarily to carry plunder; the valuables from the two grounded ships were now transferred to it.

Blackbeard then summoned Bonnet, who had been kept half-prisoner, half-guest since first joining the expedition, and informed him that he planned to retire. He intended to go into Bath, a North Carolina port on Pamlico Sound, and receive the promised pardon from Governor Charles Eden. He offered Bonnet the return of his ship but suggested that he too expurgate himself with a pardon. Then, if he wanted to resume his naval career, he could do so as a privateer. West Indian governors, anticipating an outbreak of war between England and Spain, were issuing commissions, Blackbeard informed him (correctly, as it turned out).

Bonnet, chafing in his enforced idleness, impetuously grabbed a small sailing craft and dashed into Bath for a pardon. While he was gone, Blackbeard stripped the *Revenge* of its valuables and told its crew to prepare for a privateering cruise in the Caribbean. He then selected forty of his most faithful adherents, dumped the rest on a nearby sandbar, and sailed off into Pamlico Sound.

Finding his ship intact, Bonnet at first thought Blackbeard had been as good as his word. But from his own crew and from the castaways whom he rescued, he gradually learned the full story. Instead of sailing for the West Indies, he set out after Blackbeard in the by now aptly named *Re-*

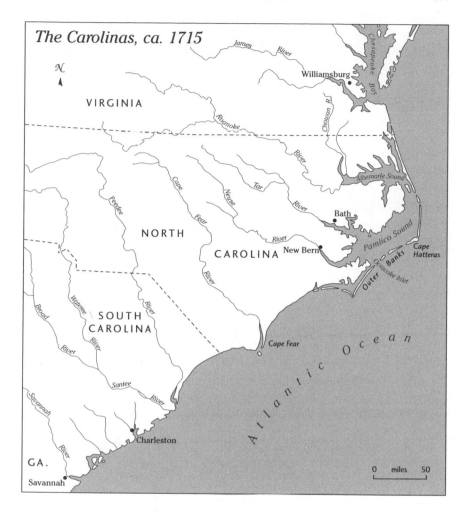

The Carolinas, ca. 1715

venge. He never found him. After patrolling the Carolina capes for three months, Bonnet encountered a warship sent out by the angry citizens of Charleston. He and his men were captured, taken into Charleston, tried, and hanged.

Blackbeard, meantime, had settled comfortably in Bath, where he received the "gracious pardon" promised by the king. It was in many ways an ideal refuge. North Carolina was in 1718 little more than a place-name. A few hundred Virginia emigres had taken up residence in the Albemarle Sound region, and there were smaller pockets of settlement on Pamlico Sound and near the mouth of the Cape Fear River. Unlike

South Carolina which centered on Charleston, North Carolina had neither capital nor commercial hub. Bath, the colony's first incorporated town, was only thirteen years old when Blackbeard arrived and boasted no more than a dozen houses. North Carolina obtained its own governor and assembly some time around 1700, but administration was casual. The governor's own plantation was the seat of authority; the assembly met in various private homes. There was, during Blackbeard's residence, not a single courthouse, jail, school, or church in the entire colony.

Blackbeard bought a house in Bath, and, before the summer was out, got married. He had already married and deserted thirteen women, most of them barroom harlots, but this union he evidently took seriously. His choice was the sixteen-year-old daughter of a Bath County planter. Governor Eden himself performed the ceremony. The marriage was a sign of his acceptance into Carolina society. Bath welcomed Blackbeard and his crew. They were brimming with hard cash and fascinating stories. Blackbeard himself entertained lavishly and once boasted that he was welcome in any house in the colony. For sleepy, isolated Bath it must have been quite a summer.

Blackbeard did not entirely abandon the sea, however. He kept his sloop and most of the crew, treating it as a private yacht. Within a few weeks he was familiar with every tidal inlet between the mainland and the Outer Banks. And gradually he returned to piracy. The sedentary life of a Bath merchant was not for him. And his crew had become a problem. All had accepted the royal pardon, but few actually reformed. When they ran out of money they became restless, eager to return to the only trade they knew. For a time Blackbeard maintained his cloak of legitimacy and satisfied his friends' lust for adventure by robbing or chasing away other pirates, all of which further enhanced his reputation.

Toward the end of the summer Governor Eden granted Blackbeard a license to trade together with a North Carolina registration for his vessel. It was a mark of respect for the pirate captain as well as a subtle effort to get rid of his crew, who had, so Eden reported to his Council, committed "some disorders" in Bath Town. Blackbeard promptly sailed off to Philadelphia, where, instead of engaging in trade, he and his men enlivened the social life of the waterfront. When the Pennsylvania governor, who evidently had little regard for royal pardons and less for North Carolina trading licenses, ordered his arrest, Blackbeard sailed for Bermuda. He apprehended a few vessels on the way but stole only necessary provisions. Toward the end of August, 1718, he came upon two French merchantmen loaded with sugar and cocoa. He captured them, put the two French crews aboard one vessel and set it free, and brought the other to North Carolina. In Bath Town, Blackbeard and four members of his crew filed affidavits that they had "found the French ship at sea without a soul on board her." The governor convened a Vice Admiralty court which agreed that the vessel was a derelict. The chief justice got twenty hogsheads of sugar in compensation for his trouble, the governor got sixty, and Teach got the rest.

During the autumn Blackbeard posted his vessel and crew at Ocracoke Inlet, while he commuted between the inlet and Bath Town. It was an ideal haven for a semiretired pirate, for Ocracoke was one of only two channels (the other being Topsail Inlet) through the long chain of sandy islands known as the Outer Banks. Blackbeard could thus monitor nearly all the traffic bound for or emerging from Albemarle and Pamlico sounds. There is no record that he actually seized any vessels, but he occasionally stopped a merchantman in order to trade for things he needed. His reputation was such that he was almost certain to get the better of any exchange. Yet even this sort of existence carried its risks. The British Empire had declared war on pirates. Woodes Rogers had cleaned out the Bahamas; South Carolina and Pennsylvania had naval squadrons on patrol. Against an ambitious colonial vigilante Blackbeard's pardon and trading license were only bits of paper. So long as he remained at sea, even in semiretirement, his odds grew shorter by the day.

The Last Fight

Toward the end of September, 1718, Blackbeard's lookout at Ocracoke spied a small fleet approaching the inlet from the South. Blackbeard recognized them as Brethren of the Coast and sailed out to greet them with gunports open. The commander of the flotilla was Charles Vane, most famous of the still unpardoned pirates. Vane, having recently been chased out of the Bahamas, was in a civil mood. He and the Brethren joined Blackbeard for what amounted to a family reunion. The merrymaking went on for days. It was certainly the largest pirate festival held on the coast of North America, and probably the last.

Repercussions of the party soon reached the mainland. Governor Eden, too weak to do anything anyway, was inclined to ignore it. As the word spread, however, the size and intentions of the pirate gathering became magnified. By the time the news reached Governor Alexander Spotswood in Virginia, the report was that the pirates were building a fort and planned to make Ocracoke into "another Madagascar." Spotswood lacked the genial tolerance of Eden. He was a soldier and a leader, the first strong governor Virginia had had since Bacon's Rebellion. And he resolved to clear out the pirate nest, which, potentially at least, was as great a menace to Virginia's trade as to North Carolina's.

Spotswood had at his command two warships of the Royal Navy, which had been dispatched to Virginia earlier in the year to aid in defense against pirates. Realizing that he had no authority to invade North Carolina, Spotswood contacted a pair of prominent Carolina planters, political opponents of Governor Eden who were anxious to see the governor discredited. These were to lead an overland expedition, manned by Virginia militia, while the men o' war approached Ocracoke by sea.

Both forces got underway on November 17. The land expedition headed for Bath, which Blackbeard was known to frequent. It found only the governor, who accepted the Virginians' presence without complaint (though after they departed he sent an angry protest to the Board of Trade). The warships meantime found Blackbeard anchored in his favorite spot on the inland side of Ocracoke Island. The pirate festival had ended. Vane and the Brethren had headed north in search of plunder, taking a number of Blackbeard's men with them. In his subsequent report of the battle Spotswood listed Blackbeard's crew at only eighteen.

Lieutenant Robert Maynard, commanding the English ships, set up a blockade of the inlet and spent a day preparing for battle. Blackbeard, so secure in his haven that he had not even posted a lookout, spent the day in his cabin drinking with the master of a coastal schooner who had stopped for a visit. At dawn on November 22, Maynard weighed anchor and proceeded cautiously through the inlet. Blackbeard, whose vessel was smaller than the warships, could easily have slipped away through the shallows of Pamlico Sound, but he elected to stand and fight. When Maynard ran the British Union Jack up his mainmast, Blackbeard fired a cannon and roared across the water: "Damn you for villains, who are you? And whence come you?" Maynard replied simply that his flag showed he was not a pirate. Seizing a bowl of liquor Blackbeard grandly toasted his foe. "Damnation seize my soul," he cried, "if I give you quarter or take any from you."

At that juncture the English vessels ran aground. While they worked to free themselves Blackbeard let fly an eight-gun broadside that killed half of Maynard's crew. Maynard ordered the rest below deck to fool Blackbeard into thinking he had killed them all. Closing in for the kill, the pirates threw hand grenades—bottles filled with powder and shot and ignited by fuses—onto the deck of Maynard's ship. The effect would have been devastating had Maynard not prudently retreated below deck. Peering through the smoke at his empty foe, Blackbeard shouted jubilantly: "They were all knocked on the head but three or four. Blast you—board her and cut them to pieces!" And so he walked into the trap. Maynard and his men leaped out of their hiding place, and in a brief but bloody scramble overpowered the outnumbered pirates. Blackbeard, swinging cutlass with one hand and firing his single-shot pistols with the other, went down before a pack of English sailors. Maynard later counted five pistol wounds and twenty sword gashes on various parts of his body.

So ended Blackbeard. So ended the age of piracy.

SUGGESTIONS FOR FURTHER READING

There are numerous, highly romanticized stories of the life of Blackbeard. The most recent and most objective biography is Robert E. Lee, *Blackbeard the Pirate, A Reappraisal of His Life and Times* (1974). Robert C. Ritchie, *Captain Kidd and the War Against the Pirates* (1986) has a treasure-trove of information on the origins of piracy in the West Indies. Shirley Carter Hughson, *The Carolina Pirates and Colonial Commerce, 1670–1740* (1894, reprinted 1971), is an old doctoral dissertation, but a good scholarly study. Cyrus H. Karraker, *Piracy was a Business* (1953), examines the role of piracy in world trade. An entertaining popular account is Robert Carse, *The Age of Piracy* (1957). The latest writings on pirates are Jan Rogozinski, *Pirates!: Brigands, Buccaneers, and Privateers in Fact, Fiction, and Legend* (1995), and David Cordingly, *Under the Black Flag: The Romance and the Reality of Life among the Pirates* (1995).

9

James Oglethorpe: Soldier Visionary

The crew of the *Anne* had never seen anything like him. He had the manners of an English country squire and the bearing of a soldier. Yet, instead of holding to his cabin in gentlemanly seclusion, he paraded around the ship, mingling freely with the tattered minions that accompanied him on the voyage. One moment he was tending the sick in the dark and noisome hold, and the next he was crouched in the ship's longboat trying to catch fresh fish for the women and children. He insisted on lights-out at eight and prohibited smoking below decks at night, yet when provisions ran short he distributed his own private stores. When a small child died on board and had to be buried at sea, the gentleman-soldier presided over the funeral. Toward the end of the service one of the passengers started

James Oglethorpe (1696–1785). The conventions of 18th-century portraiture, as shown in the mezzotint copy of an unidentified artist, obscure more than they reveal. The stiff pose, heroic gesture, and haughty glance tell us nothing of the human complexity of the man. (National Portrait Gallery, Smithsonian Institution.)

a fuss, threatening, for reasons that no one fully understood, to throw water around. While the ship's captain stood in uncertainty and the crew gaped, the gentleman-soldier slipped behind the troublemaker and, so one of the bystanders reported, "gave him a good kick on ye arse." He then ordered "a pint of Bumbo" so everyone could "Drink & be friends together."

Benign and autocratic by turns, a curious blend of military man-hunter and utopian visionary, James Edward Oglethorpe was a strange personality. So too was the colony that he and his fellow passengers on the *Anne* had set out to found in the year 1733. The American wilderness had witnessed many a social experiment in the century and a quarter since English colonization had begun. But none of them was more romantic, or more troubled, than Oglethorpe's Georgia.

The Gentle Jacobite

Moral courage, high purpose, and a fanatical sense of duty were an Oglethorpe family tradition. Theophilus Oglethorpe, father of James Edward, was a soldier in the service of King James II. When William of Orange landed to claim the English crown in 1688, Theophilus was one of the few regimental commanders in the realm who was prepared to put up a fight. He did not do battle but only because James, in flight to Paris, ordered his followers to lay down their arms. The Oglethorpes followed James to France and took up residence with him at Saint Germain. Theophilus was distressed, however, by the predominant role of Roman Catholics among the exiles at Saint Germain and offended by the none-too-subtle hints that he must convert if he wanted royal preferment. The Protestantism of his forebears, as it turned out, was stronger than his loyalty to the Stuart family. In 1696 he returned to England, took an oath of loyalty to William III, and retired to his estate in Surry. His wife Eleanor, who had once been a maid to the Duchess of Portsmouth, the favorite mistress of Charles II, remained, however, a fierce and active Jacobite. When her husband was elected to parliament in the late 1690s, Lady Eleanor established herself as a contact between the "king over the water" and his allies in London.

Born in 1696, the seventh and last of the Oglethorpe children, James Edward grew up in this atmosphere of fanaticism and intrigue. After the death of Theophilus in 1702, Lady Eleanor sent her two daughters to Saint Germain, where they converted to Catholicism and married French noblemen, and her eldest son Lewis fought in the French army during

Queen Anne's War. It was a mercy, perhaps, that, despite his Stuart name (James Edward was the name that James II had given the son that was born to him in 1688), Oglethorpe was too young to share in, much less understand, these faintly treasonous activities.

He received the education of an English gentleman, attending first Eton and then Oxford (his mother chose Corpus Christi College for its supposed Jacobite sympathies). Oglethorpe's arrival at Oxford in late 1714 coincided with the death of Queen Anne, the accession of the Hanoverian Protestant George I, and, a few months later, an uprising in Scotland in behalf of James Edward Stuart (James II had died in 1701). Lady Eleanor was up to her earrings in intrigue throughout "The Fifteen" rebellion, but Oglethorpe himself, although apparently friendly to the Jacobite cause, played no active role. He did leave Oxford for France in 1716, but not to play politics. He entered a French military academy, and after a brief stint there (all of Oglethorpe's formal education seems to have consisted of brief stints) he joined Austria's Prince Eugene in a campaign against the Turks. He fought in the bloody Battle of Belgrade (August, 1717) and emerged from the war with a reputation for military prowess. Captain John Smith, in his grave now nearly a century, would have applauded a kindred spirit.

In 1719, Oglethorpe returned to England to take charge of the family estate in Surry. One of his older brothers had died in battle; the other had become a Stuart sycophant, aimlessly following the "Old Pretender" through the chateaux of France. Lady Eleanor, though notorious for her politics, had been discreet enough in her espionage activities to avoid arrest. Oglethorpe spent the next few years quenching her fiery fanaticism and refurbishing the family name. And then in 1722 he stood for, and won, a seat in parliament. A new career beckoned.

Political Samaritan

A youth of twenty-eight, scarred by the curse of Jacobitism, could not hope to shake a complacent, and predominantly Whig, House of Commons. Nor did Oglethorpe try. He held to the secure anonymity of the back benches, served on routine committees, and awaited his opportunity. When he developed a concern for the downtrodden of English society is not exactly clear, but it was a natural extension of his family's high-minded adherence to lost causes. In 1727 he published anonymously a fifty-two page pamphlet protesting the Royal Navy's system of conscripting sailors by sending press gangs through the streets of England's cities. Oglethorpe denounced impressment as a violation of Magna Carta, and, though other concerns thereafter intruded upon his conscience, he never abandoned the cause of sailors' rights.

Patience and diligence paid off, and in February, 1729, Oglethorpe was made a committee chairman, and the charge was one to his liking. His committee was to inquire "into the State of the Gaols of this Kingdom." The assignment itself was a novel one, for parliament in those years was not known for its humanitarian concerns. Sir Robert Walpole was the king's chief minister, the dominant figure of the age, and he lacked the temperament for social experiments. Peace abroad and stability at home were his twin gods, and for nearly twenty years he kept bumptious Britain in the church of status quo.

What prompted the appointment of a prison committee is uncertain, but it may have been nothing more radical than the common knowledge that the country's jails were overcrowded. Oglethorpe did not have to proceed far with his inquiry before discovering the principal cause—the jails were full of debtors. Felons were rarely jailed for any length of time in the age of Walpole, since the care and feeding of the errant was regarded as an unnecessary extravagance. As a result, most felons were executed, maimed, or transported to the colonies. Benjamin Franklin, who objected to the latter alternative, suggested sending American rattlesnakes to Britain in return.

Imprisonment for debt originated in the medieval notion that each person ought to be bodily liable for his social obligations. Such simplistic business ethics may have made sense in the primitive world of Edward I (1285), but in the capitalized world of the eighteenth century it was a daily horror. Capitalism thrived on credit. For every investor there was a borrower, for every investment an attendant risk. Some, inevitably, were losers in the competitive game, and, with bankruptcy unknown, the insolvent went to jail. Creditors, Oglethorpe discovered, seemed to delight in sending their obligees to jail, even though the penalty actually lessened the likelihood of ever recovering the debt. And once in an overcrowded prison the insolvent was at the mercy of privileged keepers whose emoluments were related to the number of inmates.

After a year's investigation Oglethorpe's committee issued three reports detailing the loathsome living conditions of England's prisons and accusing prison officials of fraud, extortion, gross brutality, and even torture. In his final report, which exposed an attempt by government placemen to bribe the committee, Oglethorpe ominously declared, "If this be law, all England may be made one extended prison." The reports produced a public sensation, not merely because of their gory details, but because exposes of any sort were so rare. Oglethorpe became, for the moment at least, a national hero.

The Genesis of Georgia

On February 13, 1730, Viscount Percival (later the first Earl of Egmont), a man of influence at Court, power in the House of Commons, and a member of the prison committee, recorded in his diary a conversation with Oglethorpe. The two men discussed a "scheme to procure a quantity of acres either from the Government or by gift or purchase in the West Indies and to plant thereon a hundred miserable wretches who . . . are now starving about the town for want of employment; and that they should be settled all together by way of colony, and be subject to subordinate rulers, who should inspect their behavior and labour under one chief head." The idea of resettling the English poor in the New World was by no means new, nor, for that matter, was the supposition new that such colonists would require a benevolent master. All such plans had faltered, however, for want of political influence and royal attention.

The alliance of Oglethorpe and Egmont bade fair to achieve both. The committee report aroused the interest of philanthropists. Oglethorpe became trustee for various bequests in behalf of debtors. With Egmont's cooperation he reorganized the Commons committee into a board of trustees for the founding of a colony as an asylum for the poor. To name the settlement Georgia, after the king, was too obvious a gesture to require discussion. Egmont carried the idea to Sir Robert Walpole.

Walpole and his associates in the ministry felt little sympathy for the poor. Nor were they at all sure that they wanted to stimulate an exodus of able-bodied subjects from the kingdom. Yet strategic considerations of that sort also worked in favor of the Georgia project. South Carolina, which had lately developed a highly capitalized rice culture, needed a buffer. It was menaced by Indians to the west and by the Spanish in Florida. The indebted poor, sprinkled throughout the country south of the Savannah River, would do nicely. Oglethorpe's was not the first, nor the last, humanitarian scheme to slip through on the cutting edge of cynicism.

It took several suspenseful years for the colony's charter to wind its way through the imperial bureaucracy, but on April 21, 1732, King George II at last signed it into law. The Georgia charter was, to say the least, unique. It was a proprietary grant, like that of Pennsylvania, but it described Oglethorpe and his associates, not as proprietors, but as "Trustees." The distinction was a meaningful one, for Oglethorpe and his fellows were to hold Georgia in only temporary trust; after 21 years the colony was to revert automatically to the king. This neat arrangement relieved the king of the trouble and expense of colonization, while assuring him ultimate control. Only a man such as Oglethorpe, with his curious mixture of loyalty and compassion, would have accepted such a bargain. In addition, the charter spelled out the details of the Georgia government. Instead of a governor, the colony was to be ruled by a council of twenty-four, nine of whom, including Egmont and Oglethorpe, were named in the charter. That nine, in turn, were to appoint the remainder. Since it was evidently intended that the council remain in England, the entire setup spelled trouble. Finally, under the charter, the boundaries of the colony were to extend from the Savannah River to the Altamaha, and from the Atlantic Ocean to the Pacific.

With charter in hand, the trustees prepared a brochure explaining their plans for the colony and inviting applications. The trustees offered to send some colonists over on charity, but they lacked the resources to finance very many. Parliament in May, 1732, appropriated £10,000 to assist in the founding of Georgia, but it made no provision for travel grants to the poor. Oglethorpe himself seems to have lost sight of the imprisoned debtors by that date. In *A New and Accurate Account of the Provinces of South Carolina and Georgia*, which he published at his own expense, he stressed the advantages to the mother country in having a colony that produced semitropical products, such as silk, citrus fruit, and wine. If imprisoned debtors did apply for transportation to Georgia, the trustees treated them like other charity cases. The trustees, in any case, lacked the means to get debtors out of prison. Few, if any, ever went to Georgia. In the twenty years of trustee governance a total of 2122 persons were sent to Georgia on charity, and nearly half of those were foreigners from the Continent. Georgia, in short, was settled in the same way as other southern colonies, by people with enough wealth to finance themselves, and venturing in pursuit of more.

The Paternal Colonist

Never was a colony so highly publicized as Georgia. The trustees, in addition to their own printing facilities, enlisted the aid of the British press, which freely reprinted their brochures and broadsides. Applications streamed in, though the process of selection, hampered by the com-

mittee's own cumbersome procedures, was slow. In October, 1732, Oglethorpe offered to go to Georgia himself, on condition that a shipload of
emigrants be sent out at once. Since none of the other trustees was prepared to venture his life in the malarial wilderness of the American South,
and no other leader was in sight, the trustees gladly accepted Oglethorpe's
offer. The navy obligingly provided him with a 200-ton frigate, the *Anne*,
for the journey. On November 17, Oglethorpe and 116 colonists set sail.

The emigrants, under Oglethorpe's solicitous eye, fared well on that
first crossing. Although two children died, several more were born, and
the company landed more numerous than it had begun, a circumstance
rare in that age and one universally regarded as a good omen. After seven
weeks at sea the *Anne* dropped anchor in Charleston harbor. Leaving his
restless flock aboard ship (there were limits, evidently, to his faith in humanity), Oglethorpe went ashore for provisions and advice. Governor and
council welcomed him warmly, for South Carolina fully appreciated the
value to themselves of the Georgia buffer. The assembly voted to supply
him with 100 cattle, 25 hogs, a stockpile of rice, and ships to carry it all.

The South Carolinians thought the Altamaha River the best place
for a settlement, but Oglethorpe steered the *Anne* for the Savannah instead. It was closer to the protective arm of South Carolina and hopefully
less provocative to the Spanish. After an exploratory poke, Oglethorpe
selected a high bluff, about ten miles upriver from the sea. A small group
of Yamacraw Indians lived nearby, and Oglethorpe quickly made friends
with their aged leader Tomochichi. The old chief welcomed the colonists
and amiably agreed to sell enough land for a settlement. He had little
choice, for his tribe was weak and had long since become dependent on
English goods. Tomochichi's trust was well placed; Oglethorpe never violated Indian rights so long as he remained in charge of the colony.

The trustees, who took pride in their attention to detail, had directed
that Oglethorpe locate his colonists in a single town (they even provided
him with a name, Savannah), giving each family a lot in town and 45
acres on the outside to farm. The landholder was only a trustee of the
soil, however. He could not sell his property, and he could bequeath it
only to a male heir (because landholding was tied to military service, as
in feudal times). In the absence of a male heir the lands of a deceased
colonist reverted to the trustees. These restrictions, or tails, were a source
of endless trouble.

The one detail that the trustees overlooked was providing a government for Georgia. Oglethorpe had no formal authority; he had financed
his own passage to Georgia, and the trustees apparently expected him

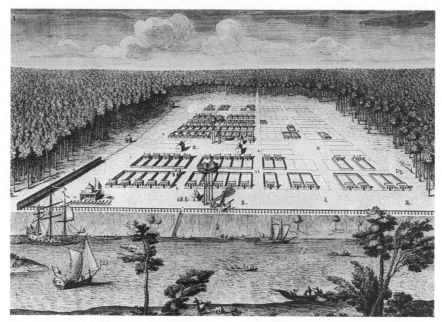

View of Savannah, 1734, with Oglethorpe's tent on the water's edge. (I. N. Phelps Stokes Collection, The New York Public Library.)

to remain there only a short time. Oglethorpe simply assumed control, and the colonists looked to him for leadership. "The general Title they give him *is Father*," reported a South Carolina visitor six weeks after the colonists' arrival. "If any of them is sick, he immediately visits them and takes a great deal of Care of them. If any Difference arises, he's the Person that decides it. . . . He keeps a strict Discipline."

Strict he was. The people, he decided after three months in Georgia, had become too dependent on him for decisions and too "impatient of Labour." The idleness, he concluded, was due to the presence of slaves, brought in from South Carolina. So he sent the blacks back to Carolina and prohibited the possession of slaves thereafter in Georgia. Then, discovering that "Some of the Silly People" had tried to trade their food, provided them out of the Trustees' store, "for a little Rum Punch," he forbade liquor in the colony and "Staved such as [he] could find in the Town." Georgia, in his image, was to be a land of sober, independent farmers. Allow rum or negroes, he told the Trustees, and "our whole design will be ruined."

He might have added lawyers, as well, to the proscription list. The one governmental agency authorized by the trustees was a town court to handle civil and criminal complaints. Oglethorpe set up the court and appointed its officers, but he prohibited lawyers from appearing before it. Self-reliant citizens were expected to plead their own causes; lawyers merely obstructed the proceedings with their Latin phrases and obscure motions. The handful of debtors among his throng no doubt agreed. What others thought of such devotion to the amateur ideal went unrecorded.

Such regulations, though they ultimately caused Oglethorpe much trouble, were not without reason. Carving a settlement out of the piney woods was no easy task. Fevers and agues (probably malaria) were endemic, the soil in many places was sandy and unyielding, and there was constant danger of attack. Discipline, in such conditions, was essential to survival, and Oglethorpe, it must be said, provided a personal model of austerity. He pitched a tent on the edge of the bluff and lived there throughout his initial stay in the colony. He was a man of simple tastes who took naturally to the pioneering life.

Shiploads of new colonists arrived periodically, some sent by the Trustees, most coming on their own. The Trustees' advertising campaign early attracted the attention of persecuted religious groups on the Continent. Oglethorpe welcomed such refugees because of their reputation for sobriety and diligence and because the English government still frowned on the emigration of its own people. Two groups of Jews, one from Germany and one from Portugal, arrived during the summer of 1733, and a shipload of German Lutherans landed in early 1734. By the time Oglethorpe returned home a little later that year, there were about 500 people in the colony sheltered in eleven fortified communities. Savannah boasted some forty houses with log frames, clapboard siding, and shingled roofs. Two strongholds, containing four cannons apiece, guarded the river. The town's water supply was pure (another Oglethorpe concern), and the people, according to a visitor, were "healthy and orderly."

The principal reason for Oglethorpe's return to England was finance. Despite small gifts from the governors of South Carolina and Pennsylvania, Oglethorpe was in chronic need of cash. He financed much of the Georgia venture out of his own pocket, and when that went bare he began writing drafts on the London Trustees. To honor the drafts, the Trustees turned to parliament with annual petitions for money, and parliament was becoming increasingly reluctant. Besides, neither parliament nor Trustees had any clear idea of what was going on in Georgia because Oglethorpe had been too busy to write. By early 1734 tempers in London were ugly enough so that even a resumption of letter-writing was not enough; Oglethorpe had to appear in person. The crisis seemed to resurrect his promotional instincts. He took with him on the royal man-o'-war *Aldborough* the ninety-year-old Tomochichi, his wife, his grand-nephew, and five Yamacraw warriors. Georgia had not yet produced the silks and wines that parliament had been promised; a touch of imperial romance would have to do.

The Paternal Warrior

By the time Oglethorpe landed, the storm of anger had turned into a shower of praise. The newspapers were filled with anonymous tributes. The founding of a new colony had captured the nation's imagination. Even Alexander Pope, the acknowledged arbiter of poetic tastes, was moved to pen a few couplets in tribute. The royal navy named its latest warship after him, and the king invited him to a special audience to pore over maps of the New World. Oglethorpe took the occasion to present the queen with a dress made from Georgia silk, which, gushed one newspaper, "was universally acknowledged to excel that of any other country."

Tomochichi and his kin fared equally well. They toured London, visited Eton and Canterbury, reviewed the horse guard in Hyde Park, and sat through a "grand entertainment" staged by the Georgia Trustees, which ended with a colossal bonfire. Invited to the royal household at Kensington, they impressed the court with their stately carriage, their tactful responses to questions, and above all, their obvious affection for Oglethorpe.

Whether intended by Oglethorpe or not, the flummery served some material purposes. The Trustees ceased their grumbling, the ministry turned sympathetic, and parliament opened its purse. In March, 1735, Oglethorpe, himself still a member of the Commons, brought before parliament the Trustees' annual appeal for an appropriation. To justify the request, Oglethorpe pointed to the threat presented by the French founding of Mobile. The new base gave the French better access to the Indian trade and posed a potential danger to the Carolinas and Georgia. The Commons responded with a generous grant of £25,800 to construct forts along the southern frontier. The Board of Trade followed suit by making him commander of the joint Carolina-Georgia militia and commissioner for treating with the Indians. The Georgia Trustees further solidified his position by enacting into law his edicts against rum and slaves.

The Trustees did make one request: that to improve his letter-writing Oglethorpe appoint a private secretary. The general's choice was Charles

Wesley, a young theologian of Oxford who, in tandem with his older brother John, had organized the Methodist movement within the Church of England. Oglethorpe had long known the Wesleys' father Samuel, as well as their mother, who was an ardent Jacobite. At the urging of his mother, John too decided to accompany Oglethorpe to Georgia in order to preach the Gospel to the Indians. The party sailed in November, 1735, after the usual delay of several weeks while they waited for favorable winds. The ship was jammed with 257 colonists, the largest party ever to sail to Georgia, and Oglethorpe had his hands full ministering to the sick, the pregnant, and the hungry. Despite an unusually stormy crossing, the band of emigrants reached Savannah without the loss of a single person, the credit for which John Wesley divided about evenly between God and Oglethorpe.

Savannah by 1736 was rich enough to rate a buffer of its own, so Oglethorpe decided to place his ship-borne comrades in a new settlement farther to the south. Characteristically, he left the main body on board ship in the Savannah River while he and a scouting party searched out a location. He selected St. Simon's island, about halfway between Savannah and the Spanish outpost at St. Augustine, Florida. Naming the site Frederica, he marked out a fortress, left careful instructions for the placement of ramparts and digging of a moat, and then went back for his sea-weary colonists.

The establishment of Frederica, together with another fortified town on the Altamaha River, angered the Spanish. Although the Spanish no longer had any interest in forming settlements of their own to the north of Florida, they worried when the British moved in on one coast and the French on the other. Florida, though it had proved to be of no intrinsic value as a colony, was of vital strategic importance to Spain. It guarded the Bahama Channel, the main artery for Spanish gold shipments, and it served as a buffer for the protection of Cuba and the Antilles. Spanish authorities had viewed the founding of Georgia with mild concern, and their concern deepened with every fort Oglethorpe erected. When, in the fall of 1736, Oglethorpe set up a new outpost at the mouth of the St. Johns River, on the very doorstep of Florida, Spain acted. The governor of Cuba revived Spain's ancient claim to the entire south Atlantic coast and sent an emissary to Savannah to demand an English withdrawal from all holdings south of Beaufort, South Carolina.

Oglethorpe received the Spanish diplomat like an Oriental potentate, but yielded not an inch. He countered the Spanish ultimatum with a demand that the Spanish abandon all claims north of St. Augustine. After intense bargaining, during which Oglethorpe paraded his Indian support,

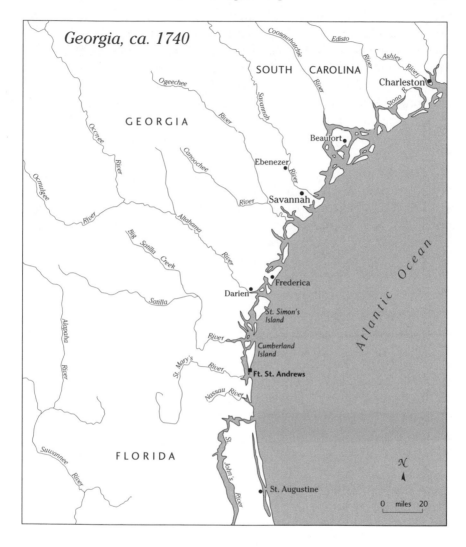

Georgia, ca. 1740

the two agreed to neutralize south Georgia. Oglethorpe promised to abandon his advance base on the St. Johns River, and in return the Spanish agreed not to enter the area. The safety of Frederica and the remaining Georgia forts was thus guaranteed; Oglethorpe, having got what he wanted in the first place, was satisfied. The Spanish envoy, after returning to Cuba with the treaty, was summoned to Madrid and hanged.

Oglethorpe realized, nevertheless, that his principal gain was time,

time to strengthen Georgia's defenses. There was increasing friction between Britain and Spain over trading rights in the Caribbean; if war came,
Georgia would be the battleground. He spent several months supervising
the construction of additional battlements at Frederica, and in November, 1736, sailed for England to secure further help. Crossing his path
in midAtlantic was a strongly worded plea from the Trustees that he return and render an accounting of his latest expenses. Charles Wesley
had quit as secretary, and Oglethorpe's correspondence had once again
fallen into arrears.

Back in London, after a terrifying journey through wintry gales, Oglethorpe managed to pacify the Trustees once again, and he secured a new
subsidy of £20,000 from parliament. He even wrung from the ministry
permission to raise a regiment of regulars for service in Georgia. It was
a measure of the extent to which Anglo-Spanish relations had deterio-
rated, for Walpole, who abhorred the fiscal waste of warfare, had strived
for years to keep Oglethorpe on a short leash.

Oglethorpe spent the next six months recruiting his regiment and
renewing his humanitarian interests. He engrossed himself in the affairs
of the Westminster Infirmary, which had placed him on its board of governors, and he underwrote the publication of a poem, *London*, by an unknown author named Samuel Johnson. In the summer of 1738 he returned to Georgia and stationed his troops at newly built Fort St. Andrews
on Cumberland Island. Situated to the south of St. Simon's Island, the
new outpost became a buffer for thriving Frederica. The Spanish might
well be pardoned for showing concern over Oglethorpe's salami-slicing
territorialism.

The first threat came, however, not from Spain, but from Oglethorpe's
own men. In November, 1738, the troops at St. Andrews developed grievances over pay and provisions and tried to take over the fort. The general,
who happened to be on hand, confronted the mutineers in person. When
one of the ringleaders raised his weapon, Oglethorpe lunged at the man
and disarmed him after taking a shot that grazed his shoulder and blew
a hole through his wig. Another mutineer fired and missed, whereupon
Oglethorpe seized a third and held him as both shield and hostage. He
offered pardons to the other disaffected troops if they would disperse,
and they did. He later interviewed each individually and promised a re-
dress of grievances. With that situation under control, he headed west
to mend relations with the Indians. The diarist who recorded the incident
at St. Andrews, did not say so, but it would have been in character had
he left behind orders that his men improve their marksmanship.

Indian relations were much in need of repair. South Carolina traders, ignoring Georgia's claim of a monopoly, as well as Oglethorpe's stringent regulations, had been cheating the western tribes with shoddy goods. Creeks and Chickasaws, moreover, were worried about French and Spanish aggression. Capitalizing on the poor reputation the South Carolinians had given English goods, the French had told the Chickasaws that British gunpowder "makes no noise," and that British musket "balls drop down as soon as they come out of the guns." The Chickasaws were also curious about Oglethorpe, having heard that his mother was a "red woman." (The enemies of Eleanor the Jacobite would have been amused at that.)

Oglethorpe countered by inviting the leaders of both Chickasaws and Creeks to Savannah. After an interview with Oglethorpe one of the Chickasaw chiefs reported to his fellows that Oglethorpe had "as white a body as any in Charles Town." Whether this was a good thing or bad is uncertain, but Oglethorpe carried the day when he replied that he really was a red man, "an Indian in my heart." He then presented his own coat to Chigilly, the principal mico of the Lower Creeks and a personal friend of Tomochichi's. The Creeks, who resided on the rivers that flowed into Mobile Bay, were the most powerful and most strategically situated of the western tribes. Oglethorpe's gesture enhanced Chigilly's standing in the tribe and wedded him forever to the English. On their departure the Indians were invited to inspect the Savannah arsenal and take whatever they wished. English-made weapons would reaffirm their own quality.

In the spring of 1739 the Indians, aware of the approach of war between Britain and Spain, became uneasy once again. The Spanish in St. Augustine made open preparations for an expedition into Georgia, and the Indians understandably wanted to side with a winner. In addition, the Creeks were having trouble with the pro-French Choctaws, and feared an attack by the French. Chigilly sent a special runner to Oglethorpe asking him to come out and "put all things in order." Accompanied by twenty-five attendants and an assortment of Indians, Oglethorpe journeyed to the Creek settlement of Coweta on the Chattahoochee River. The Creeks hospitably placed "cakes and bags of flower [sic]" in trees along the trail, so the English would not hunger along the way. Oglethorpe conferred with Creek leaders for several days, exchanged toasts with much fanfare and ritual, and returned home with everything he could wish. He patched up the differences between Creeks and Choctaws, persuaded the Creeks to abandon a preemptive strike against the French, and secured their promise of aid in the event of an Anglo-Spanish war. It was really an astonishing diplomatic achievement.

On his return to Savannah in September, 1739, Oglethorpe blandly declared war on Spain and ordered preparations for an attack on St. Augustine. The news from Europe was that Britain and Spain were on the verge of war, and he obviously wanted to strike the first blow. He was saved from a possibly embarrassing predicament when parliament issued a formal declaration in October. The pretext was the appearance in London of an English ship captain named Thomas Jenkins, allegedly carrying one of his ears in a box. The Spanish had caught Jenkins smuggling in the Caribbean and performed the severance as punishment. (Or so Jenkins and the Whig establishment claimed. Critics noted that he never opened the box or removed his wig.) Jenkins' allegations, coming on top of years of friction, was sufficient to provoke a declaration of war, a conflict ever after known as the War of Jenkins' Ear, although it eventually became merged in a general European conflagration, the War of the Austrian Succession.

The St. Augustine expedition was ill-fated from the start. South Carolina's aid was essential, but that colony was still suffering the jittery after-effects of a slave uprising among plantations along the Stono River (the worst slave revolt, in fact, of the pre-Revolutionary period). The assembly was reluctant to send its fighting men to distant fields, and when, after months of delay, it finally authorized a small contingent, it placed all sorts of restrictions on Oglethorpe's use of it. Carolina then discovered that its treasury was empty, and Oglethorpe had to loan the colony £4000 out of his own pocket to finance the expedition. In the meantime the Spanish had ample opportunity to strengthen their defenses. On April 3, 1740, the day Oglethorpe set forth, six galleys, armed with nine-pound cannon, arrived in St. Augustine from Cuba. These vessels, stationed at the harbor entrance so that they reinforced and were in return protected by the Spanish fort, thwarted the Georgian invasion.

The Walpole ministry, seeing an opportunity to expand Britain's imperial holdings, opened its well-buttoned purse in the spring of 1740, and sent Oglethorpe a small naval squadron to aid in the expedition. Oglethorpe ordered the vessels to blockade St. Augustine, while he proceeded overland with his army. He crossed the St. Johns River in early June and overran two Spanish forts, capturing a quantity of arms and ammunition. At St. Augustine, however, he found the Spanish galleys an insuperable difficulty. His naval escort refused to enter the harbor for an attack and advised instead that he lay siege to the city. And then, fearful of remaining in Florida waters during the hurricane season, they gave him until July 5 to complete the operation.

A direct frontal assault on the Spanish works might have succeeded (the Spanish commander thought so), but Oglethorpe instead elected to divide his army, placing part of it to the west of the city to keep the inhabitants from foraging for food, and scattering the remainder on various islands in the harbor. The move served only to reveal his weakness and his indecision. The Spanish took advantage of both with a surprise sortie against an isolated British detachment, killing or capturing the entire lot. For the next few days Oglethorpe moved his men about, shifting regiments from island to mainland and back, all of which quickly convinced friend and enemy alike that he had run out of ideas.

On July 3 a sloop from Cuba slipped past the British blockade with relief supplies, and the siege was over. The British squadron departed the next day; so fearful was its commander of storms that he would not even agree to linger along the Carolina coast to protect against Spanish counterattack. Oglethorpe abandoned the campaign and trudged dismally back to Frederica. A fever struck him on the way and kept him in bed for the next two months.

Discontent in Utopia

Inexperience was the principal reason for Oglethorpe's failure at St. Augustine—never before, after all, had he commanded a military expedition. But the fiasco also revealed some serious flaws in his character, flaws that hampered his civil leadership as well. He lacked, in short, a sense of proportion, an ability to distinguish the epochal from the trivial. A minor skirmish in which he captured a few guns and horses he considered a major battle, and wondered why the Spanish fort did not promptly surrender. After years of contemplating an attack on St. Augustine, he arrived in front of the fort without a single plan in mind, nor did he have the imagination to invent one as events unfolded.

His civil administration of Georgia suffered the same shortcomings. One reason he never had time to write the Trustees was that he was continually bogged in minor detail. In the summer of 1739 he had to delay his mission to the Creeks for several weeks while he resolved various problems brought to him by the citizens of Savannah. With paternal care he listened patiently to every one. Escaping at last, he stopped for the night in the frontier settlement of Ebenezer. There the local schoolmaster collared him, and while wartime alliances hung in the balance, he spent half a day listening to the complaints of a crusty old German pedagogue. In the midst of his frantic preparations for the St. Augustine expedition after he returned from the Creek country, he took time out to organize a Savannah cleanup campaign. He personally led a group that pulled all the weeds on the village common and "publick squares."

Oglethorpe was reluctant to delegate authority and rarely chose wisely when he did. At an early stage of settlement he placed Thomas Causton in charge of the colony's storehouse, from which, at least under the original plan, everyone was to be fed. Causton was so niggardly in his allocations that everyone grumbled, and then it developed that Causton kept no account of who got what. Blind to criticism, Oglethorpe loyally defended Causton, until the incompetent official was removed by direct order of the Trustees.

Oglethorpe was no better in managing finances himself. He never accounted adequately for the enormous sums given him by parliament; instead he bombarded the Trustees with requests for more. The Trustees finally lost patience in 1740, when, in the midst of his St. Augustine campaign, he concocted a scheme for improving Georgia's food production. He proposed placing a bounty of two shillings a bushel on corn and peas and one shilling for potatoes. He frankly admitted he had no idea how much the farm subsidy would cost the Trustees, and did not trouble himself with the complexities of administering such a program. Back across the Atlantic came an order transferring Oglethorpe's fiscal powers to a select committee and further limiting his civil responsibilities. From 1740 on, Oglethorpe's chief role in Georgia was military.

The Trustees' own regulations, it must be said, were responsible for much of the discontent in Georgia, but Oglethorpe was slow to recognize even that aspect of the problem. The most disastrous of these were the regulations governing the ownership and use of land. Military defense (rather than, say, efficient food production) was the Trustees primary criterion for land-use. Thus, they reasoned, there ought to be an able-bodied man on every parcel of land, and the parcels ought to be fairly close together. So they limited individual holdings to 500 acres, and each family traveling to Georgia "on the charity" received only 50 acres. Land could be passed only to a male heir; in the absence of one it reverted to the Trustees. The 50-acre parcels could not even be sold; they were simply on loan from the Trustees. Thus there was little incentive to make improvements, for one's plot might revert to the government at any time. And the family that was unfortunate enough to be granted a parcel in the pine barrens (which covered a good percentage of the landscape) was simply stuck there. Oglethorpe firmly resisted all requests to move, fearing that similar requests would follow, and the entire system would break down.

The colonists responded to Oglethorpe's rigidity by fleeing to other colonies where land was available for the taking. One band of Moravians, after struggling with Georgia sand for two years, simply packed up and moved to Pennsylvania. Amidst a cacophony of complaint, the Trustees gradually unraveled their web of regulation. In 1738 they permitted females to inherit land, and the following year men without heirs were allowed to will their lands to others. In 1741 the maximum holding was increased from 500 to 2000 acres. Oglethorpe sullenly resisted all such change. He claimed that the complaints came only from the shiftless, and pointed out that the regulations so reinforced one another that all would have to be abandoned if any were given up. As if to prove him right, the Trustees in 1742 ordered the sheriffs to cease enforcing the liquor laws, and in 1750 they eliminated restrictions on landholding and threw open the colony to slavery. Oglethorpe, mercifully, was by then long gone.

The only thing that held Oglethorpe in the colony after the Trustees sheared his political authority in 1740 was the war. The Spanish burned to revenge the attack on St. Augustine and made no secret of their preparations. They had to delay the counterthrust for two years, however, because of British naval operations in the Caribbean. Georgians, waiting anxiously for the blow to fall, looked to Oglethorpe for leadership, forgiving or perhaps forgetting the ineptitude he had shown in the St. Augustine campaign. Oglethorpe, glad of an opportunity to redeem himself, accepted the burden. This blend of faith and self-confidence allowed him to close his Georgia connection in a brief flurry of glory.

By the summer of 1742 the Spanish were at last ready to attack. Apprised of the troop buildup at St. Augustine (his intelligence network was first-rate), Oglethorpe brimmed with confidence. When the attack came, he wrote South Carolina's Governor William Bull, his Georgians would "give them a warm reception and make them sick of it." His annual message to the Trustees exhibited the same sunny optimism. The spring crops on St. Simons island, he told them, looked promising and the vineyards grew "prodigiously." "The soldiers hold the spade in one hand and the sword in the other and both successfully." He did request some naval support, but the ministry (Walpole had since yielded to the more bellicose Pelham brothers) was too preoccupied with the treasures of the Spanish Main. South Carolina also let him down. Governor Bull, misled, perhaps, by Oglethorpe's optimism and insolvent as usual, did not even summon the Carolina assembly into session until the day the Spanish landed in Georgia. Oglethorpe was on his own.

On July 5 a Spanish flotilla of 36 vessels forced its way past the British batteries and dropped anchor in St. Simons Sound. Oglethorpe, profiting by his experience at St. Augustine, destroyed the sea batteries, called in his rangers, and concentrated his troops at Frederica. The Spanish disembarked and began a cautious advance on Frederica. They numbered perhaps 2000 men, a force slightly, but probably not significantly larger than Oglethorpe's. On July 7 the Spanish commander sent two columns along separate trails in the general direction of Frederica. The columns became confused and merged their advance, but, even so, they came within a mile of the fort before being discovered by Oglethorpe's rangers. The rangers exchanged fire with the attackers and hurried to inform their commander. While the Spanish stood in momentary uncertainty, Oglethorpe impetuously rushed out of his fort and smashed pell-mell into the Spanish center. The Spanish force turned and ran. Oglethorpe followed for a mile or so until he reached a thick woods. There he deployed his men under cover along both sides of the trail and awaited the next Spanish move.

The Spanish commander, who was fighting on unfamiliar terrain without benefit of scouts, sent out a second party to cover the retreat of the first. The second group apparently missed the first altogether and ran headlong into Oglethorpe's ambush. After the initial shock, the Spanish column fought well. There were few casualties because neither side could see the other in the thick underbrush, and an afternoon thundershower dampened gunpowder. The Spanish were able to retire in good order, but their morale was crumbling. The Spanish commander drew his men into a defensive position at the end of the island and sat there uncertainly for a week. Oglethorpe marched and countermarched his men and engaged in some parade ground histrionics, but the Spanish held fast until a number of British sail were spotted on the horizon. Not knowing how large the squadron might be (there were only five vessels, as it turned out), they reboarded their ships and fled back to Florida.

The Battle of Bloody Marsh, as the rained-out ambush came to be called, lacked the drama of some of the other military confrontations of the time, such as the Plains of Abraham in 1759, but it was nearly as significant. It represented Spain's last serious threat to the British settlements in North America. Spain thereafter was on the defensive, and one by one her North American possessions were stripped away: first Florida, then Louisiana, and finally Mexico, Texas and California.

The battle also marked the end of Oglethorpe's American career. He made another unsuccessful feint against St. Augustine in 1743, but he himself seemed to realize that his American venture was over. He returned to England later that year and never came back.

Oglethorpe was only 46 when he left the Georgia scene, and much of life still lay before him. He married the following year and settled into the sedentary life of a country squire. He retained his humanitarian and literary interests, however. He became fast friends with Samuel Johnson and Johnson's worshipful biographer James Boswell. Others in his literary circle included Edmund Burke, the Whig member of parliament, David Garrick, the greatest Shakespearean actor of the day, and the portraitist Sir Joshua Reynolds, founder of the Royal Academy. Oglethorpe also retained his affection for the American colonies. During the imperial crisis of the 1770s he staunchly defended American rights; like Burke, Isaac Barre, and other liberal Whigs, he viewed the protesting colonists as "sons of liberty." And he lived to see American independence. He died in 1785 at the age of 90. With all his faults, the world was the better for him.

SUGGESTIONS FOR FURTHER READING

The standard biography is Amos Aschbach Ettinger, *James Edward Oglethorpe, Imperial Idealist* (1936). Phinzy Spalding, *Oglethorpe in America* (1977), as the title suggests, focuses on the Georgia experience. Albert B. Saye, *New Viewpoints in Georgia History* (1943), was among the first to explode the old myth that Georgia was an asylum for debtors. Daniel J. Boorstin, *The Americans: The Colonial Experience* (1958), gives a rather critical view of colonial Georgia, citing it as an example of European ideals failing in the American environment.

PART 3

Bridges of Empire

"The Security of their Freedom and their Rights is essential to the enjoyment of our own. We should never for a moment forget this important truth, that when the people of America are enslaved, we cannot be free; and they can never be enslaved whilst we continue free. We are stones of one arch, and must stand or fall together."

—John Horne Tooke, English Radical, on American Rights (1770)

10

Cotton Mather:
The Mystic as Scientist

"God's Controversy with New England" was the way one seventeenth century poet phrased it. Puritan ministers of the late seventeenth century were worried. They faced half-empty churches and a people more concerned with a fun-filled herein than a blessed hereafter. There had been backsliding, and God was certain to be angry. God, after all, had formed a covenant with their fathers. He had given Massachusetts His particular blessing, and in turn the founders of the Bay Colony had undertaken to preserve the true Church, defending it against both corruption and apostasy until worldwide justice and mercy arrived with the Second Coming of Christ. Now, it seemed, the sons and daughters had broken the covenant, the Church was defiled, and God was seeking elsewhere for a chosen people.

Among the ministers who expounded this jeremiad in the 1660s and 1670s was Increase Mather (1639–1723), himself the son of one of the Bay Colony's founder Divines, Richard Mather (1596–1669). Increase shared the notion of his father and other founders that they had been banished from the old country, chased out by a worldly, sin-ridden state-owned church. And they clung to the hope that, once God had scourged old England and purified it, they would return, in the Millennium. Despite their intense differences with the mother country, Richard and Increase Mather were still transplanted Englishmen.

Cotton Mather, Increase's son, thought more in American terms. (Indeed, he was the first English colonist to use the word "American.") He grew to maturity amidst the din of "God's Controversy with New England" and witnessed his father's declining hopes for the Church. But Cotton Mather refused to give up on his native land. He fought corruption and worldliness with efforts to expand the church, and he did this by simplifying its heady doctrines and broadening its social concerns. His simple maxim "Doing Good" was something every churchgoer could understand and follow. Community improvements, in turn, soothed the anger of God and prepared the world for the Second Coming, the Millennium, and the Last Judgment. He was the bridge between seventeenth century Puritanism and modern evangelism while conferring on his new creed a distinctively American flavor.

Born a Saint

Cotton Mather entered the world of Visible Saints on February 12, 1663. His father, who had gone to England to pursue his ministry, had returned to Massachusetts two years earlier. The religious Conformity Acts adopted by the government of Charles II forced him from his English pulpit. In Boston Increase Mather accepted a position as Teacher in the Second Church (where Richard was pastor), and there he met and married Maria Cotton, daughter of John Cotton. A son, the first of nine children, was born eleven months later. In naming him Cotton Mather they imposed a lifelong reminder of his heritage and his obligations. There were at that date four Mathers and two Cottons commanding pulpits in New England, and the women of both families were full members of the church. Visible Saints all. Indeed, Increase Mather even believed he held a special covenant with God that guaranteed the salvation of both himself and his children. All Cotton Mather needed was to recognize, through the characteristic conversion experience, his sanctified condition.

Given the expectations thrust upon the child, it is fortunate that he was precocious. The first sentences he composed were notes on his father's sermons; he could read and write before he entered grammar school. He read the Bible, at the age of seven or eight, at the rate of fifteen chapters a day, five in the morning, five at noon, and five at night. Kept at home during the cold winter months, young Mather whiled the hours in his father's library, reading history, reviewing Latin, and plunging into the mysteries of science. Increase Mather kept well abreast of the scientific and medical discoveries that heralded the dawn of the modern era. He was one of the first of New England clerics to subscribe to the Copernican astronomy that placed the sun, rather than the earth, at the center of the planetary system.

In 1674, when Cotton Mather was eleven, he was taken across the Charles River to Cambridge to be examined by the Reverend Leonard Hoar, president of Harvard College. The president examined the boy in Latin and Greek and pronounced him eligible to enter the college. Cotton was young, even by the standards of the day (the average age of his classmates was 14 or 15); indeed, he was probably the youngest person ever admitted to Harvard. Neither president nor father reflected on the social or psychological impact such an age deficiency might have. Child psychology, even the sort practiced by parental amateurs, was still in the distant future. The inevitable tension surfaced in the form of a speech impediment, a stutter that embarrassed the boy and menaced his hopes for a ministerial career.

The Harvard curriculum was a broad and demanding one for its time, modeled on the Arts program at Cambridge, England. It was, as the historian of the college has pointed out, designed to educate Christian gentlemen, not merely to train Congregational clergy. Freshmen concentrated on Greek and Hebrew. These were continued in the second year, together with logic, the latter requiring weekly public declamations in Latin. Rhetoric and the various forms of natural and moral philosophy (physical and social sciences today) were taken in the final years. The range of Cotton Mather's lifelong interests, the clarity of his reasoning, and the fluidity of his prose testify to an excellent undergraduate upbringing. He gradually overcame the stutter as well, though for years thereafter the possibility of its return haunted him whenever he stood up in a public forum. He graduated in 1681 at the age of fifteen.

Although he seemed destined for the ministry from birth, Cotton Mather remained unsure of his calling through his college years. The stutter was a worrisome handicap; more serious was his lack of a conversion experience. Without assurance of grace he could not even become a covenanted member of a church, much less a minister. So he combined, while at Harvard, his readings in theology and church history with the study of medicine. It was, given his age, a sophisticated effort to keep his career options open. The two fields, however, were not as unrelated as they often seem today. Illness, it was commonly believed, was among the afflictions visited upon humankind after the fall of Adam, and in some contexts a disease or an epidemic was considered punishment for the particular sins of individuals or groups. Thus the most common prescription for any sickness was prayer. Professional pride kept physicians and clerics apart, but a beginning student could easily keep a leg in each discipline.

In his medical studies, Cotton Mather's precociousness again betrayed him. Reading about diseases and contemplating their various symptoms sent him into periodic fits of hypochondria and melancholy. About a year after he finished college he was in the depths of one such depression when the long-awaited conversion experience came upon him. In the midst of his prayers he "sensibly felt an unaccountable cloud and load" lifted from him, and he felt his spirit transformed "by a new light, and life, and *ease* arriving to me, as the *sunrise* does change the world, from the condition of *midnight*." Mather knew full well that such an experience was entirely subjective, that it could not be submitted to external tests. He also knew that the Devil was fully capable of sending beings in the forms of angels to give men false assurances of salvation, so that he might enjoy a little joke on the Day of Judgment. The churches were full of hypocrites convinced of their righteousness while unwittingly being eternally damned.

Thus, spiritually explosive though his experience was, it did not resolve his doubts. He spent his life seeking further assurances that he had indeed been among the chosen at the beginning of time. And the search was physically and emotionally demanding. He set aside six periods in each day for solitary prayers, outcries, meditation, and psalm-singing. Most of his private devotions were carried out while he lay prostrate on the floor, abasing himself before the infinite power of the deity. He no doubt found such physical demonstrations of faith more satisfying than quiet contemplation, but they never fully relieved him. Anxiety was at the root of his psyche.

The conversion experience did, however, resolve his career dilemma. A creditable recital of it to a committee of elders was sufficient to gain him church membership, and, after another year at Harvard in which he earned his master's degree in divinity, he became his father's assistant at the North Church. He was an instant success as a preacher. Church membership grew steadily, at the rate of twenty or thirty conversions a year. In 1683 the congregation elected him its pastor (his father retained the title of teacher). By then the membership numbered over 200 (largest in Boston) and regular attendance was two or three times that number.

His popularity as a sermonizer brought invitations to visit other congregations, and within a couple of years he was preaching as many as five sermons a week, sometimes two or three in one day. Cotton Mather's pedigree, talents, and popularity, in turn, gave him political influence. Shortly after he assumed his pastorale the colony experienced an imperial crisis that presented him a rich opportunity to exercise it.

The Charter, the Dominion, and the Resistance

God's wrath at Massachusetts was nothing, compared to London's. Charles II and his entourage had succeeded admirably in reestablishing royal authority and religious conformity over Britain after 1660, but New England seemed to reject their every effort at control. Massachusetts even continued to style itself a commonwealth, a term that implied republican independence, and, as if to demonstrate its status, it confined voting and officeholding to church members, it coined money, regulated legal tender, and imperiously extended its boundaries northward into Maine. Its merchants paid no heed to imperial trade regulations, and when imperial officials complained, the colony replied with what one scholar has described as "creative transatlantic procrastination."

In 1676, the king sent Edward Randolph to investigate the transgressions of Massachusetts and bring the colony into line. Randolph arrived in the midst of King Philip's War, an Indian uprising that threatened, for a time, the very existence of the colony. The uprising was suppressed, but it left the colony in somber mood. Randolph's simultaneous appearance only reinforced the clergy's conviction that God's endorsement of their holy experiment was under strain.

A prototype of the imperial bureaucrat of a later day, Randolph was shocked by the independent atmosphere he found in the colony, and when his demands met only evasion and counterproposals, his shock turned to fury. He bombarded London with complaints and recommendations, bolstered them with a personal appearance before the Privy Council, and then returned to Massachusetts to gather new evidence. In 1680, convinced that the Puritans would never mend their ways, he recommended that the king institute *quo warranto** court proceedings to seek a revocation of the colony's charter. Then, with the colony in his own hands, the king could restructure its government with a new charter. The imperial machinery ground slowly, but in 1683 it at last came forth with a writ, and Randolph carried it triumphantly to Boston. Governor and assistants were inclined to submit, but the lower house, its courage shored by the sermons of Increase Mather, refused. With the colony in sullen repose, the court revoked the charter in October, 1684.

King Charles and his ministers had more in mind than the destruction of the Puritans' Zion. They planned to unite all the New England colonies into a single dominion, governed by an emissary of the king. This would make it easier to coordinate defense, enforce the navigation laws, and collect the customs duties. Plans for the Dominion of New England were still on the board when Charles died, but his brother James was happy to put them into effect. He even added his own province of New

---

* *Quo warranto*: "by what warrant" was the charter held? On the assumption that the terms of the charter had been violated, the court ordered the colony to show cause why the charter should not be revoked.

York to the project. He named Sir Edmond Andros, a professional soldier, as governor of the dominion, and Francis Nicholson, another soldier, was put in charge of the New York subsidiary.

Andros arrived in Boston in December, 1686, accompanied by sixty redcoated regulars, the first ever seen in the colonies. Determined to establish his position from the outset, Andros designated the Town House as a place for Anglican worship, declared that one of the Congregational meetinghouses might also be put to that purpose, and announced that his commission gave him power to appoint a new council. Accepting the challenge, Increase and Cotton Mather joined the next day with the elders of all the Boston congregations in a public declaration that they could not permit their meetinghouses to be used for Anglican services. Andros let that pass for the moment and confined his own worship to the Town House. One Puritan diarist noted scornfully that Andros' wife curtsied every time Jesus was mentioned in the service.

Increase Mather led the opposition to the new regime. Cotton was, for the moment, distracted by domestic concerns. In May, 1686, he married Abigail Phillips, daughter of one of the more prominent citizens of Charlestown. We know little of Abigail, other than the fact that she always referred to him in public as Mr. Mather. That designation was not unusual for the time, but it probably also reflected a certain awe, inspired by their age differential and his standing in the community. Mather's occasional references to her in his diary indicate that he loved her as much as he could love anything that was of this world.

Abigail gave birth to a girl in the summer of 1687; the child lived five months and then died in convulsions. Unaccustomed to tragedy, Mather felt the loss keenly. In his funeral sermon, *Right Thoughts in Sad Hours*, he sought to explain it in cosmic terms, but his emotion shone through. Ironically, the unintended blend of passion and resignation made it one of the best he ever wrote. A friend, who had lost two children in similar circumstance, financed its publication, and the two had the satisfaction of seeing it reprinted several times.

Increase Mather, in the meantime, had run afoul of Edward Randolph. In the course of one altercation he denounced Randolph as "a great knave." Randolph ignored the insult until the congregations of Boston in October, 1687, voted to send Increase Mather to London as their agent. Randolph thereupon secured Mather's arrest on a charge of defamation. In January a Boston jury acquitted Increase, and, though Randolph promptly instituted another suit, the minister-politician managed to escape. With the help of Cotton and another son Samuel, Increase slipped aboard a merchant vessel bound for England.

Though it added to Cotton Mather's responsibilities, the departure of his father set him free. He quickly took over his father's role as leader of the Opposition, while simultaneously serving as both teacher and pastor in the North Church. Pride and ambition (qualities that coexisted in tense equilibrium with his psychology of abasement) drove him swiftly into the political arena. And by the summer of 1688 Governor Andros had provided plenty for Mather to oppose. First, he threw the colony into confusion by calling into question all land grants conferred under the original charter, and compounded the error by threatening to collect royal quitrents. Then he imposed a Sunday Anglican service upon the South meetinghouse in between the morning and afternoon services of its owners. Finally, he showed a partiality for Indians, which persuaded Mather and others that he was in league with the French, especially after Indians raided the village of Northfield. In the midst of the tension, and perhaps because of it, appeared several cases of bewitchment, a malady that would spread to Salem four years later. A problem crying for ministerial attention, the witchcraft temporarily deflected Cotton Mather from the developing political crisis.

Witchcraft in Boston

A belief in witches was a natural corollary to the Puritan doctrine of "election." Just as God chose certain individuals to be Saints, Satan had his own small victories by invading the souls of sinners and making them witches. Every Puritan (with the possible exception of Anne Hutchinson) experienced periodic backsliding even when, like John Winthrop or Cotton Mather, he was convinced of his ultimate salvation. Descending to witchcraft was simply the final form of backsliding. Historian John Demos has found a total of 114 persons suspected of witchcraft in seventeenth century New England, of whom 81 were subjected to some form of legal action. Because the public records from that time are so spotty, the number of suspected witches could have been double that. Demos's collective portrait of this sample is that the witch was most likely to have been female, middle-aged, married but with fewer children than most, and involved in family or neighborhood discord. About half of all known witches were charged with other crimes, most often verbal or physical assaults on others.

Although the most famous and best documented trials were those conducted in Salem in 1692, the Salem experience was in many ways unique. Boston's experience four years earlier—and Mather's role in it—was a precursor.

The incident began in the fall of 1688 when four children of John Goodwin became afflicted with "strange fits." Mather, who appears to have been summoned to the scene early, described their behavior: "Sometimes they would be deaf, sometimes dumb, and sometimes blind, and often, all this at once. One while their tongues would be drawn down their throats; another while they would be pulled out upon their chins to a prodigious length." He went on to describe mouths seemingly pried open and then snapped shut, elbows and other joints snapped around as if unseen demons were pushing and shoving. On inquiry it developed that the oldest girl had had an argument with a neighboring woman, Goodwife Glover, over some missing laundry. Glover had cursed the girl, and the fits started shortly thereafter.

In concert with other ministers, Mather first insisted that the girls be separated to make sure that they were not influencing one another. The youngest almost immediately recovered, but the older girls continued to suffer. Most amazing of all, they underwent identical spasms, even when out of sight or hearing of one another. The ministers went on testing for weeks, but for all their scientific method they could not avoid the conclusion that it was witchcraft.

In the meantime, the magistrates located Goodwife Glover, who turned out to be a Roman Catholic from Ireland who spoke little English; under pressure she lapsed completely into Gaelic. Glover's answers to their questions, given through an interpreter, were ambiguous. At no time did she flatly deny her guilt. A search of her house unearthed several rag dolls stuffed with goat's hair. She admitted attempting to torment people by spitting on her finger and stroking the dolls. What seems likely in retrospect is that she was a simple peasant, superstitious enough to entrap herself in the leading questions of the magistrates. Cotton Mather seems to have reached this same conclusion. He visited her in jail to question her in less pressured circumstances. Without admitting or denying guilt she named four confederates. Mather kept these names to himself. Goodwife Glover was found guilty by a court and hanged on November 16, 1688. Because of Mather's judicious silence there were no other trials.

The children, predictably, were not cured by Mrs. Glover's execution. Hysteria, a craving for attention, a practical joke—whatever impelled them it was a thirst not yet quenched. Their torments in fact grew more imaginative. They were struck by invisible blows; observers claimed to see the marks on their skin. They flew about the room with "incredible swiftness," their toes barely touching the floor. Such things continued even when they were moved to other homes.

Cotton Mather, though reluctant to spread accusations of witchcraft, could not escape the conclusion that the children were possessed by the Devil. Cotton Mather's entire life was a massive struggle against evil spirits that he saw were continually trying to insinuate themselves into his soul. Because Satan was as real to him as God, he saw no reason why the deeds of the Devil could not be subjected to empirical scrutiny. So he invited the oldest of the Goodwin children, thirteen-year-old Martha, to live in his own house, not only to cure her, but to observe the extent and the limitations of the Devil's powers so he might help all of Massachusetts combat this insidious foe.

The gesture may have been a mistake, though Mather never realized it. The girl was only four years younger than Mather's wife, only twelve years younger than the minister himself. The association—and there was much physical contact as they wrestled with the evil spirits—may only have stimulated her histrionics (not necessarily consciously). For seven long days they battled Martha's tormentors, while Mather carefully recorded every experiment and every result for future publication. Not surprisingly, Mather's principal weapon was the Bible. At first she could not see the book, then could not make out the words. When prayer improved her eyesight, the spirits clamped her mouth shut when Mather asked her to read a psalm. There was a final titanic struggle in Mather's private study (where the evil spirits were at a disadvantage) after which the demons informed the girl of their defeat. After that the possessions became less and less frequent through the spring. She left the Mather household in June, 1689. Those who would explain the entire affair in sexual terms— and there were cynics in Mather's own day who suggested as much—must answer the question: Why, if there had been the least hint of wrongdoing, did he publish such a candid account of it?

Mather sent his account of the affair, *Memorable Providences, Relating to Witchcrafts and Possessions*, to a Boston printer that autumn after the governmental crisis ended. It had little impact; when witches appeared in Salem a few years later there is no evidence that anyone in that village was aware of Mather's prescriptions for healing the possessed. But a century and a half later, after scientific advances had revised substantially the relationship between the material and spiritual worlds and religious skepticism was in vogue, the work earned Mather a reputation that no sympathetic biographer has since completely overcome. Mather was naive, of course, and his scientific method had sharp limitations. But in his defense let this be noted: he was concerned with healing, not punishment, and when accusations of witchcraft were made, he suppressed them lest the innocent suffer. Ill-informed historians have sometimes accused him of fomenting the Salem witch hunt that broke out in 1692. He had nothing to do with it. Perhaps it would have been better for Salem if he had.

Resistance, Revolution, and the Charter

While Cotton Mather wrestled with Satan in the fall of 1688, Massachusetts wrestled with its governor. Andros matched his royal master, James II, in his disregard for representative government and in the tactless manner with which he let that fact be known. After a series of confrontations with the Chamber of Deputies, he dispensed with the legislature altogether and proceeded to govern by decree. In this fashion he prohibited town meetings, canceled the tax collected for the support of the clergy, forbade proclamations of thanksgiving and days of humiliation, and rearranged the method of jury selection so as to secure easier conviction. By the fall of 1688 even the council, initially submissive, had turned against him.

The popular unrest deepened through the winter as rumors trickled into Boston that King James himself was in trouble and there were plots afoot for his overthrow. On April 4, 1689, a copy of a proclamation, issued by William of Orange on the eve of his departure from the Netherlands, arrived in Plymouth. It announced his intentions and asked all English "magistrates who had been unjustly" removed from office to resume "their former employments." William was not referring to the English colonies, of which doubtless he knew little, but in Massachusetts his language was easily construed as a reference to the magistrates whom Andros had replaced. If William managed to overthrow King James, moreover, the legitimacy of Andros' rule was uncertain. The proclamation, in short, was an ideal pretext for a revolution in the name of established authority— King William's.

For the next week and more there were nightly meetings of town leaders and clergy. Cotton Mather was almost certainly among them, for he was the acknowledged author of *The Declaration of Gentlemen and Merchants*, which justified the overthrow. On April 16 Andros observed "a general buzzing among the people." On the morning of April 18, crowds collected at each end of the city; anonymous rumormongers spread the word among each that their compatriots on the other side of town were up in arms. At nine o'clock drums beat for a militia muster; simultaneously small, well-organized bands arrested Andros, Edward Randolph, the sheriff, and the jailer. The ex-officials were placed in the town jail under the eye of a new jailer, "Scales the bricklayer." At noon Cotton Mather's *Declaration* was read aloud. Mather justified the overthrow by accusing Andros of being in league with the Pope, the French in Canada, and the Indians. Then he outlined the governor's trespasses on popular liberties and appealed for a restoration of free speech, the writ of habeas corpus, and fair jury trials.

Who exactly was behind this bloodless coup remains a mystery. The "gentlemen and merchants" stoutly maintained that their chief function had been to contain popular wrath and prevent destruction of property. This may have been a front that covered their true role. On the other hand, the "leather aprons," as the town craftsmen sometimes called themselves, were perfectly capable of leading themselves, as Samuel Adams and other radical politicians discovered seventy-five years later. Whatever the case, it was generally agreed that the revolution had to preserve a placid, genteel front for the benefit of King William. To that end, the more prominent merchants and clergymen formed a Committee of Safety to preserve law and order in the governmental hiatus, and, when the success of England's "Glorious Revolution" was confirmed, they sent off an affirmation of loyalty to William and Mary.

Cotton Mather, whose pen had given both voice and tone to the revolution, was in his glory. He had successfully replaced his father in pulpit, in political precincts, and in combatting the Devil (Increase had earlier written a treatise on witchcraft). At only 26 he had many years to live and many more contributions to make, but never again would he wield so much influence in the community.

The reputation of both Mathers began to decline when Increase returned with a new charter in 1691. King William endorsed the new regime in Boston, but he had no intention of restoring the Puritan oligarchy. At the urging of the imperial bureaucracy, he insisted that Massachusetts remain a royal colony, with governor appointed by the king, and a secular one, with voting conditioned on landholding, not religion. He did, however, permit an assembly with substantial powers, including authority to set the salary of the governor, and he allowed the upper house, or council, to be selected by the lower. The latter feature, unique among the American colonies, could have been a source of considerable trouble for the

Crown, but the colonists did not exploit its possibilities until Samuel Adams appeared on the scene in the 1760s. Increase Mather's principal achievement was the insertion of a list of colonial rights in the charter. The list was not comprehensive; it involved mostly legal guarantees such as the right to habeas corpus and trial by jury. But Massachusetts was the only colony so blessed. Fifteen years earlier Virginia had tried and failed to secure just such a statement.

The Mathers pointed repeatedly to the bill of rights in defending the charter, but few were willing to listen. The triumph over Andros had raised hopes too high; the new charter was anticlimax. The outbreak of war with France shortly after William acceded to the throne further dampened spirits. The Schenectady massacre of 1690 heralded a succession of Indian raids along the entire New England frontier. Amidst the rising tension, and perhaps because of it, there was an outbreak of witchcraft in Salem village, followed by a prolonged and bloody witch hunt. To the west, in the Connecticut River Valley, the Reverend Solomon Stoddard had dispensed with some of the rigid requirements for Congregational Communion and seemed to open his church to all. Such catholicism struck at the very roots of the Covenant, to the utter dismay of the Mathers. At the beginning of the 1690s Cotton Mather thought he saw signs of the approaching Millennium. At the end of the decade he could refer to it as a time of troubles.

Of Sorcery, Physics, and History

The Salem episode began in early 1692 when several young girls, including the village minister's daughter, suffered fits similar to those that had afflicted the Goodwin children in Boston. The girls, who had been dabbling in fortune-telling and other occult practices, promptly blamed a neighborhood woman, Sarah Good, and the minister's West Indian slave, Tituba. As soon as officials questioned them, Good (who did not confess) and Tituba (who did) implicated others. The girls confirmed these and suggested some more names. As soon as Cotton Mather learned of the uproar, he suggested that Salem officials "scatter" the girls "far asunder," offering to take six of them into his own home. But by then it was too late. The girls had done their damage, hysteria had seized the village, and a search for culprits was on.

When the new royal governor, Sir William Phips, arrived in May, he found the Salem jail full of terrified people leveling accusations in all directions in desperate efforts to save themselves. By then Cotton and

Increase had concluded that only prompt judicial action could stem the tide of accusation. On their recommendation Phips created a Special Court of Oyer and Terminer to hear and determine the cases. Too ill to attend the trials, Cotton Mather wrote one of the judges to urge legal caution. He was particularly concerned about the use of spectral evidence; that is, the visual evidence of extraordinary behavior. There were two flaws in this sort of evidence. One was that the possessed person might be a fraud. The other was that, even if there were good experimental evidence that the person was indeed afflicted, it did not mean that another person was a witch. The Devil himself might be responsible. The value of such advice is perhaps debatable, but it matters little. It was completely ignored. Nineteen men and women were hanged by the end of September, and the trials continued.

During that month the two Mathers decided to write accounts of the affair. Unhappy with "the jealousies among us" that the trials had created and the number "of innocent people being accused," the two decided to condemn the procedures of the court while simultaneously defending the principle of witchcraft investigation. Increase undertook the first task; Cotton accepted the second. Each read and approved the other's manuscript, suggesting that neither saw any inconsistency in the two approaches. The public certainly did. Those who had been disillusioned by the girls' transparent excesses (they were by then accusing skeptics of being witches) hailed Increase's pamphlet as the first public voice of sanity, and the same people denounced Cotton's *The Wonders of the Invisible World*, a jeremiad that suggested New England was suffering for the sins of her people, as ministerial fanaticism.

Shorn of political influence, Cotton Mather retreated into the realm of scholarship. He continued his pastoral duties, of course, and remained a popular sermonizer, but science and history engaged his intellect. In July, 1693, he sketched an outline for what would be his greatest, or at least his most famous, work, the *Magnalia Christi Americana*, what he described as a "church history of this country." He completed it five years later, and the 850-page opus was published in London in 1702. It is tempting to scorn the *Magnalia* as escapism, a glorified reproduction of the past as a device for escaping the shabbiness of the present. And it was a jeremiad—it described what New England had once been and might yet recover. It was also hagiography, a collective biography of the Puritan saints: Endicott, Winthrop, Cotton, Eliot. But it was principally history, for Mather conscientiously strove to set down an impartial record of New England's past. As with the best of New England's historical writing, it was, finally, great literature. The theme that tied it together was one worthy of a Jeremiah: *"Religio peperit divitas, et filia devoravit matrem;* Religion brought forth *prosperity*, and the *daughter* destroyed the *mother."* Instead of bestowing reverential gratitude on a God *"who gives them power to get wealth,"* wrote Mather, "the enchantments of this world make them forget their *errand into the wilderness."* Just as the clergy had been doing in their sermons for a generation, Mather made the history of Massachusetts a cycle of progress, backsliding, divine vengeance, reaffirmation of faith, and renewed progress.

Monumental though the project was, the *Magnalia Christi* did not occupy all of Mather's research efforts. He began at this time what he hoped might be his most important bequest to posterity, the "Biblia Americana," a commentary on the Bible that ultimately became six huge volumes of manuscript. He was never able to get it published, in part because of its length, and in part (one suspects) because the witchcraft books had destroyed his credibility in the realm of Biblical scholarship. It was a pity, for Mather's mind was open; indeed, he was eager to reconcile religion and science. A decade earlier—in the year 1686 to be precise—Sir Isaac Newton had inaugurated an intellectual revolution with the publication of his *Principia Mathematica*, a dissertation on the mathematics of calculus, which he had used to deduce certain laws of physical behavior, most notably the law of gravity. In the late 1690s Mather came across the writings of a pair of English ministers who had sought to reconcile Newtonian physics and the Bible. Mather incorporated their ideas, with variations of his own, into the "Biblia Americana."

Cotton Mather had never seen any unbridgeable gap between science and religion. By the time he left Harvard he was familiar with the basic "argument from design": that the immensity of the universe, together with its rich variety of animals, vegetables, and minerals ("incredible hundreds" of "little *eels* . . . playing about in one drop of water") required a divine creator. Nothing less could have done it. "There is not a Fly," declared Mather, "but what may confute an Atheist." God, moreover, was reasonable, even though His ways might at times be beyond the comprehension of mortals. Thus a universe governed by natural laws formed as much a part of God's design as the creation of a fly.

It could be argued, as deists were beginning to, that the argument from design proved only that God created the universe (first cause in logic); it argued nothing for any subsequent intervention (Christ, revelation, miracles, etc.). This line of thought never occurred to Cotton Mather, any more than it did to Newton himself (who was, in fact, a deeply religious man). Spatial separation itself, Mather felt, demonstrated the continuous influence of God, for without Him all matter would draw together (under the law of gravity) into one massive lump. To explain God's daily intervention (in which he firmly believed) Mather distinguished between "special providences"—divine actions that did not violate physical laws—and miracles—divine interventions, such as parting the Red Sea for Moses, that were above natural law. The Puritans' God, after all, was not to be bound by laws of any sort. There remained a difference, said Mather, between the creator and the created.* God might have seen fit to create a rational universe, but his deed was "a pure act" unrestricted by any human conception of natural order. By this ingenious distinction Mather sought to reconcile the Calvinist view of an arbitrary God with the Newtonian view of an orderly universe. Although Mather developed this chain of thought as part of his commentaries on Scripture, he saw that it had independent value and published it under the title *Reasonable Religion* in 1700.

This pamphlet, however, was as close to "liberal" Congregationalism as Cotton Mather would step. Under pressure from liberals of the Solomon Stoddard variety within the church and religious rationalists (deists) from without, Cotton Mather retreated into an evangelical pietism. He built his bridge, not in the direction of the Enlightenment,** but toward the Great Awakening.***

Old Enemies and a New Piety

The Mathers' controversy with Massachusetts began with the Half Way Covenant of 1662, which Increase, along with other conservative divines, considered an official sanction for backsliding. The covenant was a compromise necessitated, not so much by backsliding, as by the increase in population and the passage of time. Massachusetts by the middle of the seventeenth century was no longer the tiny, well-knit community of saints that it had been in Anne Hutchinson's day. Nor had it succumbed totally

---

* In making this distinction Mather anticipated and answered David Hume's devastating critique of the "argument from design" in his *Dialogues Concerning Natural Religion (1779)*: that one cannot infer from a result (an imperfect universe) a cause that is better (a divine being).

** The Enlightenment is the term given to the eighteenth century's faith in reason and disposition toward scientific inquiry.

*** The Great Awakening was an evangelical religious revival that swept the American colonies in the 1730s and 1740s.

to materialism and depravity. It contained, in sum, a large number of well-disposed law-abiding people who could not convince themselves or others that they were "Visible Saints." The Half Way Covenant, while continuing to exclude such people from church membership, allowed them to have their children baptized.

Under pressure from his son, Increase Mather came to accept the Half Way Covenant, but both Mathers were determined that it not open the gates to further compromise. Solomon Stoddard, minister to the frontier outpost of Northhampton, proceeded to do just that. Stoddard admitted to full membership any person who had "a good conversation and a competent knowledge" concerning the church. In the mid-1690s he published a book defending his "catholic" (meaning in this sense open, or universal) principle. Before long, churches in the eastern part of the colony became infected with the Stoddardean virus, and in 1697 Increase Mather (who had been president of Harvard since 1685) saw fit to warn both the Cambridge congregation and the Harvard students against it. Increase's conservatism had already aroused some opposition among Harvard fellows and tutors; this pointed warning brought it to the surface. And the religious liberals had ready allies in the rationalists who were still bitter over Cotton Mather's defense of witchcraft trials. Within a year Boston was rocking with the controversy, and people were choosing sides with a zeal not seen since the departure of Anne Hutchinson.

In 1698 the liberals, joined by some of the old political enemies of the Mathers dating from the Andros regime, formed a new congregation in Brattle Street and then published a *Manifesto* of Stoddardean principles. The *Manifesto* defied the Mathers and other conservative clergy by questioning the foundation on which they had constructed their sermons. The first generation of Puritans, it suggested, far from being a model that all later ones needed to emulate, was excessively restrictive and parochial. The faith and love that united all Christians were more important than fine points of church doctrine or governance. A simple examination by the minister would be sufficient for entry into the Brattle Street Church. This was the voice of a new age.

Unsure of their popular support, the Mathers and other clergy backed away from a fight, and differences were papered over in sermons published by each side. Encouraged by that victory, the liberals set out to remove Increase Mather from the presidency of Harvard with the dual purpose of eliminating an enemy and capturing a citadel, a citadel of orthodoxy. In 1700 the General Assembly renewed Mather's appointment on condition that he reside in Cambridge. Increase had never moved to Cambridge because it would have meant abandoning his Boston pulpit. The aging cleric gave it a try, failed, and resigned the presidency of the college in 1701.

That incident ended the public role of the Mathers. Cotton Mather did not fully realize it, for he continued through that year and the next to blast his enemies in sermon and pamphlet. But his tone grew ever more quarrelsome, his arguments less and less constructive. He was ignored, and it was probably just as well. He also suffered through these months a personal trauma. Abigail lay dying of a mysterious, slowly debilitating illness, whose chief symptom was chest pains. She died in December, 1702, leaving him with three daughters and a son. The latter, Increase, was his oldest child and his biggest trial. Despite his name (or perhaps because of it) he showed no interest in the ministry and no sign of justification. Indeed, his behavior was such that he might have experienced difficulty gaining entry even into the Brattle Street Church.

In the slough of adversity Cotton Mather's religious views underwent a subtle change. He had always been an emotional preacher whose messages deeply affected his audiences. After 1700 he slipped deeper into "vital" or "experimental" religion, as he sometimes called it. The first generation of Puritans had recommended introspection as a means of checking on their saintly condition. Experimental religion asked people to examine their feelings; to be affected emotionally by the love of Christ, it suggested, was more important than a chilly commitment to an eternal covenant. Such notions, of course, were nothing new; various sects in central Europe had practiced them for centuries. Pietism is the term commonly given this form of evangelical religion. Indeed, after pondering these ideas for several years, Mather learned of the European Pietists and opened a correspondence with several of their leaders. The interchange was interesting but affected him little; Cotton Mather's New Piety was an extension of his Puritan evangelism.

As an evangelical technique it had numerous advantages. It answered the rationalists who were doubting Christianity and questioning the authority of Scripture by offering a completely subjective test for religious truth. Who could doubt the validity of an emotional experience? It appealed, moreover, to the weakest intelligence, to people who had never been able to comprehend the fine points of justification and sanctification, the nice distinction between grace and works. And, finally, it enabled Mather to undermine the catholic appeal of the liberals. He too could denounce excessive sectarianism and strike to the heart of Christianity. Eventually, in fact, he reduced Christian practice to a few simple maxims, the essence of which was "Doing Good."

Such an approach, of course, had dangers of its own. The untutored, especially, were prone to excess emotion, turning religious services into an orgy of mystical raptures. Mather drew back from such excesses, carefully avoiding the emotional anarchy that clerics and rationalists alike denounced as "enthusiasm." Yet even this vulnerability of Pietism made his pastoral job somewhat easier. He could play the role of moderate, calmly drawing his flock back from the brink of emotional ecstasy, back to the true and all-embracive love of Christ.

The New Piety was thus professionally as well as personally satisfying. He needed in fact whatever solace it could provide, for worldly Boston continued to rain abuse upon him. By 1713, "riotous young men" would gather under his window late at night to "sing profane and filthy songs," and take sticks from his woodpile to club anyone who tried to stop them. His Special Providence may have felt the world owed him an apology, for in that year too he was elected a Fellow of the Royal Society, Britain's elite scientific club. His New Piety remained a constant solace, but it did not monopolize his mind or pen. In his late years he turned, as he had in the troubled 1690s, to the pursuit of science and medicine.

The Angel and the Pox

Shortly after his wife's death Cotton Mather went through a "very astonishing trial" in the form of a beautiful woman. Characteristically he recorded every detail in his diary. She called upon him one day to tell him "that she has long had a more than ordinary value for my ministry," that she was charmed with his "person to such a degree, that she could not but break in upon me with her most importunate request, that I would make her mine." Mather, clearly flattered yet defensively sanctimonious, pointed out that his life was a joyless round of religious exercises. She came back with the unanswerable retort that such an existence would only improve her own chances for salvation—as well, she seemed also to be saying, as being something new and different. She was only twenty, and Mather was much intrigued, not only by "nature" (as he put it) but by the possibility of ushering another lamb to the seat of God. But father and friends raised a "violent storm of opposition" against the match, and he sent her away. The biographer can only sigh, for she was one of the few truly warm beings in this zealous man's life.

   He married a few months later a thirty-year-old widow who was both "honorably descended and related" (Mather was more concerned with telling us this fact than with providing us with her first name). They lived together for a little better than ten years in outward compatibility, though there is no evidence in Mather's diary of deep affection. She died in 1713 of smallpox, together with a set of twins to which she had just given birth. The death of his "dear consort" seems to have focused Mather's attention on this dread disease, which had visited Boston at something like ten-year intervals throughout his life.

   The treatment for smallpox was the same as that for measles (though similar in symptoms the two had already been differentiated)—isolation and bed rest. Such a prescription did no harm, but only the strong recovered. A black servant of Mather's suggested a new and quite startling approach. Asked if he had ever had smallpox, the black replied yes and no. He explained that in his native Guinea he had been given a small dose which "would forever preserve him from it." The black referred, of course, to inoculation and claimed it was common practice in his part of Africa. Mather stored this bit of intelligence until he came across an essay in the 1716 *Transactions* of the Royal Society. This was a report of inoculation as practiced in Turkey. Boston physicians read the report and dismissed it as "virtuoso amusement"; Cotton Mather, a layman, was more openminded. He sensed, however, that he was on dangerous terrain, and for once did not publish his information (he had not hesitated, for instance, to publish what he knew about measles in 1713).

   Nothing further came of the matter until smallpox struck again in April, 1721, brought by a ship from the West Indies. Mather watched the progress of the epidemic for a month and then addressed a letter to the town physicians suggesting the use of inoculations. The physicians publicly ignored him and privately indicated their resentment at lay interference. A month later Mather wrote to Dr. Zabdiel Boylston, submitting to him the evidence he had on the technique and suggesting he try it alone. The doctor (the term was honorary since Boylston was trained through apprenticeship, rather than through schooling—there was only one British-educated M.D. in Boston), inoculated his son and two slaves. When these survived he tried it on others, ten by the middle of July, seventeen more in the month of August.

   The public outcry was deafening, understandably enough since Boylston seemed to be spreading the epidemic. The town physicians, led by the lone M.D., denounced the practice in the newspapers. Boylston could only reply that to that point he had not lost a patient. Mather countered the physicians by lining up the clergy, including even his aged father, in public support of the practice. It was a curious, not to say unique, alignment, and there was both truth and error on both sides. The practice of instilling a live virus in a person was undeniably dangerous, and Boylston can be faulted for carelessness. He made no effort to ensure that the people he inoculated were basically healthy, he did not keep them isolated, and he did not even put them to bed.

By mid-autumn there was a full-scale newspaper war under way, and the physicians had a formidable ally in the anti-clerical *New England Courant*, published by James Franklin (whose younger brother Benjamin worked as an apprentice typesetter). Boylston calmly answered his critics by pointing out that of the 242 persons he inoculated only six died. Given his clinical procedures, even those might well have died of something other than smallpox; in any case, it was a mortality rate of only 2.5 percent. In the city as a whole, nearly half of the 12,000 inhabitants were hit by the virus and 844 died, a mortality rate of nearly 15 percent. Recognizing the importance of these statistics, Cotton Mather sent them to a friend in the Royal Society. This action itself may have been the most important result of the entire affair—it was the first use of probability statistics in the field of medicine, and it encouraged further inoculation experiments in Britain and elsewhere in the colonies.

When both the epidemic and the hysteria subsided, Cotton Mather turned to a new project, a compilation of all the medical knowledge then available. It was not intended as a textbook for students but as a handbook for everyone, a popular pharmacopeia of home remedies. It thus combined his interest in science with his pietistic zeal for "doing good." As with his history, the frame of reference was religious. Venereal disease, for instance, he considered a punishment for sin; he refused even to describe symptoms, much less prescribe remedies. Yet he also evidenced scientific detachment, as he had in his history. He described each disease, gave its particular symptoms, and offered such remedies as were known. Not surprisingly, he focused on infectious diseases and fevers. Intrigued by the phenomenon of contagion, he read the latest European essays on the subject and passed them on to his American readers. Diseases are transferred, he said, by microscopic "animals" or "insects," passed from one person to another through food and drink and through respiration. "One species of these animals may offend in one way, and another in another, and the various parts [of the body] may be various offended: from whence may flow a variety of diseases." This was one of the first expressions of what, more than a century later, would be called the "germ theory" of disease.

He named his treatise "The Angel of Bethesda," a reference to a Biblical healing pool. It stands with the *Magnalia Christi* as his most important work, but, alas, he never got it published. The reason is not entirely clear, but the enemies he made during the smallpox episode must have been in part responsible. It was also his last important work.

His final years were troubled ones. He married a third time, choosing, apparently unwittingly, a passionate woman who raged at his sexual reserve. He grew increasingly pious and self-absorbed in his last years, which only made her more frantic and more angry. He finally concluded that she was mad and apparently treated her so. She, of course, had no way of stating her case in that society, and we can only feel pity for her, wondering whether it was for good or ill that she managed to outlive him. Increase, the father, died in 1723; Increase, the wastrel son, went off to sea the following year and was never heard from again. Cotton Mather followed them both four years later. His was a curious existence. He was a man of two worlds, and his efforts to span them were both his glory and his torment. He surely transcended the medieval but somehow fell short of the modern.

SUGGESTIONS FOR FURTHER READING

Kenneth Silverman, *The Life and Times of Cotton Mather* (1984) provides a competent, full-length biography of Mather that was "badly needed" in the first edition of this book. David Levin, *Cotton Mather, The Young Life of the Lord's Remembrancer, 1663–1703* (1978), is excellent, but stops with the end of Mather's public career in 1702. Robert Middlekauff, *The Mathers: Three Generations of Puritan Intellectuals, 1596–1728* (1971) is a study of their thought, arranged topically. It is indispensable for scholars, tough going for novices. Otho T. Beall, Jr., and Richard H. Shryock, *Cotton Mather, First Significant Figure in American Medicine* (1954), overstates its case, but it contains useful information on colonial medicine. A recent effort to relate the Puritans to later strains of American thought is Sacvan Bercovitch, *The American Jeremiad* (1979). Peter Gay, *A Loss of Mastery: Puritan Historians in Colonial America* (1966), contains a splendid essay on Cotton Mather. On witchcraft, the place to start is John P. Demos, *Entertaining Satan: Witchcraft and the Culture of Early New England* (1982). Richard Weisman, *Witchcraft, Magic, and Religion in 17th-Century Massachusetts* (1984) brings an anthropologist's view to the subject. Peter Charles Hoffer, *The Devil's Disciples: Makers of the Salem Witchcraft Trials* (1996) is the most recent study of that episode.

Sewall
DIARY

11

William Byrd II:
Virginia Gentleman

My "*ancien* dominion" King Charles II had called Virginia. The occasion for this tender regard was Virginia's staunch adherence to the royalist cause during the English Civil War. Until finally subdued by a naval squadron sent over by Oliver Cromwell, Virginia and Maryland were the only bastions of Stuart loyalty in the empire after the execution of Charles I, and, so it was said, were havens for a number of royalist refugees. Two centuries later, when memories faded into legends, it was widely held that Virginia's "first families," the leaders of the slave plantation society,

William Byrd II (1674–1744). The pose tells the story. A blend of opulence and studied informality, it is the portrait of a worldly gentleman of leisure. Students of Godfrey Kneller, one of London's most prominent portrait painters, rendered this likeness in 1704, while Byrd was living the role of colonial grandee, indulging himself in the cosmopolitan capital of the empire. (Virginia Historical Society.)

were descended from these aristocrats who had fled the bourgeois tyranny of Puritans and Parliament. Cavaliers they were called, and the word evoked an image of a splendidly attired warrior, mounted on a thoroughbred, sword in hand, loyal to the end to king and country.

The American Civil War recast the symbols. Antislavery Yankees took the place of Puritan "Roundheads," hypocritical moralists whose sole passion was making money. The southern "chivalry," blue-blooded descendants of aristocrats, viewed itself as the last repository of genteel culture. Crushed by northern armies, the aristocratic life of the Old South was "gone with the wind."

Virginians today lovingly refer to their home as the "Old Dominion," but the Cavalier legend has been shattered. It withstood everything but the cold-blooded realism of twentieth-century historians. All that survives of the old tradition is the splendidly mounted gallant, attired in cloak and white-plumed hat, who patrols the sidelines during University of Virginia football games.

Thomas Jefferson Wertenbaker, a pioneer in the field of southern history, opened the assault on the Cavalier myth by demonstrating that Virginia in the seventeenth century was a society of middle-sized farmers. The grandees of Virginia's golden age, argued Wertenbaker, did not appear until the end of the seventeenth century—long after the English Civil War—and they made their fortunes in Virginia, not in England. Virginia's gentlemen, in short, were self-made men who reached their station by engrossing land and slaves.

Even so, the Cavalier myth, like most myths, was based upon an underlying stratum of truth. Virginians of 1700 believed that all men are created unequal. Some were born to lead, socially as well as politically; others were born to follow. Although their society was in fact more open, more mobile than England's, they adopted English attitudes concerning caste and class. Those who got ahead, by luck or diligence, consciously aped the social graces, the speech, and the dress of the English gentry. And, like any feudal elite, they used their riches to gain power and used their power to enhance their riches. In such an atmosphere the seeming metamorphosis that changes a self-made entrepreneur into well-mannered gentleman was not a matter of physical change but of the acceptance that comes with time. As the saying went, "It takes more than one generation to make a gentleman."

The career of the first William Byrd is a case in point. He was the son of a London goldsmith, and had he never moved to Virginia he would no doubt have pursued his father's trade. It was a promising occupation, for goldsmiths, in addition to being skilled artisans, performed rudimentary banking services. But, in Restoration England, it was not a road to power and fame. In 1670, when William was eighteen, he received a letter from his uncle, who owned an estate of 1800 acres on the James River in Virginia. Aged, lonely, and childless, the uncle offered to make William his heir if he would come to Virginia. As an added inducement the uncle no doubt mentioned also that he possessed a seat on the Governor's council and held the office of auditor-general of the colony. Offices in Virginia, as in England, were often as heritable as property. William was enterprising enough to accept the offer.

The uncle died, as if on cue, a year later. True to his promise, he left his property to his nephew, as well as a good word with the governor in the lad's behalf. Before long Byrd had a seat on the Governor's council and the office of receiver-general for quitrents. That post brought him a healthy slice of the annual rents that every planter in Virginia owed the king. In 1673 Byrd married Mary Horsmanden, the daughter of a Cavalier officer who had fled to Virginia during the Puritan regime. A widow of twenty-one, she added both her family estate and her former husband's to Byrd's growing fortune.

The wilderness lay just across the river when Byrd took up his uncle's plantation on the James. Indians were a constant menace, but they were also a source of profit. Byrd took over and expanded an Indian trade begun by his uncle. His agents penetrated hundreds of miles into the Carolina backcountry, carrying rum and firearms to the Catawba and Cherokees, returning with packs of deerskins and furs. Byrd purchased his rum and molasses from New England, other trading goods from the mother country. His plantation store became a neighborhood market, as other planters came to rely on his shipping connections. His profits were poured into the land. When Byrd died in 1704, he left an estate of 26,231 acres (had it been in a single parcel it would have made forty square miles). He was a self-made gentleman. His son, William Byrd II, was a gentleman by right of birth.

The Education of a Gentleman

William Byrd II was born in 1674, a year after his father's marriage. Before he could acquaint himself with his Virginia surroundings he was shipped off to England in company with his mother. This hasty exile was due to frontier violence, first Indian raids on the plantations of the upper James and then the militant outbursts of Nathaniel Bacon. As a militia captain the elder Byrd accompanied Bacon on his initial foray against the Indians, but he did not participate in the uprising (later known as Bacon's Rebellion). Or at least he was prudent enough to escape the vengeful attention of Governor Berkeley. When the danger ended, he recalled his family. Two trips across the Atlantic must have been just as risky for an infant as an Indian raid. The gesture shows the elder Byrd's abiding faith in the mother country.

At the age of seven William Byrd II was again consigned to London and his maternal uncle, this time for education and training in the style of an English gentleman. Uncle Horsmanden sent the boy to one of the most famous of England's grammar schools, one that had once housed the sons of Oliver Cromwell. There he was thoroughly grounded in Latin and Greek, and probably Hebrew (he read Hebrew regularly in his adult years). In 1690, at the age of sixteen, the elder Byrd sent his son to Holland "to imbibe some of the fine business sense of the Dutch." The Dutch experience was a brief one (the result, one suspects, of language problems and lonesomeness), and before the year was out the lad was attached to his father's business agents in London. In 1692 he entered the Middle Temple; the law would round out his education.

Byrd glided nimbly through the social whirl of the Inns of Court. The friendships he formed there gave him intellectual sustenance and political leverage that he drew on for the rest of his life. Through the agency of Sir Robert Southwell, an associate of his father's business agents, Byrd made other acquaintances outside the Inns. Sir Robert introduced him to Charles Boyle, son of the great Restoration physicist (Boyle's law established the relationship between pressure and volume in a gas). Later titled Earl of Orrery, Boyle remained a lifelong friend and correspondent. Southwell, for some years president of the Royal Society, also managed Byrd's election to that august group. Byrd contributed only one paper to the Society's Transactions, a 1696 description of an albino slave: "An Account of a Negro Boy that is Dappled in Several Places of his Body with White Spots," but he retained a lifetime taste for science and a talent for describing natural phenomena. None of this distracted him from his legal studies, and in 1695 he was admitted to the bar. The following year he returned to Virginia.

Gentlemen Politico

Within months of his return Byrd was elected to the Virginia House of Burgesses. A gentleman with political aspirations normally began his career with local service, either as justice of the peace on the county court or as member of the parish vestry. The prestige of Byrd's father evidently enabled the twenty-two-year-old to skip these rungs on the ladder. Fatherly influence plus his own background advanced him to the House of Burgesses. In 1697 that body sent him back to London as its agent. The lower house did not normally retain a representative of its own; perhaps it felt hard-pressed (the domineering Andros, having been ousted from Massachusetts, was now governor of Virginia). In any case, the council corrected the anomaly by making him official agent for the colony a year later.

Byrd's agency betrayed his youth and inexperience. First, he became involved in a dispute between Andros and Commissary James Blair (head of the Anglican Church in Virginia) concerning funds for the newly founded College of William and Mary. Byrd sided with Andros, who lost the argument and was subsequently replaced as governor. Byrd then got into the middle of a three-way fight between the assembly, the Board of Trade, and the new governor, Francis Nicholson. The Board, speaking for the Crown, had asked Virginia to help New York defend herself against Indian attack. Nicholson, a professional soldier, transmitted the request; the assembly balked. Byrd leaped a bit too vigorously to the assembly's defense, the Board of Trade protested to the council, and the council relieved him of duties. His father had died in the meantime, and in 1704 Byrd hastened back to Virginia to take up his inheritance.

The elder Byrd, with true aristocratic instinct, conferred his entire estate on his son. The younger Byrd's two sisters, one of whom had married and settled in England, were cut off with a few hundred pounds. The system was called primogeniture; it was a feudal relic designed to keep the landed estate intact through the generations. In Virginia a man could divide his holdings among his children by will, but Byrd chose not to.

Before leaving England, Byrd asked Queen Anne to confirm him in his father's offices of auditor and receiver-general of the quitrents. The queen was agreeable, but the Board of Trade objected that the two offices ought not to be held by one man. It was a sensible suggestion, for the chief duty of the auditor was to examine the accounts of the receiver-general. Byrd was accordingly granted the latter office only, at a salary of 3 percent of the revenue collected. The Board of Trade, still piqued apparently by Byrd's earlier transgressions, also held up his application for a seat on the Governor's council. He finally won a place on that body in 1708 and clung to it until his death in 1744. Two other marks of status were easier to attain: the governor named him a colonel of militia (though he had no military experience whatever) and the vestry offered him "the best pew" in Westover Church.

Ready at last to settle into the life of a Virginia planter, Byrd cast about for a wife. He had already experienced several torrid romances in England, but he had not been able to overcome the English prejudice against colonials, however rich they might be. In Virginia he had no such barrier; indeed, he was the most eligible bachelor in the colony. Though unusually susceptible to feminine charm, Byrd approached matrimony cautiously. He insisted on a mate of equal social station, and when his eye fell upon a damsel of satisfactory appearance he talked first with her father before courting to ascertain what portion of his estate she was to inherit.

Given these criteria, his choice was an excellent one: the beautiful Lucy Parke. Her father had left Virginia for England some years before to become an aide to the Duke of Marlborough, and he had been rewarded with the governorship of the Leeward Islands for bringing the news of the victory at Blenheim to Queen Anne. As with so many unions founded on wealth and beauty, this marriage proved a tempestuous one. Lucy Parke Byrd was spoiled and temperamental, mean to the servants, and careless with money. Their quarrels, however, never lasted long, and Byrd's diary gives evidence of genuine affection between them. She bore him four children, two of whom lived to maturity.

The Byrds took up residence at Westover, the large wood-frame house his father had built on the north bank of the James in 1690. Of farming Byrd knew nothing, since agriculture was not part of the English curriculum; he had to glean what he could from friends, overseers, and the more communicative slaves. The principal market crop of the plantation was tobacco, though it occupied only a tiny portion of the land. Tobacco was grown on a relatively small scale because it required so much labor. The seeds were planted one by one (not broadcast like grain) in newly cleared forest loam. The young plants had to be protected from the sun, a service usually tendered by the neighboring trees. In June, when the plants were four or five inches high, they were transplanted to fields, placed in rows about a yard apart. Throughout the summer they required periodic attention. Tops had to be cut off to ensure full leaves, unwanted shoots ("suckers") snipped, and worms picked off by hand. The soil had to be stirred constantly, for the plants could not compete at all with weeds. In early autumn the yellowing leaves were cut and hung in sheds to dry. This was the most delicate task of all, and a circumspect businessman, such as Byrd, soon learned to supervise it himself. When dry, the leaves were stemmed and packed in hogsheads. With the use of screws, as much as a thousand pounds of tobacco could be pressed into these wooden casks. The casks were then rolled to the wharf to await one of the many vessels that prowled the estuaries of the Chesapeake (after 1730 shipments were made from central warehouses, where the hogsheads were first inspected).

Labor, rather than land, was thus the vital element in tobacco production. The common estimate was that a single slave could tend an acre of tobacco in a season, and an average acre produced a hogshead, valued at ten to twenty pounds (the price fluctuated wildly) in English money. Even on the largest plantations, such as Byrd's, only a few acres, rarely more than a hundred, were devoted to tobacco. The rest of the cleared land was given to maintaining the human and animal population—cornfields, pasture, vegetable gardens, and small patches of flax or cotton for clothing. Uncleared woodland, often half or more of the total, was the reserve when other soils wore out.

Without fertilizing, both tobacco and corn exhausted a soil in three to five years. Because of the mild climate, there was no need to build barns for farm animals, and they roamed freely in the woods. Thus the collection of manure for fertilizer was difficult and expensive. It was cheaper to abandon worn-out fields and clear new ones. Had the planters turned their cattle onto worn-out fields, the manure thus spread would eventually have reclaimed the land. We don't know whether this alternative occurred to Byrd, but it was common practice among Maryland and Virginia planters later in the century.

Byrd continued his father's practice of consigning his tobacco to merchants in London. Unfortunately, this left him dependent on English merchants for credit and the purchase of consumer goods. Since the merchant was more interested in his own welfare than Byrd's, the arrangement often left the Virginia planter in debt at the end of a harvest year. To escape this web and expand his options, Byrd built or purchased vessels to ply the islands of the West Indies. On August 2, 1709, for instance, he recorded in his diary: "I wrote a letter to the Governor of Barbados to whom I intend to consign my sloop and cargo." Byrd did not describe the cargo; it was almost certainly not tobacco, which was grown in abundance in the islands. The products most in demand in the West Indies were food (flour, beef, and pork), lumber, and horses. The return cargo was likely to be rum, molasses, and sugar, which Byrd dispensed to his neighbors through the stores he inherited from his father. The West Indian trade also brought him cash and bills of credit, which he used to free himself from the predatory grip of London merchants.

Successful as both farmer and merchant, Byrd steadily increased his wealth, and that enabled him to maintain his interest in statecraft. When Lieutenant Governor* Nicholson left Virginia in 1709, Byrd applied for the job. However, the Duke of Marlborough, by then the dominant voice in imperial affairs, decreed that no one but professional soldiers would be sent to govern the colonies. Colonel Alexander Spotswood, a soldier who had been wounded at Blenheim, was accordingly sent to Virginia.

Spotswood proved an able, if somewhat imperious, administrator. He took over the Indian trade, placing restrictions on rum-runners such as Byrd, reorganized the militia, and tried to set up standards for the colony's tobacco exports. After Jamestown burned in 1698, the seat of government was removed some six miles north to Middle Plantation (renamed Williamsburg). Spotswood took charge of the construction of government houses, including the erection of an elegant palace for himself, surrounded by boxwood-lined formal gardens. Byrd visited the worksite and listened to Spotswood's complaints about the "abundance of faults" and the erroneous "proceedings of the workmen."

Governor and council were soon at odds, and Byrd, though on good terms with the governor at first, quickly assumed leadership of the opposition. The House of Burgesses, the only popularly elected officers in the colony, had not yet developed the authority it would wield in the days of Patrick Henry and Thomas Jefferson. Its members were drawn from the lesser families, its powers were few, and attendance was sparse. The council, though appointed by the Crown (on the recommendation of governor and Board of Trade), was the chief ruling force in the colony. It contained the greatest planters, men who also served their counties as revenue officers and sheriffs. Unless removed for cause, they served for life. There was thus more stability within the council than in the governorship, and the stability was reinforced by intermarriage. Spotswood once complained bitterly that if a cause involving a member of the Burwell family came before the General Court (the name of the council when it was functioning as supreme court of the colony), seven of the twelve members would have to disqualify themselves because of kinship. Byrd was not related to the Burwells, but he did have a marital connection with five other members of the council.

The council quarreled with every governor on the question of royal prerogative, the amount of authority the Crown and its agent the governor

* George Hamilton, Earl of Orkney, named governor of Virginia in 1704, never went to his colony, and thus Virginia was ruled by lieutenant governors until the eve of the Revolution.

had in the daily management of the colony. It was a question that would be resolved satisfactorily only by revolution. The disputes usually involved taxes or appropriations, for it was readily seen that the power of the purse was at the root of every other power. In Spotswood's term the conflict came to center on a quarrel between the governor and Philip Ludwell, the colony's auditor. The governor was trying to tighten the collection of quitrents, and Ludwell refused to show him the books. Spotswood complained to London, and Ludwell was removed from office. Anticipating that he might be next on the governor's list, Byrd sold his receiver-generalship to a fellow councillor for £500.

In 1715 Byrd took leave from the council to return to England. His excuse was personal: his father-in-law had died at the hands of a mob on the West Indian island of Antigua and left some tangled finances. But his motives were political: London was a sounder base from which to carry on a fight with a governor. The council obligingly gave him official status by naming him agent for the colony. Byrd sailed for England later that year.

London Dandy

Byrd was not happy with his father-in-law's will. Despite promises to Byrd concerning Lucy's endowment, Daniel Parke left his landed estates in Virginia and the West Indies to two other daughters, one of whom was illegitimate. Lucy was, in Byrd's view, "fobbed off with £1000" in cash. Given Parke's debts, which were attached to his landed property, an unencumbered £1000 was not a bad bequest, but Byrd, as land-thirsty as any Virginian, scorned the cash. In 1711 he had made a reckless bargain with Lucy's sister, agreeing to pay Parke's debts in return for title to his Virginia property—and that without having any clear idea of the amount of indebtedness!

On his arrival in England, Byrd learned that he had made a bad bargain. Parke's finances were more complicated than he had supposed, and the debts far exceeded the value of the Virginia lands. Realizing that he would have to remain in London longer than he originally planned, he sent for Lucy. She came, leaving their two daughters in Virginia, but she died of smallpox within a few months of her arrival, leaving him the poorer for companionship as well as wealth. Daniel Parke's debts would burden him the rest of his life.

The debts did not encumber his social life, however. Old friendships were renewed, new ones found. He adopted the lifestyle of a colonial grandee, the absentee landlord who explored the cosmopolitan delights of London with income derived from American soil and African labor. The duties of a colonial agent were neither worrisome nor time-consuming. His life by day was a series of social calls and political visits, by night a round of masquerade balls, theater, cardplaying, and periodic rendezvous with prostitutes. Using his diary as a sort of confessional, he recorded his daily misadventures in lurid detail. Byrd had a lifetime weakness for women, but never was he so intemperate, or so indiscreet, as in this London interval. Wealth, widowhood, and urban opportunities are probably explanation enough.

Throughout his five years in London, Byrd searched diligently for an heiress to marry. He conducted several romances, mostly through elaborately phrased letters, but without success. He still could not overcome English prejudice toward colonials. He explained to one prospective father-in-law that he possessed about 43,000 acres and 220 slaves, as well as "a prodigious quantity of stock of every kind," but the old gentleman simply retorted that an estate outside of England was "little better than an estate in the moon."

In Virginia the council kept up its running feud with the governor, and Byrd did his best to represent the council's point of view before the Board of Trade. The imperial bureaucracy understandably sympathized with the governor, and when Spotswood in exasperation asked that Byrd be removed from his seat on the council, the Board gave it serious consideration. Recognizing his danger Byrd in 1719 dashed back to Virginia to humble himself before the governor. Spotswood, having smashed his other enemies on the council, was in a generous mood; the two, in fact, became friends again.

Byrd thereupon returned to London and resumed his quest for an heiress. He found one at last in Maria Taylor, whom he married in 1724. She was twenty-five, he fifty. Nine months later she gave birth. The enlarged family added to his financial burdens. His daughters by Lucy had come to London in the meantime and were incurring the usual expenses of debutantes. And his plantations, suffering from the haphazard management of overseers, were no longer producing much income. Another visit to Virginia was necessary, though he expected it to be brief. Among friends, he spoke of it as a "pilgrimage to the new world." But he never returned. A Virginian he would be.

The Dividing Line

In 1726 Byrd settled once again into the routine of plantation life. His diary indicates that every day was much the same. He rose and said prayers, had boiled milk for breakfast, and "danced his dance" (a daily exercise). The morning was spent setting up the day's work schedule in the fields, settling accounts, and writing letters to the overseers on the plantations above the falls of the James. Dinner, served about one, was a substantial repast with several varieties of meat and vegetables and graced with French wine. If a ship had landed, the afternoon was spent reading letters from friends and relatives in England and sorting the new acquisitions for his growing library. In the absence of news he spent the afternoon reading, playing cards with his wife, or billiards with a friend.

Late afternoon was the occasion for a stroll around the plantation to check on the day's work. It was essential for plantation morale that the owner be in evidence. Byrd also paid a daily visit to the slave quarters to minister to the sick. Slaves were too valuable to be left unattended, and an epidemic could be financially ruinous. But Byrd was also a genuinely kind master. During the 1720s he made a habit of spending time "talking to his people," listening to their grievances and soliciting suggestions. He occasionally confessed to his diary that he had "played the fool" with some pretty young maidservant, but there is no evidence that he molested slave women or allowed his overseers to do so. He was also quite critical of slavery as an institution, not so much because of the injustice done to Africans, but because of its impact on the white population. In words that Thomas Jefferson would echo 50 years later, Byrd wrote to an English friend in 1736 that slaves "blow up the pride, and ruin the industry of our white people, who seeing a rank of poor creatures below them, detest work for fear it should make them look like slaves."

In 1727 newly crowned King George II named him one of the three Virginia commissioners who were to direct the survey of the boundary line between Virginia and North Carolina. The boundary dispute had long troubled the relations between the two colonies and created confusion among landholders. The problem originated with a discrepancy in the Carolina charters. The charter of 1663 declared that the northern boundary of Carolina would be 36° north latitude. A second charter of 1665 placed the boundary at 36°30′, some 30 miles farther north. Settlers who occupied the disputed zone refused to pay taxes to either colony; a clearly defined boundary was needed. An early effort to settle the issue failed due to the obstructiveness of the North Carolina commissioners; this time

the king empowered the Virginians, in the event of disagreements, to proceed alone. The other Virginia commissioners were William Dandridge
and Richard Fitzwilliam. The latter cut a poor figure in Byrd's journal of
the expedition because he sided with the Carolinians in every dispute.
Even so, he was a slice above the Carolinians in Byrd's estimate. Like
most Virginians, Byrd viewed North Carolina as a land populated by run-
away servants whose noses had grown flat from a steady diet of pork.

Although his fellow commissioners were also men of importance,
Byrd assumed the responsibility for administering and financing the expedition. He had been keeping a personal diary for twenty years; by habit

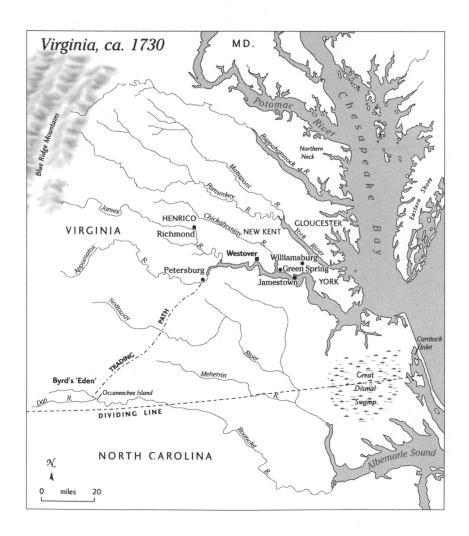

he kept a journal of the expedition, recording daily activities, personal observations, and a list of expenses. The accounts helped him obtain reimbursement for his expenditures; the journal would provide the basis for several different "Histories" of the expedition that he would write in later years.

The line was to begin at Currituck Inlet, and Byrd set out for that spot in February, 1728, accompanied by two servants and a packhorse for his camping equipment. He also took along a chaplain to provide Sunday services for the party and to baptize any denizens of the wilderness that they encountered. Byrd did not devote much time to theological meditation, but the outer forms of religion—sermons, prayer, baptism— were important to him, and he was quick to credit God with chance happenings, both good and ill.

The party assembled at Currituck on March 5, seven commissioners, forty laborers to clear the way, and four surveyors, and after a brief dispute as to the exact starting point (resolved in favor of the Carolinians) the work was begun. The countryside was heavily forested, thinly settled, and occasionally swampy, but in a little better than a week they pushed their way to the edge of the Great Dismal Swamp. As a commissioner, Byrd had no intention of risking himself in this morass, which had never been crossed. So the party split, with the commissioners and most of the laborers riding around, while the surveyors and a dozen pathmarkers waded through. Before parting, Byrd gave the surveyors a short pep talk and commended their safety to the Almighty. The speech, he noted in his journal with evident surprise, was received "very kindly," and he was given "three huzzas."

It took the surveyors a week to plunge their way through the swamp. The ground was so spongy that every footprint filled instantly with water. Had it not been an exceptionally dry spring they were sure they would not have made it at all. Once across the swamp the work proceeded rapidly, and by early April they reached the Meherrin River, seventy-three miles from the coast. The weather by then was warm and snakes were becoming troublesome, so they suspended the survey until autumn.

The expedition resumed on September 20, and in two weeks they reached the Roanoke River. The Carolinians refused to go farther because they were already well beyond the settled country. Byrd, feeling that if the job were done right it would only have to be done once, pushed on alone with the Virginia surveyors. "In justice to our Carolina friends," he noted acidly in his journal "they stuck by us as long as our liquor lasted and were so kind as to drink to our good journey to the mountains in the last bottle we had left."

Although he had never been in the wilderness before, Byrd made a fine woodsman. He enjoyed tent camping, and he took the trouble to equip himself before he left with lightweight foods, should game prove deficient. He inserted in his journal two trail recipes; one, which he called "glue broth," was simply a thick bouillon made by boiling beef juice. The other, rockahominy, was "nothing but Indian corn parched without burning and reduced to powder." It was reconstituted by adding boiling water. Ten pounds of such provisions, Byrd claimed, would last a man half a year—provided, one supposes, he also ate all the herbs and berries he could find. Byrd was also an acute observer of the landscape. His journal is filled with detailed descriptions of plants and animals, and a stop at a Nottoway Indian village gave him an opportunity to examine Indian customs and religious beliefs. Having been two months in the woods, he instantly noticed the Indian girls. "Though their complexions be a little sad-colored, yet their shapes are very straight and well-proportioned. Their faces are seldom handsome, yet they have an air of innocence and bashfulness that with a little less dirt would not fail to make them desirable." It was too bad, Byrd decided, that the first whites in Virginia had been so racially biased. If they had simply intermarried with the Indians, there would have been no frontier bloodshed, and "the country had swarmed with people more than it does with insects." With such a charitable thought it seems almost mean to point out that a swarming population would have been of immense benefit to a debt-ridden landlord.

The survey team halted at the foot of the Blue Ridge, 241 miles from Currituck. As winter was approaching, they turned and hurried for home. Even two months in the woods failed to scratch his gentlemanly veneer. When they came upon a settler's cabin, the first they had seen in weeks, Byrd rejected the owner's offer to sleep inside. He preferred instead "to lie in the tent, as being much the cleanlier and sweeter lodging."

As soon as he reached home, Byrd began expanding his rough trail notes into a report for the ministry. The report was both a propaganda tract designed to encourage emigration to Virginia and a glorification of the survey mission in the hope of wringing a financial bonus out of the Crown. Then, recognizing its narrative potential, he rewrote the story for the benefit of his London friends, sending it to them under the title, "The Secret History of the Line." This version emphasized the personality conflicts on the mission, especially the vagaries of Fitzwilliam, who was given the code-name "Firebrand" (Byrd labeled himself "Steady"). It was a witty, sophisticated discourse of the sort much admired in the London of Addison and Steele, Dryden and Swift. So well was it received that Byrd toward the end of his life undertook a new and much expanded version. This one, called *The History of the Dividing Line*, was evidently intended for publication, though it did not appear in print until almost a century after his death (The earlier "Secret History" was not published until 1929.) In this version he muted the personality conflicts, added descriptions of the landscape, expanded his scientific data, and (with an eye, no doubt, to the Virginia market) added every North Carolina joke he could remember.

The thirty-two-page propaganda piece that he sent off to the Board of Trade upon his emergence from the woods had the intended effect; the Board sanctioned an appropriation to the survey team of £1000, to be paid by the two colonies involved. Byrd's share was £142. It developed, however, that North Carolina had no cash to reimburse her commissioners; the colony offered them land instead. Byrd, who could pick out rich land as quickly as he could spot an endowed heiress, seized the opportunity. For £200 he purchased the patents of the North Carolina commissioners and surveyed for himself a tract of 20,000 acres at the junction of the Dan and Irvine rivers. The bottom land there, he had noted in his travel diary, was so rich that "a colony of one thousand families might, with the help of moderate industry, pass their time very happily." He named the place the Land of Eden, a solicitous double entendre since Charles Eden was then governor of North Carolina.

The Cultural Bridge

Shortly after his return from the back country Byrd began constructing a new mansion at Westover to replace the frame house built by his father fifty years before.* This one was to be of brick with a slate roof for fire protection. Whether or not it was completed in his lifetime, the structure reflected his desire for an architectural statement of his own magnificence, the elegant manor of a Virginia squire.

Byrd no doubt employed a master carpenter to supervise the work; architects were then unknown in America. The plans he obtained from

---

* Several historians of architecture have suggested that, while Byrd may have planned the construction of the new Westover, it was actually built by his son, William Byrd III, in the mid-1740s, shortly after Byrd's death.

English architectural handbooks, several of which graced his library. The style he chose was Baroque, an architectural fad then very popular in Britain. An extension of Palladian classicism (the dominant style in Europe in the previous century), Baroque featured curved and broken lines, walls broken into different planes, and the use of columns (pilasters) for decoration rather than support.

Byrd employed all these devices but with gentlemanly moderation. The basic structure is of classical proportions, three stories high, seven bays (that is, window or door openings) wide. The roofline is mathematically proportioned, with four chimneys visually balancing one another. There is a hint of the Baroque in the employment of Flemish bond in the brickwork, a system of laying bricks alternately by side and by end that conveys a special texture to the walls. The riverfront doorway, the most striking feature of the house, is pure Baroque. A curvilinear cornice, broken by a pineapple (symbol of welcome) is supported by pilasters with elaborate Corinthian capitals. Stark white, in contrast to the mellow red of the brick, the doorway was made of Portland stone, carved probably in England. The interior room arrangement is essentially that of an English country manor. Fireplaces, one in every room, were made of richly carved marble or wood, also probably imported from England. The result, says a modern student of architecture, is the most "thoroughly English" house built in colonial America.

The most striking feature of the interior was Byrd's magnificent library. He collected books all his life, returning from each trip abroad with boxes full. At the time of his death the collection was the largest in the colonies, numbering 3600 volumes. It is unlikely that he read them all. Many were just reference books, on law, medicine, cooking, architecture, or engineering, to be consulted when the need arose. Religious works were heavily represented. Byrd had more of these than most New England clergymen had, yet the topics also reflected Virginian taste. Most were sermons by liberal clerics of the Church of England. These divines tended to avoid theological controversy; they stressed instead proper behavior in everyday living. Byrd collected these not only for his own edification but for the benefit of his family. In Virginia, where distances were great and red-clay roads became impassable in bad weather, Sunday sermon-reading was often a substitute for church. The rest of the collection was a well-chosen sample of western culture. There were histories, biographies, travel accounts, political treatises, plays, poems, and satires. Byrd's library was the bridge between European civilization and its frontier outpost, Westover.

Neither nagging debt nor the plans for Westover curbed Byrd's appetite for land. He added steadily to his holdings, sometimes by purchase but most often through political machination. The Governor's council, especially in Spotswood's last years, seemed at times to be little more than a gigantic land office. Spotswood himself had caught the land-fever, and before he retired managed to grant himself some 40,000 acres in the Rappahannock River Valley. Discovering iron ore on his property, Spotswood built furnaces and brought in German craftsmen to work them.

In September, 1732, Byrd set out for the iron mines in the Rappahannock basin. He had some property of his own in the area that he wanted to check, and he hoped to learn something of the technology and economics of iron manufacture. He would glean what he could from former governor Spotswood. From Spotswood and others in the area he learned a good deal about the industry: the investment capital required (£12,000), the number of acres of wood per furnace for charcoal, the number of slaves needed to work the operation, and the quality of iron that might be expected. Actually, the iron that emerged from the initial smelting was too poor in quality to be usable. Called pig iron (because it was cooled in a row of connected trenches that resembled suckling pigs), it was full of carbon and very brittle. Before it could be made into tools or utensils the carbon had to be removed by remelting or hammering. Most colonial pig iron was shipped to Britain for refining, and it returned in the form of tools, cooking utensils, and weapons. An act of parliament prohibited the colonies from shipping finished iron products to the mother country, and one of Byrd's informants predicted that parliament would soon forbid the colonies from making finished iron goods of any sort. Since tool manufacture was the most profitable end of the business, Byrd decided not to invest in iron at all. Whether such trade regulations (Navigation Acts) helped or hurt the American colonies has never been fully determined, but in this instance, at least, the mere expectation of a regulation (a false expectation, as it turned out) discouraged a potential capital investment.

On his return, Byrd elaborated the notes of his journey for the benefit of his London friends, entitling it "A Progress to the Mines in 1732." As with his other literary endeavors, he did not bother to publish it. It finally went into print, along with most of his other writings, in 1841, almost a century after his death.

A year later, Byrd set forth on the wilderness pathways once more, this time to visit the Land of Eden. His account of this journey is in many ways the most entertaining and informative of his travel journals. It sparkles with vignettes of life in the backwoods:

- an overnight at one of his own plantations where Byrd had to sleep in the same room with the overseer, his wife, and their four children, "one of whom was very sick and consequently very fretful";
- the discovery one evening of a recently abandoned encampment of "Northern Indians," which "took the edge off our appetites for everything but the rum bottle";
- Byrd extracting an "impertinent tooth" from his upper jaw by tying a string around it, tying the other end of the string to a log while in a crouched position, and then leaping up;
- a pause in the surveying work for a swim, during which an Indian accompanying the party gave a lesson in the crawl stroke, "whereby they are able," said Byrd, "to swim both farther and faster than we do." (Byrd's description of his own method of swimming suggests a breast stroke.)

The journal of this expedition was likewise expanded for the benefit of Byrd's London friends and given the title "A Journey to the Land of Eden." It too lay hidden in manuscript form until 1841.

The one tangible result of his visit to Eden was the laying out of two new Virginia towns, Richmond at the falls of the James and Petersburg at the falls of the Appomatox. Because of Virginia's low-lying coastal plain, ocean-going vessels could navigate its rivers as far as the falls. Thus cities located at these strategic spots were natural marts, funnelling the commerce of the entire up-country. Planters living near the falls had repeatedly petitioned the assembly for the erection of towns on the sites, but Byrd used his influence to block such efforts. He did not want to have to sell his holding there to the colony at the colony's price. Any cities there would be built on his terms. So, at the outset of the Eden journey, he and the overseer of his plantation at "Shacco's" (Shockoe) on the James "built cities in the air" by marking out lots and streets. He then secured the assembly's permission to erect towns. In 1737 Byrd put his Richmond lots up for sale with an advertisement in the *Virginia Gazette*. The price depended on proximity to the river, and the one sale condition was that the purchasers erect houses within three years' time.

The sale of city lots enabled him at last to discharge the long-standing debt incurred from his father-in-law. By 1740 he had reduced it to £1000. He tried to borrow that sum from London friends in order to rid himself of the "usurers" who hounded him, but failed. Characteristically, he could not bear to part with any of his 179,000 acres in order to eliminate the debt altogether; its discharge by installments took him another three years.

On the death of Commissary Blair in 1743, Byrd was made president of the Governor's council. It was the highest office in the colony, except the lieutenant governorship itself, and thus a signal honor. Yet Byrd had hankered for the office for so long, while Blair, ninety and deaf, ambled on, that much of the glamor had gone out of it. Byrd himself died the following year, August, 1744. They buried him in the garden of Westover, beneath the oaks and the blue wisteria. Like his boxwood-lined garden, Byrd was a blend of cultures, "a mixture," as a recent biographer puts it, "of the gentleman-planter and the gentleman-writer, no longer quite English, not yet really American."

SUGGESTIONS FOR FURTHER READING

The Cavalier myth, as well as the modern criticism of it, are well summarized in Louis B. Wright, *The First Gentlemen of Virginia* (1940). The most recent biography of Byrd is Kenneth Lockridge, *The Diary and Life of Williams Byrd II of Virginia*. It is, unfortunately, hypercritical of the man. An earlier, but more friendly, analysis, organized by topics ("literature," "frontier," etc.) is Pierre Marambaud, *William Byrd of Westover* (1971). Byrd's own writings are still rewarding. Especially recommended is Louis B. Wright, ed., *The Prose Works of William Byrd of Westover* (1966), which contains Byrd's four major works, as well as a fine biographical sketch. The history of Byrd's "Lost History" has been expertly researched by Margaret Beck Pritchard and Virginia Lascara Sites, *William Byrd and His Lost History: Engravings of the Americas* (1993). This splendid piece of scholarship also contains new material on Byrd's political thought and artistic interests. Kevin J. Hayes's majesterial *The Library of William Byrd of Westover* (1997) thoroughly allows an analysis of the greatest library in colonial America.

12

Eliza Lucas Pinckney:
The West Indies Connection

Her words were oiled with affection and even deference, but there was no mistaking her firmness. The gentleman who desired her hand in marriage, she was telling her father, simply wouldn't do. "As I know tis my happiness you consult," she continued, "I must beg the favor of you to pay my thanks to the old gentleman for his generosity and favorable sentiments of me and let him know my thoughts on the affair in such civil terms as you know much better than any I can dictate; and beg leave to say to you that the riches of Peru and Chili if he had them put together could not purchase a sufficient esteem for him to make him my husband." In an age when marriages among the upper orders of society were often diplomatic and commercial alliances arranged by family heads, this was a remarkable statement of independence.

Eliza Lucas could afford to be independent. Her father was absent on military service in the West Indies; for some years she had been managing his South Carolina estates, making a good profit from the export of rice and naval stores. Small wonder that there was a line of suitors at her door. A wife with a business head was a prime asset for any planter. Far from being the giddy belles of the Cavalier myth, women in the colonial South played a vital role in the plantation economy. They managed the household and its servants, superintended the gardens and slaughtering pens that kept the plantation in daily fare, looked to the health of the labor force, and in some cases kept the business ledgers. The brisk self-confidence with which Eliza Lucas mastered all of these tasks bespoke a woman of uncommon wisdom and maturity. She had just turned seventeen.

From the Indies to Carolina

Eliza Lucas had, by the age of seventeen, already touched the three corners of Britain's Atlantic empire. She was born on Antigua in the West Indies, where her father, Lieutenant Colonel George Lucas, was stationed, but spent her youth in England acquiring the education and social graces thought suitable for ladies of her station in society. In 1738 Colonel Lucas moved his family to South Carolina, where he had inherited several plantations from his father. War loomed between Britain and Spain (the War of Jenkins' Ear), and Lucas apparently felt his family would be safer in South Carolina. (They were, as it turned out, due to the efforts of James Oglethorpe, although Eliza had small regard for his military capabilities.)

The family settled on a plantation overlooking Wappoo Creek, some six miles from Charleston by water. Within a year Colonel Lucas returned to Antigua to accept the post of governor, leaving his family in Carolina. Mrs. Lucas was in chronic ill health; George Lucas, Jr., was still in school in England. Management of Wappoo and its twenty slaves fell upon Eliza. In addition, she had to superintend the overseers on two other holdings, one an inland farm that produced tar and timber, the other a 3000-acre rice plantation on the Waccamaw River.

Eliza was happy with the arrangement; she had no desire to return to the Indies. Antigua was a low-lying, featureless island, sandy and dry, dependent on rainfall for fresh water. Its one asset was English Harbor, a deep, nearly landlocked roadstead large enough to accommodate the entire royal navy. Otherwise it was an unrelieved expanse of sugar plantations. South Carolina was also low-lying and level, but its landscape was broken by broad, smooth-flowing rivers and forests of live oak garbed in Spanish moss. "The country abounds with wild fowl," Eliza wrote her brother, "venison and fish, beef, veal, and mutton are here in much greater perfection than in the Islands, tho' not equal to that in England— but their pork exceeds any I ever tasted anywhere."

She also found the people "polite" and "genteel," as well she might, for most were of her own stock. South Carolina, alone among the mainland colonies, was populated principally from the West Indies. The spread of large-scale sugar planting on Jamaica and some of the Spanish islands (Cuba, Puerto Rico) undermined the economies of older, smaller, English islands (Barbados, Antigua, St. Kitts). Unable to compete, planters from these islands moved to the southernmost of the mainland colonies in the 1670s and '80s, taking their slaves with them. Because of this migration, blacks almost from the beginning of the colony outnumbered whites in low-country South Carolina.

Adapting to their new environment, the emigrants developed a flourishing trade in naval stores. The forests of long-leaf pine, which blanketed every well-drained slope in the colony, were nearly limitless sources of tar and pitch, the caulking compounds that kept wooden sailing ships afloat. And, like sugar, naval stores could be efficiently produced by gangs of semiskilled slaves. The profits from the export of naval stores, in turn, provided investment capital for the construction of rice plantations.

Rice, which was not grown in sizable quantities elsewhere in the British colonies, proved an enormously profitable crop. Parliament initially listed it among the "enumerated articles"—which meant that, like Virginia tobacco, it could be shipped only to the mother country—but after a few years, on the special plea of Carolina planters, that restriction was lifted. Able to ship their product directly to Spain, Portugal, and Italy, the planters made more profit than ever.

Wealth and the English gentlemanly ideal fostered the growth of an upper class, much as it had in Virginia, but the West Indian element gave the Carolina gentry a new dimension. There was no trace of a Puritan's conscience in South Carolina, not even a Virginian's spotty remorse. Whenever they could, Carolina planters turned their rice fields over to overseers and took their families into Charleston for a "season" of entertainment. The sprightliest town in America for its size, Charleston possessed both a music hall and a theater; its private clubs offered genteel diversions of every sort. Unlike Virginians, few Carolina planters developed any interest in politics and government. They preferred instead the dance hall and the racetrack.

This then was the environment that Eliza Lucas found so polite and genial. It was a blend of West Indian romance, English social custom, and New World riches—all resting on the sandy but momentarily stable foundation of slave labor. Nevertheless, she brought into this environment the personal work ethic of a Puritan. She arose each day at 5:00 A.M. and pursued a rigorous schedule of daily duties that included studying, supervising household servants, and providing instruction for her sister and some of the slave children. Whenever she had occasion to visit Charleston, she resisted its urbane temptations. She regretted "that giddy gayety and want of reflection which I contracted when in town." She consulted the psychological works of John Locke over and over to determine "if I was the very same self" in the city as when she was hard at work in the country.

The Business of Slaves, Rice, and Indigo

By 1739, South Carolina had not expanded much beyond the original settlements. Life still centered on the two rivers that joined at Charleston "to form the Atlantic ocean" (as Charlestonians would have it)—the Ashley and the Cooper. Both were broad, slow-moving streams, flanked by marshy flatlands ideal for rice culture. The Wappoo, where Eliza Lucas' main plantation was located, was a saltwater creek that connected the Ashley with the Stono River to the southwest of Charleston. Rice fields were laid out along the river and separated from it by a levee. The seed was broadcast over a dry field in the spring. Water was then let into the field through sluicegates. Tides helped back up the river to the level of the gates. In the autumn the field was drained for the harvest, taking advantage of a low tide. In the upper reaches of the rivers, especially on the Cooper (Goose Creek, Saint James Parish), spring floods helped flood the fields.

Rice was profitable, but it had some shortcomings, as Eliza Lucas quickly realized. The amount of land on any one plantation that could be devoted to it was sharply limited, and it required attention only in spring and fall. Slaves could be kept busy at other times of the year clearing land and repairing levees, but such tasks yielded no short-run profit. Carolina planters needed a market crop that could be grown on the uplands away from the river and one whose growth cycle varied from that of rice. The need was widely felt; a number of planters were experimenting with various seeds. George Lucas apparently brought some varieties with him from the West Indies, for as early as July, 1739, Eliza was writing her recently departed father about "the pains I had taken to bring the Indigo, Cotton, Lucern [alfalfa], and Cassada [cassava, a starchy root] to perfection, and had greater hopes from the Indigo—if I could have the seed earlier the next year from the [West] Indies—than any of the rest of the things I had tried."

Unlucky weather, stale seeds, and her own inexperience frustrated these early efforts, and Eliza turned her attention to making a profit from the crops she had. The following year she was again writing her father to thank him for sending "West India cucumber seed," and by the return vessel she shipped him two barrels of rice, two of corn, three of peas, some pickled pork, two kegs of oysters, and "one of eggs, by way of experiment, put up in salt." "My scheme," she added, "is to supply my father's [sugar] refining house in Antigua with eggs from Carolina."

Most of her rice, however, was consigned to agents in London, and from them she purchased the goods she needed, everything from a four-wheel chaise to medicine for her chronic headaches. She kept meticulous accounts of every transaction. One day a week, Thursday, was set aside for balancing ledgers, drafting instructions to overseers on the inland plantations, communicating with London, and summarizing her activities for her father. In early 1741 she wrote to a girlfriend in Charleston with evident enthusiasm, "I have planted a large fig orchard, with design to dry them and export them. I have reckoned my expense and the prophets [profits] to arise from those figs, but was I to tell you how great an estate I am to make this way, and how 'tis to be laid out, you would think me far gone in romance. Your good uncle [Charles Pinckney, Eliza's future husband] I know has long thought I have a fertile brain at scheming. I only confirm him in his opinion, but I own I love the vegitable [sic] world extreamly [sic]." By then, too, she had planted a grove of oak trees "for posterity," and her Charleston friends, the Pinckneys, were threatening to come for a visit so they could all sit and watch the oaks grow.

By 1744, indigo culture, for which she had always entertained high hopes, was showing true promise. Indigo was a broad-leafed weed, which produced a blue dye. The color blue, especially in its purple form, was in high demand in Europe because it was associated with royalty—and that perhaps because it was so scarce (red and yellow dyes abound in nature). Its preference for well-drained soils and its growth cycle (early spring to mid-summer) made it, from the planter's point of view, the perfect complement to rice. And the end product, a dry cake of blue, had relatively high value for its bulk and weight. Shipping charges, the difference often between profit and loss, were thus comparatively light, that is, compared to rice, cotton, or tobacco.

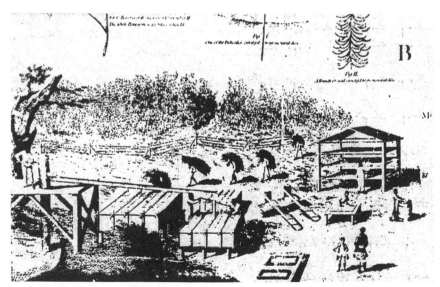

The indigo "works" on a Carolina plantation. (Charleston Library Society, South Carolina.)

It was not an easy plant to grow or refine, however, and that is largely why Eliza Lucas took so long to develop it. Like corn, it does not compete well with other weeds; the soil must be carefully prepared and constantly tended. The leaves had to be cut at just the right moment—if too early the color was poor, if too late the leaves were juiceless. The leaves were placed in vats of water where they fermented and yielded their juice. The juice was then fermented further, while being stirred vigorously with paddles until it thickened. Lime was added to precipitate the dye and the excess water poured off. The precipitate was then dried into cakes and packed for shipment.

While it was fermenting the indigo juice had to be watched night and day, for the timing of each stage was critical. In the West Indies there were professional "indigo makers" who supervised this process. When Eliza produced her first crop in 1741, Governor Lucas sent out one of these experts from the island of Montserrat. To Eliza's dismay, however, the dye he produced was so poor as to be unsalable. The overseer blamed the climate, but Eliza, who had watched the process carefully, tried it herself and succeeded. She grilled the overseer, and he confessed that he had sabotaged the process by using too much lime. Mainland competition, he had come to fear, would ruin his home island. He may also have been uneasy about following the orders of a female.

Poor seed from the West Indies wasted the next two seasons, and it was not until 1744 that Eliza produced a marketable crop. A second overseer, employed by her father, produced seventeen pounds, and Eliza sent six of it to England for trial. Her agent gleefully reported: "I have shown your indigo to one of our most noted brokers . . ., who tried it against some of the best FRENCH, and in his opinion it is AS GOOD." Parliament, he suggested by way of further encouragement, might be persuaded to subsidize Carolina indigo because the drain on Britain for the purchase of French West Indian indigo amounted to £200,000 a year.

Eliza Lucas needed no such encouragement. Providence and patriotism had already induced her to save most of the 1744 crop for seed. What she herself could not use she gave away "in small quantities to a great number of people." Simultaneously she provoked interest in the crop by publishing the report of her London agent in *The South Carolina Gazette*. In the following year Eliza made £225 on her indigo shipment to London, and at the end of that harvest a half dozen planters were offering seed of their own for sale in columns of the *Gazette*. In 1747, parliament, true to form, placed a bounty on British indigo, and the crop became a major source of income until the bounty ended with the American Revolution. In good harvests South Carolina exported as much as a million pounds of blue cake—all the result of Eliza Lucas's love for the vegetable world and eye for profit.

Crops and profits were not her sole interests, despite her determination to be a success in business. To a Charleston friend who could not imagine what there was to do in the country she described her daily routine: "In general I rise at five o'clock in the morning, read till seven—then take a walk in the garden or fields, see that the servants are at their respective business, then to breakfast. The first hour after breakfast is spent in music, the next is constantly employed in recollecting something I have learned, least for the want of practice it should be quite lost, such as French and short hand." One day a week was set aside for business affairs, and she frequently checked on the overseers of her inland plantations. Her spare time in the afternoons was devoted to "little Polly and two black girls, who I teach to read." After dinner she practiced her music again, did needlework until twilight, and spent the evening writing letters. It was a routine not unlike that of the urbane William Byrd—except for the time devoted to the education of slaves.

That project was more than an idle pastime. Her purpose in tutoring the three girls was to make them "school mistresses for the rest of the Negro children," a project so daring that she took the trouble to secure the permission of her father. The sheriff, on the other hand, does not seem to have worried her, as well he might have, for the legislature made it illegal to teach slaves to read after the Stono River uprising of 1739. Perhaps she was given a subtle caution, for there is no further mention of the education project in her letters.

Her lack of reaction to the Stono uprising is itself mute testimony to her relations with her slaves. While the rest of South Carolina writhed in fear throughout 1739 and 1740 (unable even to send troops to Oglethorpe), Eliza Lucas ignored the event. There is not a whisper of it in her correspondence even though it took place a short distance from her plantation. The one mention of slave insurrection in her letters was in 1741 when a local religious fanatic predicted that slaves would destroy the low country "by fire and sword." Even then she was less alarmed at the prospect than amused by the antics of the enthusiast who tried to part the waters of a creek with a wand and, failing, wrote a letter of apology to the speaker of the assembly. Concluded Eliza: "I hope he will be a warning to all pious minds not to reject reason and revelation [i.e., Scripture] and set up in their stead their own wild notions." Hers was the voice of cool-headed Anglicanism, confident in its faith, secure in its environment.

It was, withal, a lonely environment, but she seems to have enjoyed being alone, though she could be garrulous enough in company. She took pains to keep herself intellectually alive. She borrowed books from the Pinckneys; she employed a music master to give her lessons every Monday. She must have devoured the weekly *South Carolina Gazette*, for she commented freely on politics and war. She had the Carolinian's contempt for Oglethorpe (without realizing that South Carolina's lack of support was the root of his difficulties); she had in general little use for war and warriors. "I wish all men were as great cowards as myself," she declared; "it would make them more peaceably inclined."

When a comet swept across the southern sky in the spring of 1743 she got up early every morning to watch it. A Charleston friend told her that some thought it was a reincarnation of a hero (others thought it heralded the Second Coming) and asked her to describe it. Eliza twitted her friend for being unable to get out of bed in time but described the phenomenon in great detail. And she had to admit that the tail did resemble human dress: "I could not see whether it had petticoats or not, but I am inclined to think by its modest appearance so early in the morning it won't permit every idle gazer to behold its splendor, a favor it will only grant to such as take pains for it—from hence I conclude if I could have discovered any clothing it would have been the female garb. Besides if it is any mortal transformed to this glorious luminary, why not a woman?"

Such warmth and wit must have early captured the attention of Colonel Charles Pinckney. The Pinckneys were acquaintances of George Lucas, and after the governor's departure for Antigua, Elizabeth Pinckney befriended Eliza. Whenever Eliza visited Charleston she stayed with the Pinckneys, and their niece, Mary Bartlett, became her closest friend. Eliza's relationship with Colonel Pinckney was an intellectual one. He lent her books, and her letters to him were extended, if somewhat simple discourses on Locke, Virgil, and the novels of Samuel Richardson.

Elizabeth Pinckney died in January, 1744, and a few weeks later Colonel Pinckney proposed to Eliza. Marriage, except in response to her father's efforts, rarely entered into her correspondence. She was a self-reliant woman with exacting standards. Men she met at Charleston festivities were too often, she found, full of "flashy nonsense." But Charles Pinckney was clearly different. The two were married in May, 1744. She moved to Belmont, the Pinckney plantation on the Cooper River, leaving her own farms in the hands of overseers, and began a new life.

From Carolina to England

Charles Pinckney's father Thomas had come to Carolina in 1692. Both he and his wife, Mary Cotesworth, were from the north country of England and evidently of prominent family. Thomas Pinckney styled himself "Gentleman" whenever he signed his name. He sent his sons to England for education. The eldest inherited his English estate; Charles, the second son, inherited the Carolina properties. Charles attended the Inns of Court, practiced law in South Carolina, and added considerably to his father's fortune. He had served as speaker of the house in the assembly and was a member of the Governor's council. He was forty-five years old when he married Eliza, just about double her age.

Belmont was an imposing brick mansion on a headland that commanded a view down the Cooper River to Charleston, five miles away. Eliza briskly took charge of the household and was soon planting trees. Oaks were her favorite because they had commercial value, but she also set out some magnolias for decoration. She corresponded frequently with a friend of her husband's, Dr. Alexander Garden, a Charleston physician with an interest in botany. Garden sent samples of American plants to the Swedish classifier Carolus Linneaus, who honored him by naming one luscious flower the gardenia. Linneaus, in turn, sent European specimens for trial in America, and Garden often sent them on to Eliza Pinckney. Her arboretum was the marvel of St. James Parish.

In February, 1745, she gave birth to a son, named, with due reverence for his pedigree, Charles Cotesworth Pinckney. Childbirth, always dangerous in that age, she sustained with her customary certitude, suffering "no disorder but weakness." Three months later she proudly informed Mary Bartlett that she could see "all his Papa's virtues already dawning in him." A month after that she wrote an English acquaintance to request the purchase of a special toy so her son could "play himself into learning. . . according to Mr. Locke's method." Her reference evidently was to John Locke's *Essay Concerning Human Understanding*, one of her husband's books that she had read "over and over." Locke rejected the ancient notion that people were born with "innate ideas." The mind, he said, is a blank tablet (*tabula rasa*) on which life experience writes. His "method" of education, then, must have been a matter of "learning by doing," an interesting anticipation of some twentieth-century pedagogical techniques. Eliza was delighted with the results. A year later, when her son was 22 months old, she reported that he "prattles very intelligibly," knew the alphabet, and was beginning to spell. What the son thought of all this was not recorded until his later years when he claimed he had been nearly ruined in his youth by being pushed too rapidly in his studies. In the next few years Eliza had two more children, Harriott and Thomas (a third died in infancy).

In between motherhood and household management she managed to wedge time for agricultural experiments. Silkmaking caught her attention in the late 1740s. There had been a number of efforts to make silk in the early days of the colony, but they had been abandoned in the rush to rice. The mulberry trees were still there, however, and Eliza Pinckney had only to procure some well-bred eggs. She also viewed it as a way of employing slaves who could do no other work, which eased her balance sheet. Children gathered the mulberry leaves and fed the worms; the elderly dried the cocoons and "reeled" the silk. No one in the colony could weave silk, apparently, for she took her raw silk with her when she went to England in 1753 and had it made into dresses there. One of these she presented to the Princess of Wales, daughter-in-law of the king.

The occasion for her return to the mother country was the assembly's appointment of Charles Pinckney to represent the colony in London. A secondary motive was the desire, shared by both parents, to give their children an English education. There was still something inferior in the name "colonial."

Luckily for Eliza, a poor sailor, the passage was a swift one, a mere twenty-five days. The south coast ports of Portsmouth and Southampton were ravaged by smallpox, so their vessel sailed up the channel to London. They took a house in Richmond, a short distance up the Thames from London, and put the whole family through inoculation. Eliza renewed old acquaintances and quickly settled into a routine of social visits and sightseeing. They traveled extensively through the midlands and north country (where Charles had lands) and spent the "season" at Bath. They thoroughly enjoyed themselves, but never forgot that they were "exiles," as Eliza put it. She disliked the idleness of the English upper class and especially "the perpetual card playing." Charles, even more restless, had "many yearnings after his native land." In describing to a Carolina friend a visit to the Princess of Wales, in which the princess had dealt quite informally with the Pinckney children, Eliza added: "This, you'll imagine must seem pretty extraordinary to an American." How lightly the phrase "an American" tripped from her pen, yet it revealed much about her developing sense of national identity.

The Pinckneys departed for home in May, 1758, having resided in Britain for five years. They left the two boys in London to finish their schooling and took nine-year-old Harriott home with them. The plantations had suffered much in their absence; overseers, as every planter knew, needed constant oversight. Charles Pinckney plunged into work, but soon contracted malaria. Swamp fever was not usually fatal, but Pinckney was advanced in years and perhaps weakened by the sea journey. He died within three weeks. Eliza resumed the solitary existence she had known before.

Founding Mother

Many months later she referred to it as a time when the "lethargy of stupidity" gripped her mind and she functioned barely enough to keep alive. For more than a year after Charles Pinckney's death her letters to friends bled with misery and lament. But time healed and duty pulled her back to life. She had not only her own lands but the vast Pinckney holdings to superintend. There were thousand-acre plantations on both the Ashley and Cooper rivers, five hundred acres on the Savannah River, a sea-island near Beaufort, and an elaborate town house in Charleston. Charles Pinckney had willed all this property to his sons; it was Eliza's duty to preserve and improve it until they came of age.

Belmont, after five years of neglect, had "gone back to woods again." She threw herself into work and soon found that it had its own therapeutic value. With the help of an overseer who was both efficient and honest (because of his rare talents he was in such demand that he could choose his own employer and chose to work only for widows and orphans), Belmont was soon restored to production. By the spring of 1760 Eliza was writing to her London agent that, but for an unforeseen drought she would have produced enough to clear all the Pinckney estate's British debts. And she resumed her tree-planting. By 1761 she had a nursery for magnolia and bay trees. Her experiment with the bay tree is especially interesting, for the leaves of this West Indian tree were used as both a spice and a medicine, and cinnamon was made from the bark. And she had devised a way of packing two-year-old seedlings for shipment to friends in England.

When the day's work was done, her children occupied her thoughts. The two boys, left in vice-ridden London without parental guidance, were a particular worry. She bombarded them with letters full of homiletic advice. Whether it was her concern, or native good sense, or a combination of the two, Charles and Thomas threaded their way through Oxford and the Middle Temple without recorded difficulty. Daughter Harriott was also a source of pride and comfort. At the age of nineteen she married Daniel Horry, a rice planter with large holdings on the Santee River and a comfortable house in Charleston. By that date (1768) Eliza herself had moved into Charleston; she occupied herself through her last active years rebuilding the Horrys' garden.

In 1769 her oldest son returned home (Thomas, five years younger, returned in 1774). After completing his legal studies and being admitted to the bar, Charles Cotesworth Pinckney had journeyed to France for study at the Royal Military College at Caen. It was almost as if he foresaw that there was a new nation being born in America and that it would need soldiers and statesmen. In any case, he returned a flaming patriot, whose fight against the Stamp Act and other parliamentary impositions on the colonies had earned him the sobriquet "The Little Rebel" among Americans in London.

Both Charles and Thomas rose to the rank of general in the American Revolution, and each played a prominent role in the politics of independence. Charles Cotesworth participated in the convention that drafted the federal Constitution, and Thomas, as governor of the state in 1787, submitted the Constitution to the assembly. Each served the Federalist administrations of George Washington and John Adams in a diplomatic capacity during the 1790s, and, at different times, each was a Federalist candidate for vice president. In 1808 Charles Cotesworth Pinckney ran unsuccessfully against James Madison for president.

Eliza spent her last years in the company of her daughter and husband, rotating with the seasons between Charleston and the Santee. When President Washington toured the southern states in 1791, he made a point of stopping at the Horry plantation to visit Eliza Pinckney. An experimental farmer himself, Washington no doubt admired her as much for her agronomy as for her sons. Shortly thereafter she was stricken with cancer, a disease only recently identified and then not in all its forms. In the spring of 1793 she traveled to Philadelphia seeking treatment from a noted cancer specialist. She died there in May, 1793. At her funeral, in St. Peters Anglican Church, President Washington, at his own request, served as one of the pallbearers. In her youth she considered herself a transplanted Englishwoman; in maturity she knew herself to be an American.

SUGGESTIONS FOR FURTHER READING

Eliza Lucas Pinckney stands in need of a biographer. The only study currently available is by her great granddaughter, Harriet Horry Ravenal, *Eliza Pinckney* (1896). Pinckney's splendid letters, however, have been published by Elise Pinckney, ed., *The Letterbook of Eliza Lucas Pinckney* (1972). For the world in which she lived the following studies are recommended: M. Eugene Sirmans, *Colonial South Carolina, A Political History* (1966); Clarence L. Ver Steeg, *Origins of a Southern Mosaic: Studies of Early Carolina and Georgia* (1975); and George C. Rogers, *Charleston in the Age of the Pinckneys* (1969). Her agricultural experiments are put in context by Joyce E. Chaplin, *An Anxious Pursuit: Agricultural Innovation and Modernity in the Lower South, 1730–1815* (1993).

13

James Logan:
The American Enlightenment

"God said, 'let Newton be!' " wrote the poet Alexander Pope, "and there was light." Men of the eighteenth century believed that Sir Isaac Newton's *Principia Mathematica* (1686) had parted forever the shrouds of mystery that had veiled the workings of the natural world. By deducing mathematically laws that explained the behavior of heavenly bodies Newton showed the universe itself to be governed by rational principles, prin-

James Logan (1674–1751). This portrait by Gustavus Hesselius, one of the best-known of colonial artists, suggests a solid, successful, colonial gentleman. The Quaker "inner light" was, in James Logan, just that. His life was one of law-abiding rectitude, but seldom did he let Christian charity interfere with his drive for wealth and power. (The Historical Society of Pennsylvania. Portrait of James Logan by Gustavus Hesselius, Accession #1939.3.)

ciples that could be readily grasped by human minds. This discovery, and its applications far beyond the realm of physics, from religion to politics, came to be known as the Enlightenment. The essence of the Enlightenment was a faith in human reason. All nature was comprehensible; there was no need to explain natural phenomena in terms of miracles or revelations. God's function was only that of First Cause. Having created this natural mechanism and set it to working by certain rules, He left it alone thereafter. As one modern scholar has observed, the men of the Enlightenment "denatured God and deified nature."

It is scarcely surprising, though at first it might seem so, that one of the most articulate exponents of the Enlightenment in British North America was a Pennsylvania Quaker, James Logan. The Quakers shared the pietist vision of a blessed community in which men and women would live together in peace, simplicity, and love; but they were also shrewd, industrious, practical participants in the world as it was. To build the kingdom of God, they felt, humans must work hard, each to his or her own calling, and make resourceful use of the materials at hand. God was certain to reward the diligent and the frugal with material success, and the wealthy in turn were obliged to help others. Thus good business, social profit, and cultural enrichment went hand in hand. And no one exemplified this better than the American virtuoso, James Logan. Nor did anyone realize quite so clearly as Logan the limits of pietism in the secular, rationalist world of the eighteenth century. When his fellow Quakers drew back from the chasm of modernity, Logan pressed on. He crossed the bridge from the religious zealotry of the seventeenth century to the urbane materialism of the eighteenth. He was a true scion of the Enlightenment.

Friends and Enemies

The life of an English Quaker was difficult enough for a landed gentleman such as William Penn; it was many times worse for a poor family such as the Logans. Patrick Logan, James's father, had served as a chaplain to a noble Scottish family at Stenton, a village in East Lothian, but he was forced to give up his position when he joined the Society of Friends. The Logans moved to Ulster in northern Ireland, where Patrick obtained a job teaching school, and there on October 20, 1674, James Logan was born. The Logans had a number of children, but only two, James and William, survived.

Northern Ireland was just as poor as Scotland and even more prejudiced against Quakers. The native Irish were Roman Catholic, the emigre Scots were Presbyterian, and the ruling class was Anglican. James Logan's boyhood was a nightmare of alienation and fear. Only in his father's school did he feel comfortable and secure. Father was an inspiring teacher, son an apt pupil. James emerged with a good foundation of Latin and Greek, a start on Hebrew, and a deep fascination for mathematics. He was apprenticed to a linen merchant in Dublin to learn a trade, but that venture was interrupted by the overthrow of King James II and the ensuing war in Ireland. With the help of London Quakers, Patrick Logan secured a new post as a schoolmaster in Bristol, and the family moved to that bustling seaport in 1690.

In Bristol the religious harassment ceased, though the maturing James still had to face the subtler forms of British discrimination—exclusion from the universities, from government service, and from military service. Little was left but business, and after trying his own hand at the unremunerative occupation of teaching, James Logan became a linen merchant. He was struggling to gain a foothold in that tightly drawn guild when he received a summons from William Penn. The founder of Pennsylvania had been one of the supervisors of the Friends' school in Bristol and on occasion had visited Logan's classroom. In 1699 he was about to return to Pennsylvania. He invited Logan to accompany him as his private secretary. Logan, twenty-four years old and shy of options, accepted.

Accompanied by Hannah Penn and the Penns' daughter Letitia, they sailed on the *Canterbury*, an apt name for a ship with a cargo of pilgrims. The voyage was long (three months) and stormy. But an incident on shipboard revealed much of James Logan's character. They were nearing the American shore when a sail appeared on the horizon and gave chase. The captain of the *Canterbury* cleared the decks for a fight and gave the Quakers permission to retire into his personal cabin. They did, except for Logan, who stayed on deck to help with the guns. When the stranger turned out to be friendly, Logan went below to inform the Quakers. To his surprise Penn rebuked him publicly for participating in a potential fight. Logan angrily retorted that Penn should have thought of that earlier. He seemed eager enough to have Logan help fight the ship when he thought there was danger. This, of course, was Logan's version of the incident, but there is little reason to doubt it happened. He would be a loyal, but not unthinking servant, and he could compromise his religious scruples when he found it necessary.

The Secretary and the Democrat

Philadelphia was a proud city of 5000 souls in 1700 and growing rapidly. The Quaker migration had slowed to a trickle, but religious refugees from Germany, Switzerland, and France continued to flood into the city. Philadelphia was gaining steadily on Boston and would soon be the largest city in the British colonies. Its vessels carried wheat, flour, and lumber to the West Indies, returning with sugar and rum and bills of exchange. The latter, functioning as an international currency, were used to purchase woolens, tools, and hardware from the mother country. A few merchants had grown rich on this trade. They were all Quakers, all early residents of Pennsylvania, and most held important political positions. To them Penn and his new secretary looked for counsel and aid, not realizing that the dominant role of a wealthy few was already antagonizing the unwealthy many. Not realizing, either, that Penn's experiment in democracy had only whetted the appetites of Pennsylvania's democrats.

Penn was a democrat only in theory; he had a gentleman's manners and tastes. Logan's principal job, aside from being factotum of the Penn household, was to wring profits from Pennsylvania. Penn had sunk £25,000 into the colony and by 1700 had received no more than £1000 in return. Logan's job was to collect quitrents from those who were in arrears (each landholder owed Penn a shilling or a bushel of wheat a year for each 100 acres). It was no easy task. Surrounded by a cornucopia of land and resources, Pennsylvania's farmers could see no reason for paying rent to a distant proprietor, especially one who gave them nothing in return. The American environment was hard on Old World customs; one of its first victims was the medieval notion of quitrent. Nor did Penn make Logan's task any easier. In addition to rents, he wanted his secretary to "look carefully" at the collection of fines, forfeitures, and escheats—all outdated relics of feudalism.

Logan made little headway in debt collection, but his efforts and his transparent loyalty earned Penn's respect. When the proprietor returned to England in 1701 to parry another assault on his charter, he made Logan clerk of the council, secretary of the province, receiver-general for quitrents, and "the person particularly entrusted to take care of" the Indians. The new offices promised more labor than glory. In a final letter of instruction Penn outlined his expectations: "Get in quitrents . . . sell lands . . . Get in the taxes . . . settle my accounts, discharge all my debts . . . Get in my two mills finished . . . Cause all the province and territories to be resurveyed . . . Write to me diligently."

Logan bounded enthusiastically into his new duties, but he met no more success than before. In May, 1702, he reported dejectedly to Penn that he had collected barely twelve pounds in quitrents and less than fifty from the sale of lands, and most of it went to satisfy Penn's local creditors. Logan's strenuous efforts in the proprietor's behalf also made him enemies. He bore the brunt of popular resentment against the proprietary itself. And he suffered from the fact that there was very little money in the colony. People were simply unable to pay.

Logan, it must be said, contributed to his troubles. Despite his own humble origins, he had no sympathy for the commonalty, and he had the Briton's disdain for colonials. Thus, he was quick to resort to force. Learning, in the summer of 1702, that a New Jersey farmer had occupied one of the Delaware River islands that the proprietor had reserved to himself, Logan summoned the sheriff of Philadelphia and an armed posse to drive him off. This was too much for the city's Quakers, who brought him before the Monthly Meeting and demanded an apology for violating his faith. Logan did so, but with ill grace. His list of enemies mounted.

Logan might have survived his own errors and Pennsylvania's hard times (aggravated by the outbreak of war in 1701) had his opposition remained ill-formed and leaderless. Unhappily for him, there was an opposition leader at hand in the person of David Lloyd. Lloyd had credentials aplenty. A relative, Thomas Lloyd, had organized the first antiproprietary faction among Quakers in the 1680s. In the succeeding decade, when Penn had been momentarily deprived of his colony, Thomas and David Lloyd led the fight against royal government. David Lloyd was a gifted orator, a student of the law, and a master at parliamentary maneuver. He held the position of attorney general of the province until 1699 when Penn, under pressure from the Crown, dismissed him. Seeking revenge, he devoted the rest of his life to political war on the proprietor and all his agents.

Lloyd's motives were mixed, but there was no mistaking his power. He portrayed himself as a tribune of the people, defending their rights against the arbitrary authority of the Crown, the proprietary, and their minions. He had a ready model in parliament's struggle against the Crown in England, and he made ample use of the constitutional precedents parliament had established in the course of the seventeenth century. Lloyd's goal as speaker of the house was to make the Pennsylvania assembly a colonial House of Commons. How much of this was ideology and how much self-interest we shall never know. Perhaps it does not matter. Lloyd was a Whig of the American variety, and he had a counterpart in nearly every colony.

James Logan was no disciple of despotism. Indeed, he may have been a truer Whig* than Lloyd. English Whigs had no use for democrats or demagogues, and they did not always distinguish between the two. Like John Locke and other Whig theorists, Logan believed in balanced government that combined aristocratic and popular elements. He recognized the value of a lower house—even one controlled by a Lloyd—but he thought it ought to be counterbalanced by a strong council. Such a body, appointed by the proprietor from among the more substantial citizens of the community, would protect the interests of the executive (thereby assuring more effective government), while also serving as both rudder and anchor for the ship of state.** Since the council was in fact Logan's power base, he too was brushing his ideological landscape with the pigment of self-interest.

Penn himself triggered the power struggle when he sent over a new governor in 1704. His choice was twenty-six-year-old John Evans, whose chief credentials were that he was an Anglican and a courtier: Imperial officials approved of him as a result and expected him to cooperate with the Crown's requests for military assistance. With Evans came twenty-five-year-old William Penn, Junior, sent to Pennsylvania for such character reformation as the pristine wilderness might afford. Neither lightened Logan's responsibilities, for he was expected to serve as Evans' adviser and junior's caretaker.

For a time the arrangement worked well. Evans made Logan a member of the council (he had previously only been secretary to that body), and the three set up a bachelors' quarters in a large brick house on Chestnut Street in Philadelphia. After a time, however, young Penn returned to England, and the governor moved out in a huff after Logan suggested he might share living expenses.

The governor's move into quarters of his own was a declaration of independence. Having freed himself of Logan, he took on the assembly. He was dismayed by the assembly's habit of coming and going at will. The charter of 1701 allowed the assembly to meet and adjourn at its own volition. Controlled by farmers, the assembly had a tendency to transact its business in between chores. The urban governor found this inefficient

---

*Whigs originated during the reign of Charles II as a party opposed to Roman Catholic James, Duke of York. Whig theory stressed that there were limits on the power of the king.

** The nineteenth-century English Whig Thomas Babington Macauley once described the American government as "all sail and no rudder."

and unsophisticated; he demanded the right to summon, prorogue, or dissolve the legislature. The assembly, recognizing that an important constitutional principle was at stake, refused to change. In the resulting stalemate government drifted, even though Indians were loose on the northern border and New England was shrieking for help.

At that juncture Logan, only three years older than the governor and not a whit more tactful, injected a new issue. He was distressed that the Charter of 1701 stripped the council of its former legislative powers. He regarded the council, especially now that he was a member, as the bulwark of proprietary authority and governmental common sense. In the summer of 1704 he proposed an amendment to the charter forbidding the governor to approve laws except with the assistance of the council. His purpose clearly was to give the council a voice in legislation—a power that it had in every other colony. The assembly again objected, standing on the clear wording of the charter, and the governor himself was none too pleased. Nothing resulted from this triangular confrontation, except that the assembly marked Logan as its chief opponent.

The next move was Lloyd's. The colony's court system, established by the assembly under the Charter of 1701, had been disallowed by the privy council. The assembly had to start over, and Lloyd took advantage of the opportunity. The bill he introduced in the summer of 1706 looked to an independent judiciary. Judges would hold office during good behavior (a tenure principle adopted in England in 1702) and be removable only by the assembly. The proceeds of justice, hitherto a perquisite of the proprietor, would go to the maintenance of government. Most injurious of all, from Logan's point of view, the courts, rather than the proprietor, would settle disputes involving land titles.

If Lloyd wanted a fight, he could not have chosen a better ground. Courts were the only phase of government that touched the lives of average people. Lacking standing armies or professional police, colonial government was otherwise invisible. The courts and the attorneys that served them, moreover, were objects of suspicion. Too often they seemed to be agents of the wealthy employed to collect debts. When a mob took to the streets in early America, the law courts were a common target.

Governor and council, patching their own differences, jointly rejected Lloyd's bill. The lower house pointed out that the council had no authority to accept or reject legislation. The Council's reply, drafted by Logan with quill dipped in acid, suggested that the assembly ought to try serving the country instead of honing its parliamentary skills. Lloyd and the lower house promptly shot back a series of resolves—the first asserted the right of the assembly to impeach any official appointed by the governor, the last singled out Logan as "an enemy to the Governor and government of this province."

The threat of impeachment evoked many a ghost from the English past. Parliament's impeachment, removal, and execution of the principal adviser to King Charles I had been the opening shot in the English Civil War. Although impeachment had fallen in disuse by 1700, the threat of it was the foundation of responsible government, that is, the notion that the Crown's ministers ought to be responsible to a majority in parliament. A striking instance of this developing concept was to come in 1710 when Queen Anne dismissed her war ministry of Marlborough and Godolphin after they lost control of parliament to the Tory opposition. David Lloyd was not ahead of his time; he was simply the pacesetter. The one flaw in his position was that if the council had no power, as he maintained, a councillor such as Logan was not worth impeaching.

In the end, nothing came of it. Impeachment was simply an accusation, or indictment; removal from office required a trial and conviction of a crime. In England the trial court for such charges was the House of Lords, yet Lloyd had been arguing for years that the Pennsylvania council bore no relation to the House of Lords—indeed, that it had no function whatsoever. It was not clear in what forum the assembly wanted its cause tried. The council, seeing its advantage, agreed to a hearing, while promising Logan that he would get a speedy judgment lest his reputation be smirched by unfounded allegations. At that point Governor Evans, showing wit for a change, announced that he had no power to preside over an impeachment trial. Logan then refused to plead, pointing out that the charges against him were political, not criminal (the principal one being that he had given "pernicious counsel" to the governor). With a judge who wouldn't preside and a defendant who wouldn't admit to guilt or innocence, the trial broke up in confusion. It was never resumed.

The impeachment fiasco did not spike the rancor, however. Logan took his case to the proprietor; the assembly turned to the press. For years the wrangling continued while the government drifted. Pennsylvania contributed nothing to the war effort against French Canada; only the Iroquois buffer protected its own frontiers. Such was the atmosphere of distrust that protocol took precedence over legislation. The assembly spent the 1707 session debating whether it was obliged to assemble merely because the governor wanted to address it. In 1709 Lloyd insulted the governor by refusing to stand when addressing him, and the ensuing controversy terminated business for that session.

Foolish as all this seems, and little as either Lloyd or Logan understood it, it had a symbolic importance. Lloyd, whatever his motives, was carving an important constitutional position. He was arguing for the supremacy of the legislature, and, indirectly at least, founding its authority on the popular will. Logan, separated from Lloyd more by the heat of combat than by ideological principle, stressed instead the importance of order and efficiency, values that were more likely to accrue from the executive. Lloyd feared power; Logan feared anarchy.

James Logan, however, was at this point too engrossed in battle to see the significance of the war. Disgusted with provincial politics, worried about his own relationship with the proprietor, and alarmed by Penn's efforts to sell his province, Logan toward the end of 1709 returned to England. Whether he would ever come back was problematical. He was not yet an American.

An Interlude of Peace

The London that James Logan saw in that year of political crisis, 1710, was the same London that William Byrd adored, but one would scarcely know it. Like Byrd, Logan toured the coffeehouses and absorbed himself in weekly issues of the *Tatler*. But he had no use for the sensuous haunts that attracted Byrd. He spent his days touring bookstores, his evenings in the company of Quaker friends.

Logan also traveled some, using letters of introduction to pass from one wealthy Quaker family to another. On one such visit he fell in love and suffered the humiliation of being rejected by the young lady's family because he lacked wealth and social position. The setback forced him to take stock. The problem of wealth he could remedy, though not in Britain. He would have to return to Pennsylvania and direct his energies to his own interests rather than someone else's. He might then be rejected as a provincial, but at least he would be a wealthy and powerful one.

He set out on his way to wealth as systematically as he did everything else. Land was the first prerequisite, and of that there was plenty in Pennsylvania. Obtaining it, for one in Logan's straightened circumstances, was another problem. The proprietor, curiously, was no help. Penn had too many debts of his own to be generous with his lands, and in any case he had always been inclined to reimburse Logan with gratitude rather than money. Nevertheless Logan soon found a way. Some wealthy English Quakers had purchased land in Pennsylvania but had never moved to the colony. Logan purchased a number of these "old rights," totaling some 7000 acres, at bargain prices. Since the rights were not attached to specific parcels, Logan, on his return to Pennsylvania, was free to pick and choose. His long and largely unrewarded service to the proprietary land office would be useful in that regard. He then renewed his arrangement with the Penns, taking care this time to assign a fee schedule for each office he held, and sailed for Philadelphia in December, 1711.

David Lloyd's power had waned in Logan's absence. The people he relied upon for support, small farmers and city shopkeepers, had little political staying power. Their first concern was making a living. They participated in politics only when hard times or other emergency summoned them. By 1710 Pennsylvania's economy had recovered from the first shock of war, and business was flourishing. Quaker merchants and wealthy landowners, alarmed at Lloyd's class appeal, regrouped. In the fall election of that year not a single member of the assembly that had tried to impeach Logan, David Lloyd included, was returned to office. Lloyd eventually regained his seat, but he was elected speaker only once in the next ten years. In 1714, when Lloyd's court reform measure was disallowed in London, the assembly let the governor set up a court system.

The political calm suited Logan splendidly. He needed time to make his fortune. Land was only one of the avenues he developed in Britain; the other was the fur trade. He had contacted British merchants to arrange a market for his furs and a supply of trade goods. In Pennsylvania he turned a haphazard enterprise into an effective system. He organized the rough traders who toured the backwoods and dealt with the Indians, offering them both credit and supplies in return for pelts. He soon found, as John Jacob Astor did in a later generation, that by extending his traders more credit than they could repay he kept them in his service. He also found that rum was a prime vehicle for exchange, even though Pennsylvania law prohibited the sale of liquor to Indians. Fortune hunting had perceptibly dimmed the inner light. But he did make money. By 1715 he was sending to London furs valued at £1000 a year.

Wealth and comfort, to say nothing of approaching middle age, rekindled his interest in marriage. He made his choice with customary speed and finality; Sarah Reed was less than half his age, lacked wealth or social position, and possessed only the rudiments of education. But she was a Quaker and she was willing. They were married in December, 1714. Within two years she bore him a daughter, Sarah, and a son, William. A second daughter, Hannah, was born in 1720. For the first time in his life James Logan was secure and content.

He was also able to devote more time to his books. In 1708 he procured a copy of Newton's *Principia Mathematica*, the first copy of that work, so far as is known, to appear in America. Without any instruction or support, he mastered Newton's abstruse equations, annotating with suggestions of his own Newton's calculations for the orbit of the moon and other bodies. In his time of political troubles he had used mathematics as an escape. Now that his life was serene he took up science more seriously. He wrote to his business agents in London, Amsterdam, and Hamburg for more books on physics and astronomy. "It may appear strange to thee perhaps," he confessed to his Hamburg agent, "to find an American bearskin merchant troubling himself with such books, but they have been my delight and, with my children, will, I believe, continue to be my best entertainment in my advancing years."

Physics led him to the medieval Arab astronomers. He examined their religion, reading the Koran, and branched from them into Hebrew and back to the Greek and Roman classics. Even Scandinavian history and the Icelandic sagas of the discovery of America caught his attention. He eventually accumulated a library that ranked with William Byrd's. But Byrd was essentially a collector; Logan was a scholar.

The Paper Money War

Hard times returned in 1720 and with them political turmoil. The South Sea Bubble—a misguided and highly speculative effort to set up a British colony in Panama—burst in that year, triggering a financial panic in London. But there must have been other factors in the depression, among them a resettling of trade patterns after nearly a quarter century of intermittent warfare. The West Indies trade collapsed, and with it went Pennsylvania's main source of hard money. Even the market for Logan's furs declined drastically. Side effects rippled from Philadelphia into the hinterland. Farmers could not sell their products or borrow money to tide themselves over. The assembly election of the autumn of 1721, Logan noted, was "very mobbish and carried by a leveling spirit." Seats were won by men who had not been seen since the impeachment assembly of 1709.

From Logan's standpoint the situation was doubly dangerous, for the deputy governor, William Keith, appeared to side with the debtors. Keith was an able administrator and well liked. Whether he espoused the popular cause from conviction or opportunism cannot be said. Logan considered him a cheap demagogue, but Logan was hardly an unbiased source.

Among those elected to the 1721 assembly was Francis Rawle, a long-standing member of the popular party and disciple of David Lloyd. Earlier that year Rawle published an essay on the money problem. His "Remedy" was the creation of a land bank with authority to issue paper currency. If backed by the security of land, the currency would hold its value, said Rawle, especially if issued only in limited amounts. It was not a very radical proposal, for Rawle did not envision debtor relief through depreciation; he only wanted to replace the gold and silver that no longer flowed from the West Indies.

Though not radical, the scheme was certainly novel. Previous issues of paper money, in Pennsylvania and elsewhere, had occurred only in wartime; they were forms of public finance, a "national" debt to be retired as soon as the emergency ended. Rawle's proposal had nothing to do with military necessity; it was simply an effort to expand the money supply. Debtors, of course, would benefit some from the availability of currency, but so would farmers and merchants. And if the money did not depreciate in value, creditors would have no cause to complain.

It was an ingenious argument and a sensible one. It touched Quaker feelings, moreover, because it was easily cast in the form of aid to the suffering poor. Logan and other conservative merchants had misgivings, however. The beneficiaries of such legislation were a political majority, and there was nothing to prevent them from issuing excessive amounts or failing to retire the paper when the depression ended. Logan's argument was that of a conservative who apprehended change and of a wealthy man who had something to lose. The poor, in any case, Logan contended, did not deserve such a windfall. "Commonly people became wealthy by sobriety and industry," he said, whereas the poor become "poor by luxury, idleness, and folly." Logan's argument may have lacked the compassion expected of a Quaker, but it rested squarely on Quaker individualism. It was a distillation of the Protestant ethic, as stark and chill as Andrew Carnegie's "Gospel of Wealth" essay a century and a half later.

The arrogance of Logan's argument was also patent, and it hurt his cause in class-conscious Philadelphia where the skilled artisans—the "leather aprons" as they proudly called themselves—had a tightly knit political organization. The governor joined in, poking fun at Logan's effort to equate the laws of credit with the laws of Newton, and the newly formed alliance of plebes and politico was overwhelming. The assembly created a land bank, authorized triple the amount of paper that Rawle had recommended, and cut interest rates from 8 percent to 6 percent.

Logan decided it was time to visit Britain again. He had other concerns besides paper money. Immigrants from Germany and Ireland were flooding into the western valleys, alarming Indians and rekindling the old border conflict with Maryland. The Baltimore family, moreover, had resurrected its ancient claim to Delaware. The Penn proprietary was threatened and the Penns seemed more feckless than ever. After the death of the founder there had been a long court fight to ascertain the ownership of the proprietary. William the wastrel son died in the interim; Hannah and her younger sons refused to go to the colony. So oblivious to their interests did the new proprietors seem, that Logan could see no alternative but to present the situation in person. Hastening his departure in the fall of 1723 was the news that Governor Keith had appointed David Lloyd chief justice of the colony, and the assembly had unanimously elected Lloyd its speaker.

The Mellowing

Logan's second homecoming was quite different from the first. He did not, in fact, any longer regard Britain as home. He returned, not as an imperial foundling insecure in his roots and unsure of his future, but as a prosperous and influential American. He glided comfortably through London's drawing rooms and coffeehouses, trading ideas with the scientific virtuosi of the day. He attended a session of the Royal Society and met its venerable president, Sir Isaac Newton, "bending so much under the load of years as that with some difficulty he mounted the stairs of the Society's room." He was introduced to Edmund Halley, the Royal Astronomer, and managed to obtain a copy of Halley's unpublished astronomical tables. Most important he met Peter Collinson, a Quaker cloth merchant with international connections. Collinson was soon to become the hub of the Atlantic intellectual community. He was a collector of people, whose circle of acquaintances included, besides Logan, Sir Hans Sloane (founder of the British Museum), Carolus Linneaus of Sweden, the American botanists John Bartram and Alexander Garden, and of course Benjamin Franklin. It was Collinson who purchased and sent to Franklin the equipment for his experiments with electricity. Collinson was the pollinator of the Enlightenment, Logan his first transatlantic contact.

The interview with the Penns was also successful. Hannah Penn, managing the province until her sons came of age, was at first inclined to dismiss Keith when she heard of the governor's transgressions and replace him with Logan. Aware of his unpopularity in the province, Logan vetoed that idea. Indeed, after looking over the assortment of placemen and court gossips that surrounded the Penns, Logan decided that Keith, after all, might be the ablest executive available. He needed only to be brought to heel. So, at Logan's instigation, Hannah Penn wrote a stiff letter to Keith, instructing him to mind the proprietary interest, to follow the advice of the council, and to reinstate Logan as secretary and clerk of the council. Thus armed, Logan returned to Philadelphia in May, 1724.

William Keith was not one to be put under collar and leash. He had had a grand time in Logan's absence, signing a bill tripling the amount of paper money in circulation and packing the council with his followers. He denounced Hannah Penn's instruction as a violation of the colony's charter and an encroachment on popular rights. He showed the instructions to the assembly so it might vent its dismay, and the assembly obligingly published them for the benefit of all. Chief Justice Lloyd then entered the war against Logan and the proprietary with a broadside, *A Vindication of the Legislative Power*.

Faced with that formidable alliance, Logan went back to the source. He had made a mistake, he wrote Hannah Penn. Keith was incorrigible and would have to be removed. A new governor, Patrick Gordon, arrived in 1726. The fall elections that year were critical, and both sides strained every resource. Logan masterminded the strategy of the proprietary party and took credit for its victory. The return of prosperity—abetted, ironically, by the infusion of paper money—was probably equally important. The ex-governor managed to secure election to the assembly, but he left the colony soon thereafter.

Logan was weary of party warfare and ready to retire. Hannah Penn died the following year, and a British court declared her sons John, Thomas, and Richard Penn to be Proprietors and Governors of Pennsylvania. The boys, still reluctant to venture into the wilderness, asked Logan to continue collecting debts and rents, but Logan flatly refused. He was tired of serving others; he had assembled fortune enough to serve himself. A fall on the ice in the winter of 1728 left him with no choice. A broken leg bone failed to heal properly; he was a cripple ever after with little strength for either business or politics.

Although slowed, Logan did not shun public life altogether. He continued his running boundary dispute with Maryland authorities. Shortly before he died, a British court accepted his claim as to the location, a settlement that permitted a precise survey by Mason and Dixon in 1767.

He also continued to serve as the colony's Indian agent. As heir to Penn's reputation he managed to maintain good relations with the Indians, though he had neither Penn's principles nor his conscience. During the 1730s Logan cleared the Indian title to most of the land east of the mountains. Small and weak tribes, such as the Christianized Conestogas, were allowed to retain patches of ground in the east; the rest were simply pushed into Ohio. Those who balked were removed by threats and trickery. When a small group of Delawares refused to sell their ancestral lands at the forks of the Delaware River, Logan shamed them into moving by summoning other Indians who called them old women for not wanting to live in the western woods. When another tribe agreed to a "walking purchase" on the upper Delaware, Logan hired specially trained runners and cleared a path through the woods for them to obtain maximum mileage (one of his runners covered sixty miles in a day and a half).

On the death of his old enemy David Lloyd in 1731, Logan was made chief justice, a position that was more honorable than onerous. It enabled him to spend most of his time with his garden and his books. The previous year he had completed Stenton, a brick mansion northwest of Philadelphia on the Germantown Road. Though a handsome structure, it lacked the up-to-date Baroque qualities of William Byrd's Westover. With classic lines and gabled roof, it was more in the seventeenth century style of Christopher Wren. Logan's library, numbering several thousand volumes, was the centerpiece of the house; it stretched across the entire second floor front.

Country life awakened a new scientific interest—botany. One of his gardening books made the suggestion that plants seemed to have male and female parts, just as humans do. This excited his curiosity and he resolved to investigate. He examined the stalks of Indian corn in his garden and discovered on the tassels "a kind of adventitious dust, scarce belonging to the plant, as if lodged there like dew from the air." The kernels of corn resembled eggs, he thought, and he wondered if the "farina" as he called the pollen, had something to do with the reproductive process.

The following summer he planned an experiment. He stripped one patch of corn of its tassels, he covered another group of plants with cloth, and left a third group alone as a control. The result was clear. Those plants that had been detasseled or covered had undeveloped ears. "It is very plain," he wrote, "that the farina emitted from the summits of the [tassels] is the true male seed, and absolutely necessary to render the uterus and grain fertile." The corn silk, he correctly surmised, was the tube by which the farina penetrated to the kernels.

He promptly shared his discovery with scientific friends and was dismayed to learn that European botanists had known of plant sex roles for many years. No one, however, was quite sure of the mechanics of reproduction. Logan continued his experiments for several years, using different plant species, and in 1735 sent his findings to Peter Collinson. Collinson published an abstract of them in the Royal Society's *Transactions*. The Royal Society, with customary disdain for colonial achievement, ignored the discovery, but botanists on the European Continent saw its importance. Within a few years Logan's essay on corn pollenization was being cited in botanical treatises as the standard authority on the subject.

The publication in the late 1730s of a Dutch treatise on optics rekindled Logan's old interest in mathematics. He reviewed the Dutch scientist's rules for finding the foci of lenses and devised geometrical proofs that were much clearer and simpler than the original. He then went on to work out mathematically a law for the aberration of light when passing through a sphere, even though Newton himself had thought it impossible. Through the help of Collinson these findings were published, together with an expanded version of his corn experiments in Leyden, Holland, in 1741.

These demonstrations established Logan as the foremost mathematician in America. He could easily be considered the foremost classicist, as well. He had always kept his Latin, Greek, and Hebrew in working order, translating passages from each language into the other, as well as into English. For the benefit of his children he translated the "Distichs of Cato," a collection of Latin homilies which Logan put into poetic couplets. Benjamin Franklin, always looking for ways to enhance Philadelphia's reputation for culture, published the piece in 1735. A few years later Logan translated Cicero's essay on old age, the *Cato Major*. This too Franklin published, taking special care with the artistic composition, type, and binding. With characteristic blend of booster spirit and American patriotism, Franklin expressed the hope that the work was "a happy omen that Philadelphia shall become the seat of the American muses."

Logan had been acquainted with Franklin, Philadelphia's other virtuoso, for some years. He advised Franklin on book selection for the Philadelphia subscription library, the first such city project in America. In 1749, when Franklin conceived the idea of a nondenominational college for Philadelphia, Logan gave it enthusiastic support. He agreed to serve as one of the trustees, though recurrent fits of palsy prevented his active participation. He died in 1751, the year the college opened its doors.

SUGGESTIONS FOR FURTHER READING

The writings of Frederick B. Tolles will tell most readers all they wish to know about James Logan and colonial Pennsylvania. Especially recommended are *James Logan and the Culture of Provincial America* (1957), and *Meeting House and Counting House: The Quaker Merchants of Colonial Philadelphia, 1682–1783* (1948, reprinted 1963). Carl and Jessica Bridenbaugh, *Rebels and Gentlemen, Philadelphia in the Age of Franklin* (1942, reprinted 1968), is an excellent portrait of the leading colonial city. Gary B. Nash, *Quakers and Politics: Pennsylvania, 1681–1726* (1968), details the conflict between proprietor and assembly.

Epilogue

From Colonies to Revolution—Spanning the Generations

James Logan and Benjamin Franklin were men of different generations confronting different patterns of history. Logan was a cultured provincial, a member of the imperial court circle; Franklin was a philosopher-statesman of a new nation. Logan pursued learning for its own sake; Franklin exploited it for its value to the community. They were both self-made men of humble backgrounds, but Logan came to scorn the multitudes. Franklin tolerated them, patronized them, and came to use them.

Yet both were faithful Whigs. They detested arbitrary government and feared mob rule. Each could honestly subscribe to the Whig slogan "Liberty and Property!" Only the emphasis was different. Logan, like William Byrd II, cherished order and moderation. Liberty, both feared, tended to degenerate into anarchy. Property and status, represented in the upper house of the legislature, were the proper ballast for government. In the next generation their views would be echoed by John Adams and Alexander Hamilton. Franklin and his earlier counterpart, David Lloyd, drew on a tradition that stretched back to Nathaniel Bacon and even William Bradford. It cherished liberty of all things and worried that excessive concern for property and place might lead to despotism. Thomas Jefferson would pick up their torch in the next generation.

Such subtle shades of ideology, magnified by party combat, would divide Americans for years, even generations, to come. But there also were sources of unity. By the end of Logan's life Americans were developing a sense of common purpose, a feeling of national identity. The new creed was a mixture of missionary zeal and self-interested enterprise. Benjamin Franklin was its chief apostle.

Franklin spent his childhood in Cotton Mather's Boston and his adulthood in James Logan's Philadelphia. The wisdom that he passed on to contemporaries and to posterity was a cautious blend of the two. In the

Almanac that he began publishing in 1733, Franklin distilled into memorable aphorisms the virtues that composed the Protestant ethic. "Lost time is never found again" celebrated diligence. "A penny saved is a penny earned" made frugality more palatable. " 'Tis hard for an empty bag to stand upright" memorialized self-reliance. Franklin offered a homiletic digest of "doing good," without Cotton Mather's apocalyptic vision, and he epitomized the "inner plantation" without the Quakers' humble piety. (Franklin admired both humility and piety, but rarely practiced either.) The amalgam was a powerful ethos, one that helped create a new nation and a new culture. It shaped a people that conquered a continent and built an empire—proud to the point of overbearing, diligent to the point of rapacious, self-reliant to the point of self-interested, philanthropic to the point of pretentious—yet one that, withal, seldom did harm knowingly.

Index

BAKER & TAYLOR